A GUIDE TO THE
JAPANESE STAGE

A GUIDE TO THE
JAPANESE
STAGE From Traditional to Cutting Edge

KODANSHA INTERNATIONAL
Tokyo • New York • London

CONTEMPORARY THEATER

Aoi no ue
"Lady Aoi" written by Mishima Yukio, acted and directed by Miwa Akihiro (left).

Aohigekō no shiro
"Bluebeard's Castle" written by Terayama Shūji, directed by Ryūzanji Show.

Ronald Cavaye
Paul Griffith
Akihiko Senda

Foreword by Mansai Nomura

CONTENTS

KYŌGEN

Susugigawa
The mother-in-law (center) stands between the fearsome wife (left) and her henpecked husband.

Tōzumō
The Japanese wrestler (left) fights a Chinese wrestler.

Gansaku sakura no mori no mankai no shita

"A Fake: Under the Cherry Forest in Full Bloom," written and directed by Noda Hideki.

Ninagawa's Hamlet

The famous tragedy directed by Ninagawa Yukio was a hit in London, too.

Kawa no hotori

"The River's Edge," Dairaku-dakan's performance.

FOREWORD

by Nomura Mansai

As a professional of the Japanese theater I would like to say how pleased I am to see the publication of *A Guide to the Japanese Stage*. The world of Japanese theater today presents a very complex picture. With their beginnings in Gagaku and Bugaku, whose traditions stem from the Asian continent, the classical performing arts developed with Nō, Kyōgen, Bunraku, and Kabuki, from which many new theatrical styles, such as Western-style drama and the so-called underground theater, have evolved. Each,

Nomura Mansai as Tarōkaja in *Suō otoshi.*

while maintaining its own tradition, coexists in a mutually influential way. The publication of a book that can take an overview of this context in an easily understandable manner is of great significance both in Japan and abroad.

Nomura Mansai as Kurokusa no Tarōkaja (center) in *Machigai no kyōgen*.

Many overseas visitors to Japan have the impression that Japanese theater is all about Kabuki. I would like to dispel that myth. There is, in fact, a wide variety of performing arts staged in all kinds of theaters, large and small, mostly centered on Tokyo. Through appreciating the many-faceted attractions of Japanese theater, I hope people from around the world may also get a feeling for what Japanese culture is really like today.

Of course, irrespective of whether audiences are Japanese or from different cultural backgrounds, we writers, directors, and performers must direct our efforts into ensuring that we present works of high quality. One area in which we must strive to do this is by creating joint productions that surpass each individual genre. At my own base of activity at the Setagaya Public Theatre I try to embrace many different methodologies and talented people in order to foster new mutual exchanges. I can liken my policy to weaving the vertical "warp" of the established Japanese performing arts with the horizontal "woof" of the emerging talent, and gradually I hope to reflect this in my performance programs.

Nomura Mansai as Oedipus Rex in *Oidipusuō*.

The relationship between actors and audiences is paramount. When I wonder why it is that people gather at a theater, I feel sure it must be for some essential purpose that many theater forms have in common. One could say it is a kind of "truth." And whether it is the minimalism of Nō and Kyōgen, for example, or the striking ornamentation of Kabuki, or even the provocative performance styles of the avant-garde, one of Japanese theater's most powerful weapons is its wide range of methods of approach. This not only guarantees diversity of expression, but also allows it to meet the diverse needs of audiences. This has ultimately enabled it to be sent out and understood throughout the world.

The theater of Japan is, even now, evolving by the moment. Through the publication of this book, I hope that readers will acquire an appreciation of our country's performing arts as well as of its artists, and that it will encourage you to visit the theater to witness this evolution for yourself.

Nomura Mansai is a Kyōgen actor and artistic director of Setagaya Public Theatre.

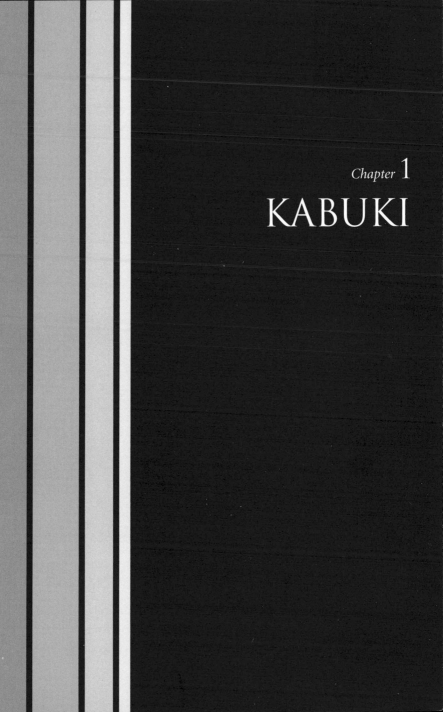

Chapter 1

KABUKI

KABUKI
SONG, DANCE, AND ACTING

The Kabuki theater has been at the forefront of Japanese popular culture for four hundred years. Some existing works date as far back as the late seventeenth century, but the major part of the repertoire was written and first performed in the eighteenth and nineteenth centuries. Performance styles vary between the older, stylized period dramas and the more realistic plays portraying contemporary life in feudal Japan. Some works are pure dance and others pure dialogue, while many are a combination of the two.

Kabuki is played solely by male actors and most of the plays and dances in the

Ichikawa Danjūrō VI as Omasa's elder brother Ganpei. By Utagawa Kunimasa I, 1797. (P. Griffith Collection)

classical repertoire are performed to on- and offstage musical accompaniment. One may also see more recent, or even brand new, realistic dramas with either pre-recorded music or no music at all. In its essence, however,

Ka-bu-ki (歌舞伎), written today with the three characters that mean "song," "dance," and "acting," is an art form combining very different disciplines that would in most other cases be performed separately.

SONG

Kabuki's roots lie in musical theater. Evidence of this ranges from the onstage accompaniment by singers and players of drums, flutes, and, most importantly, of the three-stringed shamisen, to the subtle offstage background music provided by the *geza* musicians who add immeasurably to the atmosphere and emotion of any scene. Kabuki actors of rank receive strict musical training from early youth and, while they may not need to sing or play instruments on stage themselves except in very special cases, this background is considered essential to a proper understanding of the art. In the case of dances, of course, music and especially song are of vital importance.

DANCE

Often from as young as three, Kabuki actors also study traditional Japanese dance called *Nihon buyō*. Dances make up around one third of the existing repertoire, and while some are more skilled than others, all Kabuki actors are to some degree also dancers. Kabuki, in fact, began as dance and the earliest records, dating from a little after 1600, show troupes of female entertainers dancing in a circle. Over the years, Kabuki evolved away from these primitive entertainments into a highly complex and sophisticated art.

A characteristic of most Kabuki dances we see today is their specific dramatic content. Many were created as parts of longer plays, and in some way they reflect the stories of these plays in their subject matter. Even when there is no particular story to tell, the dancer will still be in character, portraying a wide variety of people, from the great court lady to the humble street peddler. While the beauty of pure form and melody is also very important, the existence of song lyrics ensure, most of the time, that there is also something for the dancer to enact. For this reason, there is a very close connection between dance and the literal meaning of the text, and Kabuki dance is never entirely divorced from acting.

ACTING

The remaining two thirds of the repertoire is made up of plays, and Kabuki is above all a theater of its actors. One never forgets the actor behind the role. Perhaps one of the most remarkable features for the first-time spectator is the *onnagata*— male actors who specialize in female roles. As part of their training, all young Kabuki actors have to learn the basic movement patterns, postures, and speech

Shinodazuma nagori no kowakare, staged at the Ichimura-za. Kuzunoha: Segawa Rokō III (Kikunojō III). By Utagawa Toyokuni I, 1802. (P. Griffith Collection)

of typical male and female roles. While some versatile actors continue to perform both male and female characters later on in their careers, most specialize in one or the other. A similar tradition of men playing women's roles also exists in China and other countries such as India, and in Japan, too, it continues to flourish as a high art form.

Kabuki, the theater of the ordinary townspeople of feudal Japan, continues today to draw large and appreciative audiences both at home and on tour abroad.

HISTORY

OKUNI AND *ONNA KABUKI*

For over four hundred years Kabuki has remained a major form of artistic expression for Japan's mercantile, urban societies. Essentially it has always been a popular theater, reflecting not just the fashions and cultural tastes of the people, but also the political and socioeconomic conditions of each age through which it has evolved.

Following centuries of civil war that ravaged the country, the ascendancy of the Tokugawa shogunate at the beginning of the seventeenth century at last brought peace in the form of a centralized military dictatorship. The shogun maintained his power by an unforgiving, hierarchical control of nearly all aspects of Japanese society. With the samurai at the top, the class system descended through farmers and craftsmen and finally to merchants, the latter despised particularly for their association with such vulgar matters as usury and trade.

Below even the merchants, however, came an underclass known as *hinin* ("non-humans"), or *kawara mono* ("objects of the riverbed"). These were people who had either dropped out of society or whose professions were concerned with matters which were considered unclean, such

Painted screen of *Okuni Kabuki*. Early 17th century. (Kyoto National Museum)

as butchers or tanners. Actors and prostitutes were included in this underclass as they, too, were thought to be no better than social pariahs.

Shrines and temples had traditionally sent out groups of priests and nuns for the purpose of spreading religion and collecting funds. By the end of the sixteenth century, however, groups of these nuns had degenerated into traveling entertainers, and some were also involved in prostitution.

A performance in 1603 on the dried-up riverbed of the Kamo River in Kyoto is the first record we have of a woman by the name of Okuni, reputedly a *miko* or shrine maiden from the great shrine at Izumo, and her troupe of female dancers. Illustrations on painted screens show such troupes dancing in a large circle in a secularized version of *nenbutsu odori*, an older and joyous form of a Buddhist prayer dance. Okuni was also socially provocative in that she sometimes dressed as a man, and seems to have worn elements of Portuguese dress adopted from early missionaries and even a crucifix.

Music at this stage was fairly primitive, the instruments consisting originally of hand drums and stick drums borrowed from the Nō theater. In time, the performers also adopted the new three-stringed instrument called the shamisen, imported from China about fifty years earlier.

This early period of Kabuki is known as *onna kabuki* ("women's Kabuki"), or *yūjo kabuki* ("prostitute Kabuki"). As well as dances, simple skits also appear to have been performed showing the process of negotiating with a prostitute. The erotic overtones of these early Kabuki performances were a deliberate attempt both to titillate the audience and to advertise the girls themselves.

At the time, *kabuku* was a word employed to describe something considered slanted, offbeat, and eccentric. The overall strangeness of these early Kabuki performances was such that they came to be described as *kabuku* or *kabuki mono* ("strange things").

WAKASHU KABUKI

The shogunate considered the great popularity of these performers a threat to order in the public realm as well as within their own ranks, and in 1629 they prohibited women from appearing on the stage.

Troupes of young boy entertainers were also in existence as rivals to *onna kabuki*, their performances characterized by simple skits, dances, and acrobatics. In feudal Japan the coming-of-age for a young man was signified by shaving the forelock and setting the hair in the samurai style of the day. With the disappearance of women from public performances, boys who still possessed their forelocks now took center stage, and this period has come to be known as *wakashu kabuki* ("young men's Kabuki").

The most significant development during this period was the need for some of the actors to play the female roles. This saw the early beginnings of the art of the *onnagata* female role specialists. However, the natural beauty of some of the young boys made such specialization far easier at this time than it was soon to become.

There was certainly a homoerotic element to these performances and once again, in 1652, the shogunate prohibited their appearance. Homosexuality was officially forbidden but traditionally tolerated. However, the reason for the government's ban was the threat to public order caused by the large numbers of men who gathered to admire the boys and, perhaps, to pay for their services.

YARŌ KABUKI

The prohibition did not extend to more mature men with shaven forelocks, and so Kabuki continued from this time with just the older male actors. This period of mature male Kabuki came to be called *yarō kabuki* and it marked the beginning of a slow and gradual change from review-like dancing and skits toward greater emphasis on serious drama. Homoerotic elements did not, of course, disappear, but a move toward real artistic content became necessary.

The original makeshift river bed stages also gradually developed into purpose-built theaters, initially very similar to those employed for Nō.

By the end of the seventeenth century we see clear divisions between the *onnagata* actors and the male-role players. Even within these broad categories there was increasing specialization, with certain actors playing, for example, elderly women, clowns, or villain roles almost exclusively.

The art of the *onnagata*, in particular, developed out of necessity as the older actors could no longer rely solely on their youth and beauty, and adopted stylized gestures and a falsetto vocal production in imitation of real women. The first great *onnagata* was Yoshizawa Ayame I (1673–1729), and from contemporary writings both by and about

him we know a lot about these early actors. Many, including Ayame, lived their lives both on and off the stage as women—even, it is said, entering the female side of the public bathhouse!

Dance had been one of the mainstays of Kabuki ever since the time of Okuni. After the development of *yarō kabuki*, it increasingly came to be the province of the *onnagata*, for whom dancing was considered central to the expression of femininity and even eroticism. Furthermore, in plays, just as in life, female characters tended to be modest and self-effacing, playing a secondary role to their male counterparts. As many of the *onnagata* were both popular and excellent actors, the audiences desired to see them in more prominent positions, and so dances became one area in which *onnagata* could come to the fore.

KAMIGATA AND EDO

In the Kyoto–Osaka region, also called Kamigata, or Kansai, the great actor Sakata Tōjūrō I (1647–1709) established an acting style known as *wagoto*, which applies specifically to a type of leading male role. Tōjūrō emphasized the need for actors to tread the fine line between realism (imitation of the real world) and artistic interpretations of this on stage. Many of the plays in which Tōjūrō starred were stories centering on the hedonistic "floating world" (*ukiyo*) to be found in the licensed pleasure quarters.

While Kabuki was born in the

Kamigata region, it developed a distinctive form in Edo, the old name for Tokyo. While Kyoto had been the home of the refined and cultured imperial court since the end of the eighth century, Edo became the center of the military government under the Tokugawa shogunate, and this essential difference is reflected in the new style of acting that emerged from Edo in the second half of the seventeenth century. A young actor by the name of Ichikawa Danjūrō I (1660–1704) borrowed from the wild antics of a puppet character called Kinpira and made popular the exotic and exciting style of acting known as *aragoto*, or "wild warrior" style. Danjūrō's popularity in Edo grew to such heights that he and his son Danjūrō II (1688–1758) enjoyed a massive following, and on occasion their performances seem to have inspired semireligious fervor.

BUNRAKU AND KABUKI

Ningyō jōruri, the combination of storytelling, music, and puppetry known today as Bunraku, developed toward the end of the sixteenth century. This fusion of three distinct arts created a single new form that reached great heights of artistic achievement. Some of its finest plays were written by the man widely lauded as Japan's greatest playwright, Chikamatsu Monzaemon (1653–1724). Early in his career Chikamatsu also wrote for Kabuki, and between 1693 and 1702

he worked closely with the actor Sakata Tōjūrō. His puppet dramas, however, became very important for both Bunraku and Kabuki.

Takemoto Gidayū (1651–1714) perfected the *ningyō jōruri* style of dramatic narration and singing in which the narrator is accompanied by the shamisen and, together with Chikamatsu, he founded the Takemoto-za puppet theater in Osaka.

At the end of the seventeenth and the beginning of the eighteenth centuries there was a growing preoccupation with realism on stage. This went hand in hand with certain developments in playwriting that saw a vast improvement in the quality of the texts as well as in the basic structure of plays. In this respect, Chikamatsu's contribution was hugely important, and there are even records left by contemporary Confucian scholars that praise his writing for its literary merit.

The Bunraku and Kabuki theaters existed in close proximity and vied

A portrait of Chikamatsu Monzaemon drawn by a pupil just before his death.

with each other for the custom of the townspeople who were their principal supporters. Kabuki also began to adopt the dramas that had been written for the puppets, and these Kabuki adaptations came to be known as *maruhonmono*, or "scroll plays," after their original scroll format.

The practice of coauthorship also became common, and the three full-length dramas (*tōshi kyōgen*) today frequently referred to as the "three great plays" of the Bunraku and Kabuki repertoires—*Sugawara denju tenarai kagami* (1746), *Yoshitsune senbon zakura* (1747), and *Kanadehon chūshingura* (1748)—were written by Takeda Izumo II (1691–1756), Miyoshi Shōraku (1696–1772), and Namiki Senryū (1695– 1751) in collaboration.

Inevitably, Kabuki itself changed under the influence of the puppets. For the first Kabuki performance of *Yoshitsune senbon zakura* at the Naka-mura-za in Edo, the theater even hired puppeteers and musicians from Bunraku to help in rehearsals. The result was that the style of performance in the puppet theater affected that of Kabuki, especially in its timing and movements, and even such things as the stage machinery were copied. Perhaps most importantly, however, the *jōruri* style of musical narration was also adopted by Kabuki for all plays taken from the puppet theater.

Perhaps the most important writer after Chikamatsu Monzaemon was Namiki Senryū. Originally known as

Namiki Sōsuke, he was the leading playwright of the Toyotake-za until 1741, but then he joined the Takemoto-za and changed his name to Namiki Senryū. It was during this time that he collaborated with Takeda Izumo II and Miyoshi Shōraku, and although Izumo was actually the leading writer of the Takemoto-za, it is thought that Senryū had a strong influence on their compositions. Apart from the three great plays mentioned earlier, other works that this group produced include *Natsu matsuri Naniwa kagami* and *Futatsu chōchō kuruwa nikki*. In 1750, Senryū returned to the Toyotake-za and changed his name back to Namiki Sōsuke, and in the following year, 1751, he wrote the masterpiece *Ichinotani futaba gunki*.

The writing style of playwrights such as Namiki Senryū was important because it successfully mixed together the tradition of epic narrative with the idea of living drama. Historical characters were treated with greater psychological depth and were brought to life in a more convincing manner than before. In many of these works we see the very real emotional struggle and self-sacrifice that was demanded by the military dictatorship in pre-modern Japan.

The next great playwright was Chikamatsu Hanji (1725–83), who became a pupil of Takeda Izumo II at the Takemoto-za but who gradually rose to prominence in his own right, becoming the leading playwright of that theater in 1762. From his pen came such masterpieces as *Honchō nijūshikō* and *Imoseyama onna teikin*. Despite these successes, however, the puppet theater declined in popularity toward the end of the eighteenth century, ultimately giving way to the dominance of the Kabuki theater.

THE GOLDEN AGE

The latter half of the Edo period (1603–1868) was a golden age for Kabuki. During this relatively peaceful era in Japan's history the townspeople, despised by the samurai class, became increasingly powerful in economic terms. Kabuki actors, too, though still officially "objects of the riverbed," had become wealthy stars admired for their skills and personalities.

When the Osaka playwright Namiki Gohei I (1747–1808) moved to Edo in 1794, he introduced several innovations to that city's theater, including the custom of separating the day's program into two distinct plays, the first a *jidaimono* and the second a *sewamono*, as well as a more concise writing style than was usual in Edo. He helped to raise the status of playwrights and his works displayed a greater realism and rationality than had been seen before. From his brush came such masterpieces as the influential *Godairiki koi no fūjime* of 1795.

The most celebrated playwright to emerge during this time was Tsuruya Nanboku IV (1755–1829), whose works exploited Kabuki's potential to the full. Writing for the finest actors,

Nanboku is credited with developing the *kizewamono* category of plays portraying the decadence, harshness, cruelty, and sensuality of the lower stratum of Edo period society. He also popularized stage tricks (*keren*) such as flying, and the *kaidanmono* category of ghost plays.

The wealth of the theaters meant they could afford lavish costumes and sets, and both actors and playwrights became more daring in what they attempted to achieve. This in turn increased the audience's expectancy.

Traditionally, star actors had always had great influence on the plays in which they performed, and some such as Danjūrō I, even wrote their own scripts. In 1840 Ichikawa Danjūrō VII (1791–1859) produced a play called *Kanjinchō*, which was the first of the *matsubamemono* adaptations of plays from Nō and Kyōgen. This formed the beginning of his collection of plays known as the *kabuki jūhachiban*— "eighteen favorite plays"—which celebrated the achievements of his family acting line. This also established the precedent for later collections by other star actors.

Later in the century, the works of Kawatake Mokuami (1816–93), in particular, were to be extremely influential in broadening the Kabuki repertoire. Mokuami was a prolific playwright who is most celebrated for his creation of the *shiranamimono* genre which portrays, and even glamorizes, the lives of thieves. His contribution to the world of Kabuki dance lyrics is also very important, although frequently overlooked.

DEVELOPMENTS FROM THE MEIJI PERIOD (1868–1912) TO THE PRESENT

With the overthrow of the shogunate and restoration of the emperor in 1868 came a surge of interest in the modern, largely Western-influenced cultural world. The destruction of the old feudal class system left both Nō and Kyōgen bereft of their daimyo and samurai patrons. Kabuki, however, remained as popular as ever, and its actors found new status and modern-day stardom. Edo period audiences had clamored for new and exciting plays, and the theater was an integral part of the lives of many men and women. In the new modern world other excitements were to be found, but Kabuki continued successfully under its new guise as part of Japan's national heritage and as one of its "classical" theaters.

While the established dances and dramas remained the principal bulk of the repertoire, new plays were also added with varying degrees of success. In the Meiji period some attempted a new realism but these never achieved great popularity. In the early twentieth century a movement known as *shin kabuki*, or "New Kabuki," did, however, make a significant contribution to the repertoire through the works of playwrights such as Tsubouchi Shōyō (1859––1935), Okamoto Kidō (1872–1939),

and Mayama Seika (1878–1948).

Edo had been famous for its three great theaters known as the *Edo sanza*, but all were destroyed. The Nakamura-za burned down in 1893, the Great Kantō Earthquake of 1923 destroyed the Morita-za and the last, the Ichimura-za, was also destroyed by fire in 1932. The Kabuki-za became the main Kabuki theater until it too was leveled by the firebombing of World War II, and it was not rebuilt until 1951.

Under the American occupation following the war, all vestiges of the Edo period feudal system were treated with great suspicion because of the influence they were considered to have had on Japan's militarist government. Kabuki at first came under strict censorship for what was perceived as its idealization of this feudal system, but was soon allowed to continue when its true artistic standards came to be understood and appreciated.

Although Kabuki had previously traveled abroad (notably to Russia in 1928), a tour of the United States in 1960 was groundbreaking and led to numerous international tours, all performed to great critical acclaim. The appreciation of Kabuki by foreign audiences and scholars has contributed to its position as one of the world's great theatrical arts.

KABUKI TODAY

Today Kabuki flourishes in the hands of many fine actors, and classical Kabuki is very well-attended both in

Japan and on foreign tours. In addition to the standard repertoire, some actors are making serious and scholarly efforts to revive plays from Kabuki's earlier years. Nakamura Ganjirō III has dedicated a major part of his career to performances and revivals of the classical works of Chikamatsu Monzaemon, and his theater troupe operates in a variety of venues under the title of the *Chikamatsu-za*.

At the other extreme, in 1986 the popular and renowned actor Ichikawa Ennosuke III launched his so-called "Super Kabuki," which has had considerable success with people who are not usually attracted to classical theater. These plays, mostly rewritings of traditional themes or stories, are all designed to highlight Ennosuke's talents, often in many different roles within the same play. They use elaborate costumes and modern recorded music, and are in a mixture of styles with heavy Chinese, Indian and other Asian influences. The first was *Yamatotakeru*.

The leading *onnagata* Bandō Tamasaburō V has also shown himself receptive to foreign influences, both traditional and new. While preparing for the modern play *Gensō to Yōkihi*, staged at the Shinbashi Enbujō Theater in 1987, Tamasaburō traveled to China to study under one of Peking Opera's most famous female role specialists, Mei Bao Jiu, who taught him the well-known role of Yōkihi. After the great success of Tamasaburō's performance of this in Tokyo, he commissioned a brand new dance called *Yōkihi* featuring the same character and incorporating aspects of Peking Opera's costumes and techniques, though mixing it also with more traditional aspects of Kabuki, which has now become an established part of the Kabuki repertoire.

Not to be outdone, Nakamura Kankurō V, from a long line of actors and managers, and soon to succeed to his father's highly prestigious name, Kanzaburō, has revived the Nakamura-za theater troupe. Under the name Heisei Nakamura-za, their performances in Tokyo are staged in a small portable marquee, attempting to give modern audiences a taste of the atmosphere of Edo period Kabuki, albeit with some surprising and experimental touches. Kankurō took this theater and troupe to New York in 2004.

More recently, the playwright and director Noda Hideki, from outside the world of Kabuki, has also achieved great popular success with his adaptations of Kabuki plays. His *Noda-ban Togitatsu no utare* and *Noda-ban Nezumi Kozō* have brought a new avant-garde flavor to staging and sets. Meanwhile, the Kabuki actor Matsumoto Kōshirō IX has also had critical acclaim with the *Rien-za* series about the legendary actor, Nakamura Nakazō I.

Treated with some disdain by traditional Kabuki fans, the ultimate fate of these hybrid productions remains to be seen. The immediate future of classical Kabuki, however, does seem assured.

KABUKI IN PICTURES

Wagoto
Disowned by his family, Izaemon is reduced to wearing a paper kimono stitched together from old love letters in the play *Kuruwa bunshō*. Fujiya Izaemon: Bandō Mitsugorō IV. Performed at the Nakamura-za in the 9th month, 1832. By Utagawa Kunisada I. (Tokyo National Theatre)

Aragoto
The captured Heike general Kagekiyo breaks out of prison and defeats a group of enemy men in the *kabuki jūhachiban* play *Kagekiyo*. His makeup, costume, and wig are all typical of the *aragoto* performance style. Kagekiyo: Ichikawa Danjūrō V. From a series of portraits of famous actors past and present, 1863. By Utagawa Toyokuni III. (P. Griffith Collection)

Jidaimono

The magic fox Genkurō (left) is drawn by the sound of the drum in Act IV of *Yoshitsune senbon zakura*. The actor jumps out of a shamisen played by the onstage *gidayū* musician, an example of *keren* stage trickery. Genkurō fox: Ichikawa Kodanji IV; Shizuka: Bandō Shūka; Yoshitsune: Ichikawa Danjūrō VIII. Performed at the Ichimura-za in the 3rd month, 1848. By Utagawa Toyokuni III. (P. Griffith Collection)

Sewamono

The merchant Jirōzaemon murders Yatsuhashi, the courtesan he once loved, with the sword named *Kagotsurube* in the final scene of *Kagotsurube sato no eizame*, performed at the Chitose-za in the 5th month, 1888. Sano Jirōzaemon: Ichikawa Sadanji I; Yatsuhashi: Nakamura Fukusuke IV. By Toyohara Kunichika. (Tokyo National Theatre)

Sawamura Sōjūrō III as the Satsuma retainer Gengobei, the hero of *Godairiki koi no fūjime*. One of the most famous actors of his day, Sōjūrō died in the 3rd month, 1801 and this print, with a poem by his wife, must have been published shortly after as a memorial. By Utagawa Toyokuni I. (P. Griffith Collection)

The hero Danshichi Kurōbei, stripped to his loincloth and showing his magnificent tattoos, fights and kills his evil father-in-law Giheiji in the final scene of *Natsumatsuri Naniwa kagami*. Danshichi: Onoe Shōroku II. No. 12 of the series *Gendai butai geika* ("Flowers of the Modern Stage"), 1955. By Ōta Gakō, also called Masamitsu. (P. Griffith Collection)

Shosagoto

The *hengemono* dance *Shiki no nagame yosete mitsudai*, performed at the Nakamura-za in the 3rd month, 1813 by Bandō Mitsugorō III. The entire dance included twelve sections each representing a different month of the year, and the first six are shown here. By Utagawa Toyokuni I. (P. Griffith Collection)

A pair of *shishi* lion spirits dance with branches of peony in the snow. *Yuki no shakkyō* represented the twelfth of twelve months in a *hengemono* dance called *Hana kyōdai nenjū gyōji* performed at the Ichimura-za in the 3rd month, 1840. Red-haired *shishi*: Ichimura Uzaemon XII; white-haired *shishi*: Nakamura Utaemon IV. By Utagawa Kunisada I. (P. Griffith Collection)

Dressed in her finery, the "wisteria maiden" makes an outing to view the blossoms. One of five sections in the *hengemono* dance *Kaesu gaesu o-nagori Ōtsu-e*, this was the first performance of *Fuji musume* at the Naka-mura-za in 1826. The wisteria maiden: Seki Sanjūrō III. By Utagawa Kunisada I. (P. Griffith Collection)

The barrier guard Sekibei (in reality the evil courtier Ōtomo no Kuronushi) points at the lovely figure of Princess Komachi during the *mondō* "question and answer" section of *Tsumoru koi yuki no seki no to*, performed at the Kabuki-za in the 2nd month, 1897. Sekibei: Ichikawa Danjūrō IX. By Toyohara Kunichika. (P. Griffith Collection)

Kabuki Jūhachiban

Benkei hides the fake subscription scroll from Togashi as Yoshitsune looks on nervously at the start of the improvised "reading" in *Kanjinchō*, performed at the Kabuki-za in the 4th month, 1907. Yoshitsune: Nakamura Shikan V; Benkei: Ichikawa Komazō VIII; Togashi: Ichimura Uzaemon XV. By Baidō Hōsai. (R. Cavaye Collection)

The handsome dandy Sukeroku arrives in the pleasure quarter sporting his purple *hachimaki* headband. The actor's dance-like entrance along the *hanamichi* includes a series of magnificent poses with the umbrella. *Sukeroku yukari no Edo zakura* was performed by Ichikawa Danjūrō IX at the Kabuki-za in the 4th month, 1896. By Torii Tadakiyo. (R. Cavaye Collection)

Dōjōjimono

During the solemn "bell" section of the dance *Musume Dōjōji*, the spirit of Kiyohime listens to the toll of the temple bell. Kiyohime: Onoe Kiku-gorō VI. Painting on silk by Natori Shunsen. (P. Griffith Collection)

In the play *Narukami*, the high priest of that name is tricked by the court lady Taema and vows to transform into a bolt of lightning to get his revenge. Narukami: Ichikawa Sadanji III, from the series *Shunsen nigao-e shū*, 1926. By Natori Shunsen. (P. Griffith Collection)

Kaidanmono

The ghost of the murdered serving lady Okiku returns to haunt her former master in the play *Sarayashiki keshō no sugatami*, performed at the Kabuki-za in the 10th month, 1892. Okiku: Onoe Kikugorō V; Asayama Tetsuzan: Ichikawa Danjūrō IX. By Toyohara Kunichika. (P. Griffith Collection)

The grotesque apparition of Princess Osakabe appears before the brave warrior Takakage at Himeji Castle, the ghost scene from the play *Matazoro Shōroku Osakabe banashi*, performed at the Ichimura-za in the 5th month, 1814. Osakabehime: Onoe Shōroku I; Hayakawa Takakage: Ichikawa Danjūrō VII. By Utagawa Kunisada I. (R. Cavaye Collection)

Shiranamimono

The thief Benten Kozō reveals himself to be a man with bright tattoos on his left arm as he declares his true identity in the play *Benten musume meo no shiranami*, performed at the Kabuki-za in 1995. Benten Kozō: Onoe Kikugorō VII. By Tsuruya Kōkei. (R. Cavaye Collection)

Katsurekimono

Actor and theater reformer Danjūrō IX strove for historical accuracy and greater realism in his *katsureki* ("living history") plays such as *Momoyama monogatari* performed at the Ichimura-za in the 8th month, 1869. Katō Masakiyo: Kawarasaki Mimasu (Danjūrō IX). By Toyohara Kunichika. (P. Griffith Collection)

Shin kabuki

Yodogimi, widow of warlord Toyotomi Hideyoshi, becomes increasingly mad as her family line is wiped out in *Hototogisu kojō no rakugetsu*. Playwright Tsubouchi Shōyō was influenced by Western theater, and especially by Shakespeare plays like *Macbeth*. Yodogimi: Nakamura Utaemon V, from the series *Shunsen nigao-e shū*, 1926. By Natori Shunsen. (P. Griffith Collection)

Aragoto

The young superhero (left) challenges the evil courtier who plans to take over the country, a *kugeaku* role type, in an unstaged version of the play *Shibaraku*. Two of the most famous actors of their age and fierce rivals in real life, Ichikawa Danjūrō VII poses with Onoe Kikugorō III, c. 1825–28. By Utagawa Kunisada. (P. Griffith Collection)

Jitsuaku

The evil retainer Nikki Danjō exercises occult powers as he plots to overthrow his lord in the play *Meiboku sendai hagi*. The actor nicknamed Hanataka Kōshirō, "big-nosed Kōshirō," made this role his own and to this day many actors still wear a mole on their foreheads in his honor. Nikki Danjō: Matsumoto Kōshirō V. From a series of portraits of famous actors past and present, 1863. By Utagawa Toyokuni III. (P. Griffith Collection)

Iroaku

The wicked yet handsome Tamiya Iemon (right), who poisons his own wife, is an example of the *iroaku* role type in *Tōkaidō Yotsuya kaidan*, performed at the Kabuki-za in the 6th month, 1983. Tamiya Iemon: Kataoka Takao; Naosuke Gonbei: Onoe Tatsunosuke I. By Tsuruya Kōkei. (P. Griffith Collection)

Nimaime

An example of a *nimaime* role, the gentle and handsome Akaneya Hanshichi commits a lovers' double suicide with the geisha Sankatsu, leaving behind his loyal wife Osono, in the play *Hadesugata onna maiginu*. Hanshichi: Nakamura Ganjirō I, 1920. By Yamamura Kōka, also called Toyonari. (P. Griffith Collection)

Wagoto

The *wagoto* character Chūbei returns to his home, the snow-covered village of *Ninokuchi*, as he escapes from the authorities with his lover in the *Ninokuchi mura* scene from *Koi bikyaku Yamato ōrai*, performed at the Kabuki-za in the 11th month, 1982. Kameya Chūbei: Nakamura Ganjirō II. By Tsuruya Kōkei. (P. Griffith Collection)

Sabakiyaku

Judge Katsumoto, an example of a *sabakiyaku* role, displays shrewd intelligence and tact as he exposes Nikki Danjō's evil plot. From Act IV of *Haji momiji ase no kaomise*, commonly called *Date no jūyaku*, performed at the Kawarasaki-za in the 7th month, 1815. Hosokawa Katsumoto: Ichikawa Danjūrō VII. By Utagawa Kunisada I. (P. Griffith Collection)

Jitsugoto

An example of a *jitsugoto* role, chief retainer and leader of the forty-seven rōnin, Ōboshi Yuranosuke, leaves his master's estate and secretly vows to take revenge in Act IV of *Kanadehon chūshingura*. Ōboshi: Ichikawa Sadanji III. No. 9 of the series *Gendai Butai Geika*, 1955. By Ōta Gakō, also called Masamitsu. (P. Griffith Collection)

Akahime

One of the three most difficult *akahime* "princess" roles in Kabuki, Yukihime holds a sword in a brocade cover that is her family's heirloom in the *Kinkakuji* scene from *Gion sairei shinkōki*. Yukihime: Nakamura Utaemon VI, 1951. By Kawase Hasui. (P. Griffith Collection)

Baba

One of the three greatest "old woman" roles (*sanbaba*), Mimyō clutches her deceased husband's sword as she upholds her family's honor in *Moritsuna jinya*, an act from *Ōmi Genji senjin yakata* performed at the Kabuki-za in 1986. Mimyō: Jitsukawa Enjaku III. By Tsuruya Kōkei. (R. Cavaye Collection)

Akuba

Wearing the typical costume and hairstyle of the *akuba* role type, the evil woman Ohyaku grasps a kitchen knife in the play *Zenaku ryōmen komete gashiwa*, performed at the Ichimura-za in the 5th month, 1867. Dakki no Ohyaku: Onoe Kikugorō V. By Toyohara Kunichika. (V. L. Durham Collection)

Keisei

The *keisei*, "high-ranking courtesan," is the most spectacular of *onnagata* roles. In the play *Dannoura kabuto gunki*, the brave Akoya, lover of the Heike general Kagekiyo, is captured and interrogated by the enemy. Matsue performed the role at the Nakamura-za in the 9th month, 1814. From the series of stage successes *Ōatari kyōgen no uchi*, published c. 1815. Akoya: Nakamura Matsue III. By Utagawa Kunisada I. (R. Cavaye Collection)

The *keisei* Yatsuhashi begins to laugh at the countrified merchant Jirōzaemon as she parades through the streets of the Shin Yoshiwara pleasure quarter, the opening scene from the play *Kagotsurube sato no eizame*. Yatsuhashi: Nakamura Utaemon VI. No. 2 of the series *Gendai Butai Geika*, 1954. By Ōta Gakō, also called Masamitsu. (P. Griffith Collection)

Nyōbo

The fox Kuzunoha takes on the guise of a loyal and industrious wife, the *sewa nyōbo* role type, until circumstances force her tragically to reveal her true identity and return to the wild. Act IV of *Oku zashiki*. Kuzunoha Kitsune: Segawa Kikunojō III. From a series of portraits of actors past and present, 1863. By Utagawa Toyokuni III. (P. Griffith Collection)

A loyal samurai's wife, Tonase, takes over responsibility for her daughter's marriage as she grasps her husband's sword in Act IX of *Kanadehon chūshingura*, performed at the kabuki-za in the 11th month, 1984. Tonase: Nakamura Utaemon VI. By Tsuruya Kōkei. (P. Griffith Collection)

Musume

A famous *machi musume*, "town maiden" role, the greengrocer's daughter Oshichi started a fire that nearly consumed the city of Edo in order to be with her lover Kichisaburō. This was one of Hanshirō's most celebrated triumphs which he first performed at the Morita-za in the 3rd month, 1809 in *Sono mukashi koi no edozome*. From the series of stage successes *Ōatari kyōgen no uchi*, c. 1815. Yaoya Oshichi: Iwai Hanshirō V. By Utagawa Kunisada I. (P. Griffith Collection)

Yakusha-e

Kabuki *yakusha-e*—literally, "actor pictures"—are one of the main subjects depicted in *ukiyo-e*, or "pictures of the floating world." *Yakusha-e* artists were an integral part of the world of Kabuki. For centuries the theater provided stories and star actors to be illustrated, as well as a ready market for their pictures among the theater-going public. *Yakusha-e* also served as vital publicity for the theater.

While in exile, Lord Sugawara Michizane (also called Kan Shōjō) learns details of his enemy's plans to usurp the throne. In his rage, he undergoes a frightening transformation as he vows to ascend Mt. Tenpai and become a thunderbolt so that his spirit can return to the capital. This is the fourth act of *Sugawara denju tenarai kagami*. Kan Shōjō: Sawamura Sōjūrō V, from a series of portraits of famous actors past and present, 1860. By Utagawa Toyokuni III. (P. Griffith Collection)

PLAYS

The simple skits of early Kabuki gradually developed into real plays largely through the work of two great actors: Sakata Tōjūrō in the *Kamigata* region and Ichikawa Danjūrō in Edo.

WAGOTO

Some of Kabuki's earliest skits had portrayed the ruinously expensive fashion of visiting the pleasure quarters and hopefully gaining the favors of a high-ranking courtesan (a practice known as *keiseikai*, literally "courtesan buying"). Tōjūrō capitalized on the public's fascination with *keiseikai* and, with his *wagoto* style, he portrayed the sort of young and handsome men who could afford this extraordinary indulgence. These men were often also rather foppish, pampered, slightly effeminate, and faintly comical. The stories about the celebrated courtesan Yūgiri, in particular, were very popular and the role of her lover, Izaemon, became Tōjūrō's most celebrated.

Wagoto costumes and makeup are simply stylized versions of real life, and the action portrays the emotions of a young man in love. *Wagoto* men also have a comic side, which can be seen in the petty jealousies and mock anger that Izaemon displays when things are not going his way. The great *wagoto* play is *Kuruwa bunshō*, and Jihei from *Shinjū ten no Amijima* is another famous *wagoto* character.

ARAGOTO

Meanwhile, the favorite of the citizens of Edo was the young actor Ichikawa Danjūrō I. He called his exotic and exciting style of acting *aragoto* (short for *aramushagoto* or "wild-warrior style"), and is said to have based it on a puppet character called Kinpira, whose violent antics were very popular. Some of the fearsome poses he adopted when playing *aragoto* characters were almost certainly also influenced by Buddhist statuary like the frightening deity, Fudō Myōō.

Danjūrō used the style to portray superheroes and villains, and he made his whole performance—costume, makeup, vocal delivery, and acting style—larger than life. Typically, *aragoto* characters paint their faces with broad lines of makeup called *kumadori* to increase their fearsome appearances, and some wear outlandishly large padded costumes and fantastic wigs. At the same time, Danjūrō also invented wildly exaggerated modes of acting such as the glaring, stop-motion poses called *mie*, and the dramatic, swaggering entrances and exits called *roppō*.

Aragoto heroes behave as one would

Kabuki jūhachiban

In 1840 the popular actor Ichikawa Danjūrō VII produced and starred in a play that he advertised as *jūhachiban no uchi*—"from the eighteen favorite plays". This play, *Kanjinchō*, became the first of a collection that Danjūrō based on the Ichikawa family's acting traditions. These plays were to be representative of the *ie no gei* or "family art" of the Ichikawa line. Naturally, most of the plays he chose are in the *aragoto* style and were first performed by Danjūrō I, II, and IV. The most popular of the *jūhachiban* still regularly performed are *Kanjinchō*, *Sukeroku*, *Shibaraku*, *Narukami*, *Uirō uri* and *Yanone*. Most of the original scripts of these plays have been lost and the majority was revived (in part rewritten) during the twentieth century.

Later, other actors followed Danjūrō's example with the *Shin (new) kabuki jūhachiban* of Danjūrō IX (consisting, in fact, of thirty-two works in total and including the dances *Kagami jishi*, *Funa Benkei*, and *Momijigari*,) and the *Shinko engeki jusshu*, "Ten Types of Old and New Plays" of Onoe Kikugorō V and VI (including *Tsuchigumo* and *Ibaraki*).

Although these lists of plays may be the specialties of a particular acting line, it is not uncommon for actors from other families to perform them.

PLAY TITLE	FIRST STAGED
Fuwa ("Fuwa Banzaemon")	1680
Fudō ("The Deity Fudō")	1697
Gedatsu ("The Release of Kagekiyo's Soul")	1760
Jayanagi ("The Snake Weeping Willow")	1763
Kagekiyo ("General Kagekiyo")	1732
Kamahige ("Scythe Beard")	1774
Kanjinchō ("The Subscription Scroll")	1702
Kan'u ("General Kan'u")	1737
Kenuki ("The Tweezers")	1742

PLAY TITLE	FIRST STAGED
Nanatsu men ("The Seven Masks")	1740
Narukami ("The Thunder God")	1684
Oshimodoshi ("Devil Pusher")	1727
Shibaraku ("Wait a Moment!")	1697
Sukeroku yukari no Edo zakura ("Sukeroku, Flower of Edo")	1713
Uirō uri ("The Medicine Peddler")	1718
Uwanari ("Jealousy")	1699
Yanone ("The Arrow Head")	1729
Zōhiki ("Pulling the Elephant Apart")	1701

expect of virtuous supermen. Supporting justice and the underdog, even their vocal delivery is hugely distorted as they confront their adversaries with screams of rage. One of the greatest plays in the *aragoto* style is *Shibaraku*, and its central character, now called Kamakura Gongorō Kagemasa is one of the most fantastic. Most of the *kabuki jūhachiban* plays are in the *aragoto* style.

JIDAIMONO, SEWAMONO AND SHOSAGOTO

While *wagoto* and *aragoto* are historically the oldest form of original Kabuki, as the repertoire broadened it became the practice to divide Kabuki plays into one of three principal types: plays set in Japan's historical or legendary past, called *jidaimono*; plays set in a contemporary setting known as *sewamono*; and finally the very important dance category, known as *shosagoto*. Between these three categories there is some overlap, and sometimes all three genres can be seen within the same play. There are also several important subcategories.

JIDAIMONO

Jidai means "period" or "era," while *mono*, "thing," here refers to a play. *Jidaimono* are period plays set in Japan's real or legendary past prior to the Edo period (1600–1868). The "three great plays" of the Bunraku and Kabuki repertoires all fall into this category. With the exception of

minor roles such as servants, farmers, or townspeople, their main characters are almost exclusively upper class nobles, samurai, or priests. When the main characters are seemingly ordinary people, they usually turn out to be important figures in disguise. The sushi shop apprentice Yasuke in *Yoshitsune senbon zakura*, for example, is actually the Heike general Koremori.

Because of the strict censorship imposed by the shogunate, playwrights were forbidden to dramatize real contemporary events that involved the upper classes and that could be interpreted in any way as political. To overcome this they set such stories in previous epochs, one of the most famous examples being the play *Kanadehon chūshingura*, which portrays an incident that in fact took place in 1701–1703 but is set in 1338. Little effort, however, seems to have been exerted to disguise the true source. The fictional name Ōboshi Yuranosuke, for example, would hardly have been a successful camouflage for the historical character, Ōishi Kuranosuke.

Jidaimono sets and costumes are generally colorful and sometimes spectacular, while the acting style is less realistic and more stylized. Characteristic Kabuki conventions such as *mie* poses are also common. Unlike the spoken language used in *sewamono*, which is basically that of the time in which it was written, the spoken language of *jidaimono* is more classical and formal.

A full-length *jidaimono* play usually consisted of five acts and took the greater part of a day to perform in its entirety. Today, while full-length dramas (called *tōshi kyōgen*) are still occasionally staged, the practicalities of modern-day theater-going have made the performance of just individual acts far more common. Acts such as *Kumagai jinya* from *Ichinotani futaba gunki*, for example, may be performed very successfully on their own, even if a certain knowledge of what happened in previous scenes would certainly be useful.

SEWAMONO

Written by Chikamatsu Monzaemon in 1703, *Sonezaki shinjū* is generally credited as being the first *sewamono* or "domestic play" written for Bunraku. It was set at the time of writing and dealt with a true incident from the everyday life of its principal audience, the *chōnin* or townspeople of feudal Japan. The play was adapted for Kabuki in 1719. While some earlier seventeenth-century Kabuki plays set in the pleasure quarters could also be called *sewamono*, they depict nothing of the more difficult or sordid sides of real life and were only concerned with the floating world (*ukiyo*) of the pleasure quarters.

Stage sets in *sewamono* are more realistic than in *jidaimono* and speech is typical of the spoken language of the time. Despite some degree of stylization being retained, *sewamono* brought a new level of realism to Kabuki.

As *sewamono* were often inspired by real events that achieved notoriety, murders and violence are sometimes depicted. Among the many famous plays that depict this side of Edo period life are *Shinjū ten no Amijima*, *Natsu matsuri Naniwa kagami*, and *Yowa nasake ukina no yokogushi*, commonly called *Kirare Yosa*.

Sewamono may be further divided into subcategories depending on their subject matter, such as plays dealing with lovers' double suicides, for example, and plays about thieves.

SHOSAGOTO

Often performed in gorgeous costumes and against backdrops of great beauty, dances can be the most visually spectacular items on a Kabuki program. At the same time, with their combination of movement, music, and acting, they can also be profoundly moving, and works such as *Sagi musume* or *Sumidagawa* have attracted worldwide praise for their depth and emotional impact.

Most Kabuki actors begin learning dance before the age of ten and continue to take lessons until they are mature. During this time they will come across nearly every work in the vast repertoire, and it is arguable whether a Kabuki actor trained in this way is ever completely free from the influence of dance movement. Dance is an especially important part of the *onnagata*'s art, and all the top-ranking female role specialists in Kabuki must spend a great deal of time dancing as well as acting.

The Language of the Body

Over hundreds of years, movement in Kabuki dance has developed into a highly expressive language with its own unique vocabulary. Broadly speaking, it can be divided into three basic categories described as *mai*, *odori*, and *furi*, and although these three elements are all usually integrated in any performance, an understanding of these basic principles is useful.

Mai, simply meaning "dance," is a type of movement that can be traced back to the ancient art of Bugaku, the slow and dignified form of dance that accompanies Gagaku music. Bugaku and Gagaku were introduced from China during the eighth century, and reached their greatest popularity with the Japanese aristocracy between the ninth and eleventh centuries. *Mai* is also the principal movement style in the Nō theater, and it is through the influence of Nō that it came to be a major component in popular Kabuki dance. *Mai* refers essentially to circling or rotating movements and is often slow and deliberate. The body is kept rather stiff in a fixed position, with the arms held slightly away from the torso and hips. The body's center of gravity is kept low, with the knees slightly bent, and at least part of the sole of the foot always in contact with the floor. This makes the performer walk by sliding his feet along the ground (*suriashi*). This strong relationship between the dancer and the earth is further emphasized by occasional stamping, another common characteristic that has its roots in ancient religious ceremonial dances in which stamping on the earth was believed to drive away evil spirits and to call forth the gods.

Odori, another word for "dance," refers to a much looser kind of movement in which the body breaks out from the constrictions of *mai*. The arms can swing about more freely, the body can make small jumps, and the movements are generally faster, lighter, and more rhythmical.

Furi refers to gesture and mime. Traditional Japanese dance is performed not just to music, but specifically to song. Lyrics are very important, and the dancer must interpret both the melody and the literal meaning of the sung text. A large vocabulary of gestures has been developed to enable the actor to mime the most common themes found in dance lyrics. The regular spectator soon comes to recognize the gestures for scattering petals or for writing a letter, but a great many other miming gestures exist that are extremely subtle and therefore easily missed.

Not all gestures have a literal meaning, however, and far more important than the "reading" of every action is an appreciation of the delicacy and flow of movement as a whole. In this respect, the dancer's hands are very important.

In particular, for an *onnagata* the hands are considered very expressive of feminine charm, and many dances contain at least one section in which the skillful use of hands is highlighted.

For other sections, dancers will frequently perform with props such as a silk cloth, an umbrella, or most importantly, a fan. Fans of various shapes and sizes are used when miming, or else are thrown up and spun around simply for visual effect. For this purpose the traditional Japanese dance fan has special metal weights inserted at its base. Along with other props, fans also serve to extend the dancer's physical space. The narrow, tubelike Japanese kimono is a physically restricting garment and, with its long sleeves and hem, limits the amount of movement possible. Dancers use props as aids to extend the lines created by the arms and hands, thereby overcoming the physical restrictions of the kimono.

The Lyrics

Dance lyrics are not always great literature, but their wit and frequent allusions to classical poetry and Nō texts attest to a highly refined literary sensibility. The lyrics are the product of an educated urban society that enjoyed the idea of such elegant pursuits as banquets beneath the spring blossoms, or trips to view the autumn moon. The townspeople were sensitive to every passing season and, typically for those in the cities of Edo, Kyoto, or Osaka, they had a somewhat idyllic vision of the countryside. For this reason, most dances are filled with the rich imagery of nature, ranging from the ubiquitous cherry blossom, so often a symbol of life's transience, to the rising autumn mists, or flocks of wild geese alighting in a field, evoking a feeling of loneliness at the end of the day. The vision is usually romantic, and the imagery is often imbued with very human feelings, for it acts as the backdrop against which the human drama of the dance unfolds.

Hengemono

Such was the virtuosity of Kabuki dancers that *hengemono*, or "transformation pieces," became very popular. These consisted of multiple short dances performed by the same actor in quick succession. Early examples, such as *Nanabake kyōshi*, performed by Mizuki Tatsunosuke (1673–1745) in 1697, featured a supernatural character changing into a variety of forms, and it is from this idea of magical transformation that the *hengemono* category gets its name. By the early nineteenth century, however, *hengemono* had broken away from this supernatural theme and the multiple short dances came to be grouped under some other unifying concept. A group of four dances, for example, might illustrate the four seasons, a group of five, the five annual festivals. *Hengemono* reached their height of popularity in the first half of the nineteenth century when rivalry between the actors Bandō Mitsugorō III (1775–1831) and Nakamura Utaemon III (1778–1838) led to the creation of works containing as many as twelve sections. The genre greatly influenced the development of different musical styles, and such conventions as the *hayagawari* "quick-change" of costume. Today, many of these original sections survive as independent dances, such as *Sagi musume* and *Fuji musume*. *Rokkasen*, however, which is made up of five sections, is an example of a *hengemono* still performed in what is close to its entirety.

SOURCES OF PLAYS

Kabuki actors and playwrights found inspiration in a very wide variety of sources. These ranged from major works of classical literature such as the *Heike monogatari* ("The Tale of the Heike"), dating from the early thirteenth century but later much embellished, to contemporary scandals taken from real life. Original plays composed either by the early actors or later playwrights were, however, supplemented by works that were borrowed—often with very little adaptation—from other theater forms such as Bunraku and also Nō and Kyōgen.

ORIGINAL KABUKI

This term refers to a very broad spectrum of plays, covering almost the entire period of Kabuki's history,

which were written originally for Kabuki and do not have their origins in Bunraku, Nō, or Kyōgen. In the early years plays were created either by a single actor, or possibly several working in collaboration, and later by either one or several playwrights.

Examples of original *jidaimono* include the *aragoto* plays *Shibaraku* and *Yanone* (both also included in the *jūhachiban* collection). Original *sewamono* include *Aoto zōshi hana no nishiki-e*, *Kagotsurube sato no eizame* and *Yowa nasake ukina no yokogushi*. Many *shosagoto* (dances pieces) such as *Rokkasen* and *Sagi musume* are also original to Kabuki.

Ichikawa Danjūrō IX as scar-faced Yosa in *Kirare Yosa*. By Toyohara Kunichika, 1898. (P. Griffith Collection)

The Meiji Restoration of 1868 brought with it a dramatic increase in the knowledge of, and interest in, Western theater. Realism took on greater importance, and this resulted in a crop of original new plays largely devoid of the stylizations found in Bunraku, Nō, and Kyōgen derivations. Supported by the intelligentsia of the day, *katsurekimono*, or "living history plays," were created by Ichikawa Danjūrō IX (1838–1903). These plays aimed to present works that were historically accurate as an alternative to the rather fanciful *jidaimono* of classical Kabuki. They were sustained solely by Danjūrō's acting and have been largely forgotten since his death.

The end of the feudal era also saw the abandonment of the shaved crown and topknot hairstyle of the samurai. In Kabuki a further new category of plays known as *zangirimono*, "cropped hair plays," deliberately featured the new Western hairstyles. These plays, performed by Onoe Kikugorō V (1844–1903), were never very popular and none were written after about 1882. Curiously, even though the actors are supposed to be sporting "modern" hairstyles, they still wear wigs and never appear on stage without one. *Katsurekimono* and *zangirimono* are performed only very occasionally today.

MARUHONMONO

These are plays that were originally written for Bunraku and later adapted for Kabuki. The first great commercial success of such an adaptation that led to the practice becoming widespread was that of Chikamatsu Monzaemon's *Kokusenya kassen* in 1716. *Maruhonmono* are usually very similar to the original Bunraku play and always employ the *gidayū* narrator and shamisen player which accompany the puppets. The repertoire is very extensive and includes *Kanadehon chūshingura*, *Sugawara denju tenarai kagami* and *Yoshitsune senbon zakura*, as well as such well-known plays as *Heike nyogo no shima* (commonly known by the name of its principal character, *Shunkan*), *Honchō nijūshikō*, *Ichinotani futaba gunki*, and *Imoseyama onna teikin*.

MATSUBAMEMONO

The play *Kanjinchō* was not only the first of the *jūhachiban* collection, it was also the first Kabuki play to be copied from a Nō play (*Ataka*) with conscious imitation as a motivating factor. It was also the first to make use of the unchanging Nō set of a flat backdrop on which is painted a great pine tree (*matsu*), and gave rise to a new genre of plays called *matsubamemono*, which are all based on Nō or Kyōgen, and which all have the same set. Some of these adaptations are among the most popular plays in the repertoire and most were written during the Meiji and Taishō periods. Examples include *Tsuchigumo* (Nō), *Funa Benkei* (Nō), *Migawari zazen* (Kyōgen), and *Tsuri onna* (Kyōgen).

SHIN KABUKI

This is a general category of mostly original plays written during the Meiji and Taishō eras. Either created specifically for particular Kabuki actors or for publication in literary journals, most of these plays shun Kabuki's more traditional acting conventions such as *mie* poses, *roppō* exits, and *kumadori* makeup.

Famous plays of the type include Okamoto Kidō's *Shuzenji monogatari* (1911) and *Toribeyama shinjū* (1915), and Mayama Seika's *Genroku chūshingura* (1935)—a more realistic version of the *Kanadehon chūshingura* story. Later plays such as Funabashi Seiichi's *Genji monogatari* ("The Tale of Genji," 1951) are also sometimes classed as *shin kabuki*.

THEMES

Kabuki plays often share a common theme or are classed together under a specific genre.

DŌJŌJIMONO

As its name suggests, these plays (or more commonly dances) are based on the famous story about Dōjōji temple. A girl falls in love with a priest of the temple. When she is rejected, however, she becomes consumed with jealousy and, turning into a serpent, winds herself around the great temple bell under which the priest is hiding, and melts it. The most famous example is the greatest dance in the Kabuki repertoire, *Kyōganoko musume Dōjōji*.

Nakamura Shikan IV (right) and Sawamura Tosshō II in *Musume Dōjōji*. By Toyohara Kunichika, 1870. (P. Griffith Collection)

ENKIRIMONO

Enkirimono, or "plays of separation," were also popular. These tragedies feature scenes of rejection (aiso zukashi), in which two characters, usually lovers, separate. Often the female character is forced to revile her lover because of pressures brought about by their circumstances. The emotional heartache of the scene is sometimes enhanced by the plaintive strains of the bowed instrument called kokyū. A famous example is Kagotsurube sato no eizame.

KAIDANMONO

Although ghosts and spirits appear in the much earlier Nō, it was the Kabuki playwright Tsuruya Nanboku IV who made the genre more overtly horrific and bloodcurdling. Ghost plays are called kaidanmono, and by far the most famous ghost story in Kabuki is that of the murdered Oiwa in the play Tōkaidō Yotsuya kaidan. Other plays (also by Nanboku) in which ghosts appear include Tenjiku Tokubei, and the dance Kasane in which a murdered girl of that name becomes horribly disfigured through a ghost's possession.

KIZEWAMONO

Kizewamono is a genre made popular by Tsuruya Nanboku. These plays portray the depravity, bleakness and cruelty of life in the lower stratum of Edo period society in a more realistic way than ever before. Examples include the famous ghost play, Tōkaidō Yotsuya kaidan.

MIGAWARIMONO

Migawarimono feature the substitution of one character for another, often to avoid capture. Perhaps the most famous example is the substitution of Matsuōmaru's son Kotarō for the young lord Kan Shūsai in the Terakoya act of Sugawara denju tenarai kagami.

OIE SŌDŌMONO

These are plays about clan (great house) disputes. The townspeople were all too keen to hear of disputes and scandals concerning their aristocratic masters and, usually with some attempt at disguising the real incident, portrayed them on the stage. The most famous example is Meiboku sendai hagi.

SHINJŪMONO

Another important genre is the shinjū-mono, or "lovers' suicide play." Chikamatsu Monzaemon's Sonezaki shinjū, was the first play to deal with the phenomenon of lovers' suicide. The rigidity of the feudal class system, economic pressures, and the conflicts between one's feelings of obligation (giri) and personal love or desires (ninjō) saw a rash of young lovers hoping, through death, to be reunited in the next life. The shogunate tried to outlaw this practice, but Kabuki seized the opportunity of portraying it on stage. Chikamatsu's *Shinjū ten no Amijima* is another famous example.

SHIRANAMIMONO

Tsuruya Nanboku's *kizewamono* were later supplemented by the *shiranamimono* plays created by Kawatake Mokuami (1816–93) to portray the lives of thieves. *Shiranami*, meaning "white waves," is based on an old Chinese term for robber. This type of play was made very popular by Mokuami and its "heroes" tend to be rather human characters who often repent of their deeds,

either when captured, or sometimes before taking their own lives. Two of Mokuami's most famous *shiranamimono* are *Aoto zōshi hana no nishiki-e*, commonly known as *Benten kozō*, and *Sannin kichisa kuruwa no hatsugai*.

SOGAMONO

The famous story of the vendetta carried out by the Soga brothers to avenge their father's murder was a popular source of inspiration, and such plays as *Kotobuki Soga no taimen*, *Yanone*, and *Sukeroku yukari no Edo zakura*, are all classed under the general title of *sogamono*, or "Soga plays."

ACTORS AND ROLES

Although there are some versatile actors who regularly perform both male and female roles (*kaneru yakusha*), in practice most specialize in either one or the other.

TACHIYAKU

Tachiyaku is the general term for all male roles and there are several categories within this which may occasionally entail further specialization.

ARAGOTO

Aragoto roles are those performed in the wild *aragoto* style. The vocal delivery employed by *aragoto* actors is often loud and forceful, and the strain on the

voice can be considerable, requiring many years of training. The archetypal *aragoto* superhero is Kamakura Gongorō Kagemasa from *Shibaraku*. The role of Narukami at the end of the play of the same name is also performed in the *aragoto* style.

WAGOTO

In sharp contrast to *aragoto*, *wagoto* roles are gentle, refined, and rather soft. *Wagoto* heroes are usually in love, and this provides the opportunity to portray them with a slightly comic element. The most celebrated *wagoto* character is Izaemon from *Kuruwa bunshō*.

Occasionally the characterizations between the role types may be somewhat blurred. Sukeroku, for example, in the play of the same name, is performed with elements of both *aragoto* and *wagoto* in his character. He wears a very subtle *kumadori* makeup called *mukimi guma* and, although an obvious hero, he also has a gentle side to his character that makes for a more rounded human being than the typical *aragoto* superhero.

NIMAIME

Meaning literally "second flat thing," *nimaime* refers to the boards (*kanban*) displayed outside theaters to advertise the names of the actors. The second row was originally reserved for those actors playing handsome young men. While similar to *wagoto*, *nimaime* denotes a broader range of mild-mannered and rather more realistic characters, some of whom may be suffering at the hands of fate, such as Chūbei from *Koi bikyaku Yamato ōrai*, or the young lord Kamo no Yoshitsuna from *Shibaraku*.

SANMAIME

This refers to the third row of the *kanban*, which was reserved for comic roles. Sometimes called *dōkegata*, famous comic roles include Sagisaka

Bannai from *Kanadehon chūshingura* and Hayami no Tōta from *Yoshitsune senbon zakura*.

JITSUGOTO

Jitsugoto is a term employed for "real" men who may even have actual historical precedents. *Jitsugoto* men are often samurai of impressive strength of character, but may also be subject to the sway of strong emotional ties. Genzō from *Terakoya* and Ōboshi Yuranosuke from *Kanadehon chūshingura* are fine examples of the *jitsugoto* role.

SHINBŌYAKU

Characters in the category known as *shinbōyaku* are generally mild-mannered, somewhat refined men who must endure prolonged cruelty and bullying from villains. A perfect example is Lord Enya Hangan from the third act of *Kanadehon chūshingura*, who is the object of terrible insults from Kō no Moronō.

SABAKIYAKU

Known for their good judgment, these characters are wise, thoughtful, and level-headed men who can distinguish between right and wrong. They are often judges, and good examples include Katsumoto from *Meiboku sendai hagi* and *Date no jū-yaku*, and Shigetada from *Dannoura kabuto gunki*.

As in most theaters, the conflict between good and evil is an integral part of Kabuki. *Katakiyaku*, the general term for villains, come in a variety of guises, from petty criminals to evil aristocrats.

KUGEAKU

The most impressive *katakiyaku* are the *kugeaku* aristocratic court nobles, such as Takehira from *Shibaraku* and Shihei from *Sugawara denju tenarai kagami*. *Kugeaku* sport magnificent robes, and their blue *kumadori* makeup symbolizes the coldness of the blood that runs through their veins. Their wigs, too, are waxed into mane-like styles that increase their forbidding demeanor. *Kugeaku* are often largely immobile characters whose lackeys do everything for them. *Kugeaku* may, like Shihei, also possess supernatural powers.

JITSUAKU

Jitsuaku are cold-blooded, evil samurai who are usually plotting the downfall of their lord or clan. In contrast to the fantastic, make-believe natures of *kugeaku* villains, *jitsuaku* are more realistic and often display a frightening degree of sadistic cruelty. Nikki Danjō from *Meiboku sendai hagi* is a good example.

IROAKU

While on the surface these characters may resemble the handsome young *nimaime* roles, they in fact possess an immoral and cruel streak that often leads them to betray their unsuspecting wives and lovers. Tamiya Iemon from *Tōkaidō Yotsuya kaidan* is one example.

AKATTSURA

A further subcategory of villain is the *akattsura*, which literally means "red face." These men wear a broad covering of dark red base makeup and generally threaten or intimidate good characters. Narita Gorō from *Shibaraku* and Iwanaga from the *Akoya kotozeme* act of *Dannoura kabuto gunki* are famous examples.

Haradashi

Haradashi is a subcategory of *akattsura*. The name means literally "potbellies," and the characters' large stomachs and rather dim-witted behavior make them some of the most amusing of the *aragoto* villains. *Haradashi* can be seen in the entourage of Takehira in *Shibaraku*.

ONNAGATA

The art of the *onnagata* derived from the need for mature male actors to create artistically believable female characters. They did this by inventing stylized techniques that would give them not only a plausible female appearance, but also enable the creation of a psychologically convincing woman. From the banning of the *wakashu* in 1652, this process took just fifty years, and by the end of the seventeenth century a clear division occurred between male role actors and female role specialists.

While the training to become an *onnagata* requires many years, the basic principal is that the stereotypical Japanese female (with the exception of the majestic courtesans and some of the high aristocracy) should take up as little space as possible and be generally self-effacing and modest. Physically this can be achieved by bending the knees to reduce height, walking with the knees together and slightly pigeon-toed, keeping the shoulders down and, when seated, at a slight angle so as to appear narrower, keeping the hands, elbows, and arms close to the body, and speaking in a falsetto. The principal *onnagata* role types are the following.

AKAHIME

The *akahime*, or "red princesses," are not the offspring of royal blood, but rather the pampered daughters of daimyo and ranking samurai. They are so named after their bright red long-sleeved kimono and glittering silver tiara. *Akahime* are usually played as rather static characters, who often sit with their left hand withdrawn inside their kimono sleeve, which is held out to the side, and their right sleeve held across their chest. They tend to be rather reticent girls who speak only rarely, until passion and a sense of duty move them to heroic heights.

The three most famous *akahime* roles (known as *sanhime*) are Yaegaki-hime from *Honchō nijūshikō*, Toki-hime from *Kamakura sandaiki*, and Yuki-hime from *Kinkakuji*.

AKUBA

Akuba are evil women from the lower classes of late Edo period society and are found in later *sewamono* plays. Also known as *dokufu*, their vampish smart-talking talents make them particularly effective as criminals, so that extortion or even murder scenes are typical for this role type. These characters are often recognizable from their *uma no shippo*, or "pony-tail" hairdo, and their stylish, checker-patterned short coats called *hanten*. Famous examples of *akuba* include Dote no Oroku from Tsuruya Nanboku's *Osome Hisamatsu ukina no yomiuri*, and the "scar-faced" Otomi from Kawatake Mokuami's *Kirare Otomi*.

BABA

The three most famous *baba* "grandmother" or "old woman" roles are collectively known as *sanbaba*. They are Kakuju from *Sugawara denju tenarai kagami*, Koshiji from *Honchō nijūshikō*, and Mimyō from *Moritsuna jinya*. Typically these women are widows who, having taken over as defenders of their family honor, exhibit unswerving loyalty and determination, often at great personal sacrifice. Although the stylization employed by *onnagata* means that these roles may be played by actors of any age, in practice they are usually performed by older *onnagata*.

KATAHAZUSHI

This category refers to high-ranking serving ladies in the homes of the nobility, and the word *katahazushi* actually refers to the complicated asymmetrical knot in which their hair is tied. Without doubt the greatest role in this category and one of the most taxing of all *onnagata* roles is Masaoka from *Meiboku sendai hagi.*

KEISEI

The most majestic and spectacular of the *onnagata* roles is unquestionably that of the high-class courtesan. The general term for these women is *keisei*—literally, "castle toppler"—although the very highest rank of courtesan is also known as *tayū*. After around 1760, though, the *tayū* rank seems to have died out and the broader term *oiran* was employed. As in life, Kabuki plays featuring courtesans tended to be accurate in distinguishing between these ranks. Uncommonly for females in feudal Japan, high-ranking courtesans had a certain amount of power and could rebuff any man they did not like. However, even the *keisei* were bound to a cruel life of servitude in the pleasure quarters and, despite the trappings of luxury that

surrounded them, often led pathetically unhappy lives. Agemaki from the play *Sukeroku*, Yūgiri from *Kuruwa bunshō*, and Yatsuhashi from *Kagotsurube* are three of the finest *keisei* roles.

MUSUME

Musume are the daughters of farmers or townspeople. Characteristic of this role type is a sense of innocence coupled with a precocious, often seductive, charm. Chidori from the play *Shunkan* is a typically spirited country girl, and Osato from the "Sushi Shop" act of *Yoshitsune senbon zakura* is an example of a *machi musume*, or "town maiden."

NYŌBO

Nyōbo are the wives of either samurai or townsmen. While this covers a broad range of characters, most wives are industrious women devoted to both their husbands (and their husband's lord or clan) and to their children. Tonami, the wife of Genzō from *Terakoya*, and Tonase, the wife of Kakogawa Honzō from Act IX of *Kanadehon chūshingura*, are famous *nyōbo* roles.

Kōken and *Kurogo*

Both male- and female-role actors are often attended on stage by assistants known as *kōken* and *kurogo*, who are usually the students (*deshi*) of the main actor.

Kōken are formally dressed and discreetly assist the actors in both plays and dances by handing them props or adjusting their dress, makeup, or wig. *Kōken* normally kneel behind the performing actor, at the rear of the set, and only move to assist when required.

Kurogo are similar to *kōken* but are usually dressed completely in black, including a black hood and veil, to signify that they are invisible. If the scene is of water or snow, they may also be dressed entirely in blue or white so as to blend in with the background.

The role of the *kurogo* is less formal than that of the *kōken* and is more one of keeping the stage tidy. They remove items no longer required and, crouching low behind the actor, may hand him objects or place a small stool beneath him when he seats himself.

Kōken

Kurogo

ACTING FAMILIES

SHŪMEI

Kabuki is a hereditary art, passed down from father to son or from uncle to nephew. When an actor is childless, however, an especially talented student (*deshi*) may occasionally be chosen as his heir. Kabuki stage names are handed down through the generations and the process of taking a new, higher-ranking name is called *shūmei*. Age and talent are the deciding factors in how far any particular actor may progress in the line open to him.

To take the present Danjūrō (born the son of Danjūrō XI in 1946) as an example, he made his debut under his real name of Horikoshi Natsuo in 1953 and took the Kabuki name of Ichikawa Shinnosuke VI in 1958. After the death of his father he became Ichikawa Ebizō X in 1969, and in 1985 finally succeeded to the most prestigious name in Kabuki history, becoming Ichikawa Danjūrō XII.

The ceremony of taking a new name involves making a formal stage announcement called a *kōjō*. There are two types of *kōjō*. The simplest occurs during the performance of an actual play, usually to introduce a child actor to the audience. The senior actor will stop the performance and, kneeling and bowing, the young actor will be introduced. The more formal *kōjō* are reserved for major *shūmei* name-taking ceremonies. Announced as part of the program, all the high-ranking actors performing that month kneel in one or two rows on the stage, dressed in formal *kamishimo* costume of stiffened vests and wide *hakama* trousers. Each

offers his congratulations, often coming up with some personal anecdote about the actor who formerly held that name. Finally the actor succeeding to the name also speaks, and asks the audience for their patronage.

YAGŌ AND KAKEGOE

All Kabuki actors, whether by direct descent or through close association, belong to one of several "acting houses." As well as their Kabuki stage names, all actors also possess an "acting house name," known as *yagō*. This term dates from the days when some actors adopted a name because of a business association or a particular connection with a place. The *yagō* of the Ichikawa Danjūrō line of actors, for example, is Narita-ya because of the first Danjūrō's association with the temple at Narita.

The origins of many *yagō* are very obscure, and there are numerous subbranches to these main families that employ different *yagō*. *Yagō* are most commonly heard in the theater as *kakegoe*.

Kakegoe is a form of encouragement and appreciation called out to the actors by knowledgeable members of the audience at carefully timed moments during the play. Most commonly called are an actor's *yagō* and his "generation number." Ichikawa Danjūrō XII, for example, would receive calls of "Narita-ya," his *yagō*, or "*Jūni-dai-me!*" ("The Twelfth!"), his generation number. The calling is

kōjō

▪Current *yagō*

YAGŌ	ACTOR'S NAME	BORN	DATE OF SHŪMEI	FAMILY RELATIONSHIP
Akashi-ya	Ōtani Tomoemon VIII	1949	1964	First son of Jakuemon IV
Harima-ya	Nakamura Kichiemon II	1944	1966	Younger brother of Kōshirō IX
	Nakamura Matagorō II	1914	1921	
Kaga-ya	Nakamura Kaishun II	1948	2002	
	Nakamura Tōzō VI	1938	1967	
Kinokuni-ya	Sawamura Tanosuke VI	1932	1964	
	Sawamura Tōjūrō II	1943	1976	
Kōrai-ya	Matsumoto Kōshirō IX	1942	1981	Elder brother of Kichiemon II
	Ichikawa Somegorō VII	1973	1981	Only son of Kōshirō IX
	Ichikawa Komazō XI	1957	1994	
	Matsumoto Kingo III	1942	1965	
Kyō-ya	Nakamura Jakuemon IV	1920	1964	
	Nakamura Shibajaku VII	1955	1964	Second son of Jakuemon IV
Matsushima-ya	Kataoka Nizaemon XV	1944	1998	Younger brother of Gatō V and Hidetarō II
	Kataoka Gatō V	1935	1971	Elder brother of Hidetarō II and Nizaemon XV
	Kataoka Hidetarō II	1941	1956	Elder brother of Nizaemon XV
	Kataoka Takatarō I	1968	1973	Only son of Nizaemon XV
	Kataoka Ainosuke VI	1972	1992	Adopted son of Hidetarō II
	Kataoka Shinnosuke I	1967	1971	Only son of Gatō V
Mikawa-ya	Ichikawa Danzō IX	1951	1987	
Miyoshi-ya	Kamimura Kichiya VI	1955	1993	
Nakamura-ya	Nakamura Kanzaburō XVIII (formally Kankurō V)	1955	2005	
	Nakamura Kantarō II	1981	1987	First son of Kanzaburō XVIII
	Nakamura Shichinosuke II	1983	1987	Second son of Kanzaburō XVIII
Narikoma-ya	Nakamura Shikan VII	1928	1967	
	Nakamura Fukusuke IX	1960	1992	First son of Shikan VII
	Nakamura Hashinosuke III	1965	1980	Second son of Shikan VII
	Sakata Tōjūrō IV (formally Ganjirō III)	1931	2005	
	Nakamura Ganjirō IV (Nakamura Kanjaku V)	1959	2005	First son of Sakata Tōjūrō IV
	Nakamura Senjaku III	1960	1995	Second son of Sakata Tōjūrō IV
	Nakamura Tamatarō IV	1966	1976	First son of Tōzō VI

YAGŌ	ACTOR'S NAME	BORN	DATE OF SHŪMEI	FAMILY RELATIONSHIP
Narita-ya	Ichikawa Danjūrō XII	1946	1985	
	Ichikawa Ebizō XI	1977	2004	Only son of Danjūrō XII
Omodaka-ya	Ichikawa Ennosuke III	1939	1963	Elder brother of Danshirō IV
	Ichikawa Danshirō IV	1946	1969	Younger brother of Ennosuke III
	Ichikawa Kamejirō II	1975	1983	Only son of Danshirō IV
	Ichikawa Ukon I	1963	1975	
	Ichikawa Emiya II	1959	1981	
	Ichikawa Emisaburō III	1970	1986	
	Ichikawa Danjirō I	1969	1988	
Otowa-ya	Onoe Kikugorō VII	1942	1973	
	Onoe Kikunosuke V	1977	1996	Only son of Kikugorō VII
	Onoe Shōroku IV	1975	2002	
	Bandō Hikosaburō VIII	1943	1980	
	Bandō Kamesaburō V	1976	1982	First son of Hikosaburō VIII
	Bandō Kametoshi I	1978	1989	Second son of Hikosaburō VIII
Tachibana-ya	Ichimura Kakitsu XVII	1949	1967	
	Ichimura Manjirō II	1949	1972	
Takasago-ya	Nakamura Baigyoku IV	1946	1992	
Takashima-ya	Ichikawa Sadanji IV	1940	1979	
Takino-ya	Ichikawa Monnosuke VIII	1959	1990	
	Ichikawa Omezō VI	1967	2003	Only son of Sadanji IV
Tennōji-ya	Nakamura Tomijūrō V	1929	1972	
Yamato-ya	Bandō Tamasaburō V	1950	1964	
	Bandō Mitsugorō X	1956	2001	
	Bandō Yajūrō I	1956	1973	
Yorozu-ya	Nakamura Karoku V	1950	1981	Elder brother of Kashō III
	Nakamura Tokizō V	1955	1981	Elder brother of Shinjirō I
	Nakamura Kashō III	1956	1981	Younger brother of Karoku V
	Nakamura Shinjirō I	1959	1964	Younger brother of Tokizō V
	Nakamura Shidō II	1972	1981	

"Narita-ya!"

An *ōmukō-san* performs *kakegoe* from the top floor of the theater.

usually timed to an actor's entrance, exit, or to the subtle and important pauses during a speech. They can also be heard during dramatic *mie* poses. The callers are almost exclusively male and, while they receive no official payment for their services, some gain a free pass to the theater in order to perform this service for the actors and to create a lively atmosphere in the audi-torium. They are called *ōmukō-san*, "great distant people," because they traditionally call from the cheapest seats on the third or fourth floor fur-thest from the stage.

MON

Many Japanese families possess a fam-ily crest—a *mon*—and those of Kabuki actors serve as a constant reminder of who is playing a particular role in this actors' theater. The most prominent *mon* is on the sleeves of Kamakura Gongorō's costume in *Shibaraku*. Held out tight by bamboo struts, this crest of the *mimasu* "three rice measures" is the personal crest of Ichikawa Danjūrō, and reminds us that both the play and

▪ *Mon*

Bandō Hikosaburō	Bandō Mitsugorō	Bandō Tamasaburō
Ichikawa Danjūrō	Ichikawa Danshirō	Ichikawa Ennosuke
Ichikawa Sadanji	Kataoka Nizaemon	Matsumoto Kōshirō
Nakamura Ganjirō	Nakamura Jakuemon	Nakamura Kankurō
Nakamura Kichiemon	Nakamura Shikan	Nakamura Tokizō
Nakamura Tomijūrō	Onoe Kikugurō	Sawamura Tanosuke

the character are the artistic creation of the Ichikawa Danjūrō line of actors.

Similarly, during the scene of passionate entreaty known as a *kudoki* from the dance *Kyōganoko musume dōjōji*, the actor dances with a *tenugui* cloth that is decorated with his own personal crests.

More subtly, small crests of either the actor or of the character may be seen on the lapels and sleeves of many formal kimono. Onstage musicians and puppeteers in Bunraku also display crests in this way, although the crest displayed by musicians is that of the principal actor rather than their own.

COSTUMES, MAKEUP, AND WIGS

ISHŌ

Costumes are called *ishō* and, depending on the type of play, range from the simple, even somewhat drab, everyday wear of the Edo period townspeople to one of the most extraordinary and outlandish costumes in the history of world theater in the *aragoto* play *Shibaraku*.

The range and variety of Kabuki costume is remarkable, but most male and female costumes are some form of kimono which, at its simplest, covers the whole length of the body in a restrictive, tubelike wrap. Three important features of the kimono are the wrapping direction, which must always be left over right (the other direction being reserved for the dressing of the dead); the collar, which in the case of ladies of the pleasure quarters can be erotically low at the back; and the *obi*, or sash, which encircles the body several times and may be tied with a variety of complicated knots. The

knot of a courtesan's *obi* is tied at the front and, often made of the most luxurious heavy brocade, is one of the most distinguishing features of her costume.

Examples of realistic Edo period style costume can be found in most *sewamono* plays, particularly when worn by the supporting players. The farmers who come in to pick up their children from school in *Terakoya* wear typical country folk costume, and roles such as those of Okaru's mother and father in *Kanadehon chūshingura* also demonstrate the dress of the time.

A rise in social status brings a corresponding increase in style, and the roles of the schoolmaster Genzō and his wife Tonami, also from *Terakoya*, are typical. Both wear simple but elegant kimono with *mon* crests on the upper chest and sleeves. Tonami wears the plain kimono known as the *kokumochi*.

A real increase in the splendor of Kabuki costumes can be seen in

Nakamura Ganjirō III as Masaoka (right) and Sawamura Tanosuke VI as Sakae Gozen in *Meiboku sendai hagi*. Sakae wears the costume and the *kasshiki* hairstyle of high-ranking ladies.

Bandō Mitsugorō III as Kawagoe Tarō wearing the official *daimon* costume with trailing *nagabakama*. By Utagawa Kunihisa I, 1804. (P. Griffith Collection)

jidaimono such as *Ichinotani futaba gunki* or *Meiboku sendai hagi*. The standard male formal attire here is the *kamishimo*, which consists of wide skirt-like *hakama* trousers, and a vest-like upper section characterized by the wide and stiffened shoulder wings (with crests on them) called *kataginu*. This dress is also worn by all the musicians who appear onstage as well as by the *kōken* stage assistants.

In *Ichinotani*, the role of Kumagai shows a samurai of very high rank and, despite being at the scene of battle, his costumes are always resplendent. His wife, Sagami, and their mistress, Lady Fuji, show us examples of the splendid but tasteful robes worn by high-ranking ladies of the period.

In *Meiboku sendai hagi*, Masaoka, the nursemaid who is the heroine of the play, wears over her kimono the splendid *uchikake*, the standard outer robe worn by most high-ranking serving ladies of the *katahazushi* type. In most *jidaimono*, all the female costumes, even those of the humble ladies-in-waiting, are of the highest quality and opulence. This applies also to high-ranking male characters, an example being the casual outer robe of heavy brocade stiff stand-up collar called *omigoromo* that is worn by Yoshitsune in the fourth act of *Yoshitsune senbon zakura*.

Some *jidaimono* costumes may appear totally impractical for everyday living. The extremely long trailing trousers called *nagabakama*, for example, are typically worn by daimyo when in castles or palaces. The evil Kō no Moronō in the palace of the Shogun flicks his *nagabakama* in the face of Enya Hangan while insulting him in *Kanadehon chūshingura*.

We also sometimes see a kimono supposedly made of paper, called a *kamiko*. Sukeroku, in the play of the same name, is made to wear this by his mother in order to prevent him from fighting. In the *wagoto* play *Kuruwa bunshō*, Izaemon, disowned by his family and reduced to poverty, wears one that is stitched together from the love letters he received from his beloved Yūgiri.

The ladies of the pleasure quarters were famed for dressing in the finest costumes to attract their customers.

The women of quarters like Gion in Kyoto (which still exists) and the Yoshiwara in Tokyo (which finally faded away towards the end of the nineteenth century) ranked from common prostitutes to the high-class *keisei* or *oiran* who were queenlike courtesans. Even within the more realistic *sewamono* category of plays, courtesans wear some of the most splendid of Kabuki costumes. These women, too, always wear gorgeous *uchikake* outer robes when dressed in full regalia, and the skillful handling of these garments to display the beauty of line and pose is another of the great difficulties for the *onnagata* actor.

The category of *aragoto* plays presents extremes in costume just as it does in other aspects such as vocal delivery and acting styles. The costume of Kamakura Gongorō is described in some detail in the synopsis of the play *Shibaraku*, and other fantastic *aragoto* costumes are worn by the warrior Otokonosuke in *Meiboku sendai hagi*, by the triplets Matsuōmaru, Umeōmaru, and Sakuramaru in the *Kuruma biki* act of *Sugawara denju tenarai kagami* and by Soga no Gorō *in Yanone*.

KESHŌ AND *KUMADORI*

The term for normal makeup is *keshō*, while *kumadori* refers to the specialist makeup employed for *aragoto* roles. Makeup styles are very wide-ranging, and vary from the realistic to the extraordinary and exaggerated. As one might expect, the more realistic styles are to be found in modern works or in *sewamono* plays.

Pure white skin has traditionally been a sign of refinement and social status in Japan, the logical reason being that aristocrats do not work out in the sun and so do not get tanned. White is also associated with purity, and so many heroes and heroines, even in more realistic plays, have a general base makeup of pure white. In the days before electricity, the white base also helped to give the face more definition.

Kabuki actors apply their own makeup. Having covered the hair with a cloth called a *habutae* (which also prepares it for the wig), the first step in the process is to obliterate the fea-

Ichikawa Ebizō V (Danjūrō VII) wearing *sujiguma* makeup in a version of *Shibaraku*. By Utagawa Toyokuni III, 1863. (P. Griffith Collection)

tures totally with a pure white base called *oshiroi*. The makeup covers the face completely and extends as far down the neck and back as will be visible, which is often quite far down for a female kimono with a very low back collar line. Eyebrows are either shaven or are pasted over, and the lips, too, lose their definition under the thick layer of white. In many *onnagata* roles, pink is painted under the white to suggest a feminine blush.

For both male and female standard roles, the main process is then to add definition around the eyes, paint on the lips, and finally add the eyebrows. The shape of the eyes is made by drawing in the outline, then usually highlighting the outer corners with either red or black. The shape and size of the lips and mouth for roles of both sexes are set by tradition, according to the role. For young women, the mouth will become a small pouting feminine bud, and for male roles it will be given an exaggerated downward curve indicative of a serious nature.

Eyebrows for female roles tend to be higher than natural, and some married woman roles do not have eyebrows at all since it was the fashion to shave them. It was also the custom in the Edo period for married women to blacken their teeth and this can still be seen on the stage.

Kumadori is the most distinctive makeup style and was possibly invented by Ichikawa Danjūrō I for his *aragoto* characters, although its origins are unclear. *Kumadori* is applied over a base of either white or pink and uses bold lines of red, blue, or brown, with some black. The purpose of the lines is to exaggerate the facial muscles that make general expressions more clearly defined, once again helpful in the days before electricity. The sharp lines are applied with a brush and then the actor deliberately smudges them with his finger to blend them into the base color. This makes for a more "realistic" line, which is said to resemble the veins. This is a possible explanation of the colors of *kumadori* as the red color employed by heroes looks like a flush of righteous indignation, while the villainous blue makes the character seem cold-blooded.

Unfortunately none of the *kumadori* styles used by Danjūrō I have survived. The oldest one we know about, and which is still in use, is the *saruguma* that was worn by the actor Nakamura Denkurō I when playing the character Asahina in 1690 at the Nakamura-za in Edo.

One of the most subtle styles is the *mukimiguma* worn by Sukeroku. Sukeroku has a very human side to his character and so this makeup is less fantastic than some, highlighting just the lips and around the eyes.

The makeup of Kamakura Gongorō and his adversary, Takehira, from *Shibaraku* are perfect examples of *kumadori* at its most eccentric. Gongorō wears the red *sujiguma* style of the super-hero, while Takehira wears the blue *hannyaguma* style typical of *kugeaku* aristocratic villains.

While red and blue (always with a little black at certain points) are the main colors, demons such as the spider in *Tsuchigumo* and the demoness from *Momijigari* have brown *kumadori*.

■ **Styles of *kumadori* makeup**

kaenguma

kugeare

mukimiguma

sujiguma

saruguma

taishaguma

Oshiguma

The name *oshiguma* literally means "pressed *kuma*," *kuma* being an abbreviation of *kumadori*. After a performance, an actor will return to his dressing room where he may press his face carefully against a white silk cloth to create a printed image of his makeup. He will then sign the cloth with brush and ink and seal it, perhaps also writing on it the name of his role as well as the theater and play in which it was performed. Occasionally, he may even compose a suitable poem to accompany the image. The completed *oshiguma* will then be given away to an eager fan as a memento, or else sold to the public, usually in aid of a charity for actors.

Despite the long history of the *kumadori* style, the practice of taking an *oshiguma* appears to be fairly recent, having been started by Ichi-kawa Danjūrō IX in the Meiji period. Today, only two *oshiguma* made by Danjūrō IX are known to exist, one in the National Theatre and the other in the Danjūrō family collection. It is said to have been the chance pressing of a cloth onto Danjūrō's face to remove his makeup after a performance of *Shibaraku* that inspired him to begin this custom. Attempts may possibly have been made by earlier actors to take *oshiguma*, but it was not until the Meiji period that the quality of the makeup itself improved enough to enable the makeup to stick and then dry satisfactorily to form a picture. Many Kabuki fans are avid collectors of such face prints for, in a way no photograph can equal, they are highly personal images bringing one into extreme closeness with the actor.

Onoe Shōroku II as Kagekiyo in *Nanatsu-men*, 1983. (P. Griffith Collection)

Nakamura Utaemon VI as the lion spirit in *Kagami jishi*, 1951. (P. Griffith Collection)

Nakamura Utaemon VI (above) and Matsumoto Kōshirō VIII in *Musume Dōjōji*, 1960. (P. Griffith Collection)

KATSURA

Onoe Shōroku IV as Soga no Gorō wearing the *kuruma bin* wig in *Yanone*.

Katsura is the name for a wig, and Kabuki actors never appear on stage without one. In the early days of *wakashu kabuki*, however, actors appeared with their own hair. It was the government regulation that actors shave the crown of their heads in the customary adult hairstyle which had the effect of forcing adolescent males off the stage. Initially the "mature" actors took to covering their bald crowns with a patch of purple silk called a *murasaki bōshi* to give the semblance of hair. This can still be seen today, incorporated into the front part of the wigs of some female characters as a charming reminder of the past. Real wigs, influenced by Nō, first appeared for female characters around the years 1651–55.

Today actors cover their real hair with a tight cloth called a *habutae*. The wig consists of a copper base (*daigane*) that is moulded to the exact shape of the individual actor's skull and onto which the hair is attached.

MALE WIGS

The usual wig for male characters consists of a back hair section and side-locks that are dragged back and tied into a forward-facing topknot (*mage*). Even though the actors had shaven pates, it was thought necessary to cover this with the *habutae*, which may either be a pale color, or a darker blue to indicate the need for a fresh shave. This and any other signs of dishevelment to the topknot or sidelocks are usual indications of mental distraction or of a rather disreputable character.

Ichikawa Ebizō (Danjūrō V) wearing the *chikara gami* in *Shibaraku*. By Utagawa Toyokuni I, 1796. (P. Griffith Collection)

Ichikawa Omezō I wearing the *sakaguma*, "thatched bear fur," wig used for villainous samurai. By Utagawa Kunimasa I, 1803. (P. Griffith Collection)

Ichikawa Omezō I as Lord Kudō Suketsune. By Utagawa Kunimasa I, 1803. (R. Cavaye Collection)

Hair that has grown back completely is an indication that the character is either ill, or has too many cares to attend the barber. Certain masterless samurai (*rōnin*) such as Sadakurō from *Kanadehon chūshingura* are depicted in this way, as are thieves and other lowlife characters. Another stylized version of this is the *gojū nichi*, or "fifty day" wig, worn by the ailing hero Matsuōmaru in *Terakoya*. An even more exaggerated form of male hairstyle with a large bushy growth on top and voluminous side locks that hang down over the chest is the *ōji*, or "prince" wig, worn frequently by villainous lords in *jidaimono*. Examples include Matsunaga Daizen in the *Kinkakuji* act of *Gion sairei shinkōki*, and Noritsune, Lord of Noto, in the closing scenes of *Yoshitsune senbon zakura*.

The presence of any forelock, such as that seen on the wig of Kamakura Gongorō from *Shibaraku*, is an indication that the shaving ceremony held usually at the age of sixteen to enter adulthood formally has not yet taken place and so the character is still a youth. The triplets in the *Kuruma biki* act of *Sugawara denju tenarai kagami* all have this forelock.

Perhaps the most spectacular of the male wigs is that of Gongorō from *Shibaraku*. The wig, which incorporates a small hat and bow tied under the chin, has its forelock of hair parted in the middle. A hugely exaggerated stiffened paper bow called *chikara gami*, or "strength paper," sticks up at the back of the wig and is a symbol of his physical power, while the sidelocks have been separated out and stiffly oiled like the spokes of a wheel. This gives the wig its name of *kuruma bin* —literally, "wheel locks." Wigs with stiff, flat sidelocks as worn by the *haradashi* in *Shibaraku* are known as *ita bin*, or "board locks."

▪Male Wigs

The *namajime* style for samurai in *jidaimono*.

The *mushiri* style for rogues and romantic scoundrels.

The *happōware* style for strong warriors and *aragoto* heroes.

Female wigs are categorized by age and social status, based on whether a woman is unmarried or married, young or old, as well as whether she is low class, middle class (townswomen), or high class, a princess (*akahime*), lady-in-waiting, or a courtesan (*keisei*). The introduction of an oil-based dressing enabled women to mold and hold their hair in the complex knots and styles reflecting their status. Pins and other ornaments are also important parts of the wig.

The typical style of a middle-aged woman is the *takashimada* as worn by maid servants in the houses of the nobility, while the *fukiwa* is worn by the girls of high birth known as *akahime*. The diver girl Chidori from *Heike nyogo no shima* wears the *uma no shippo*, or "ponytail" wig.

Masaoka's wig in *Meiboku sendai hagi* and Sagami's wig in *Kumagai jinya* are known as *katahazushi*, and

Nakamura Ganjirō III as the nurse Masaoka wearing the *katahazushi* wig used for serving ladies of rank.

Sawamura Sōnosuke I as the courtesan Umegawa wearing the *shimada* hairstyle in *Ninokuchi mura*. By Yamamura Kōka, also called Toyonari, 1922. (P. Griffith Collection)

are representative of upper class serving ladies in the household of the nobility. Noble ladies themselves, however, often wear their hair parted down the middle, pulled back and tied loosely in a ponytail that hangs down their backs. This hairstyle is called *kasshiki* and it is seen for the role of Lady Fuji in *Kumagai jinya* and for Sakae Gozen in *Meiboku sendai hagi*.

The most spectacular of all the female wigs is the elaborate and extremely heavy *date hyōgo*, replete with tortoiseshell hairpins, combs, coral beads, and other ornaments of the finest quality, worn by high-ranking courtesans such as Agemaki from *Sukeroku* or Yūgiri from *Kuruwa bunshō*.

▪Female Wigs

The *fukiwa* style for *akahime* roles.

Ichikawa Ennosuke III as the boatwoman Oen wearing the *uma no shippo*, hairstyle in *Kaminari sendō*. By Tsuruya Kōkei, 1997. (R. Cavaye Collection)

The *katahazushi* style for serving ladies of rank.

PERFORMANCE

While Kabuki often impresses the newcomer as an exotic spectacle with its sets and costumes, there are in fact many unique conventions and stylizations, depending on the type of play, which can be very meaningful when recognized and which can add greatly to the audience's enjoyment. For convenience we have divided some of these conventions into aural and visual groups. While some of them may at first appear somewhat strange, it is worth remembering that Kabuki was originally the theater of the ordinary townspeople—just as vaudeville was in the United States, or Edwardian music-hall was in Britain, in the early part of the twentieth century. Even the most unusual of Kabuki conventions were designed to be understood by everyone. With a little knowledge, the gap of three to four hundred years that separates us from Kabuki's earliest fans can be easily bridged. Kabuki fans look forward to these stylized moments, which also give the actors an opportunity to show off their skill.

THINGS TO SEE

HAYAGAWARI, HIKINUKI, AND BUKKAERI

We have seen that costumes in Kabuki can be impressive. However, equally spectacular are the quick changes of costume and sometimes makeup when actors play more than one role in the same scene. These quick changes are called *hayagawari* and can be either same–sex or male–female, female–male transformations. *Hayagawari* are less an attempt to deceive the audience than a demonstration of an actor's

virtuosity. Ichikawa Ennosuke III has revived many plays that make much use of quick-change techniques. A highly skillful exchange of an outer robe and an umbrella between two actors in *Date no jūyaku*, for example, takes only two and a half seconds and is done in full view of the audience. At other times an identically dressed substitute actor will appear without showing his face to enable the main actor to change quickly offstage. By methods such as this, an actor may even appear to fight with himself by playing first one character and then the character's opponent. A particularly famous example

Hayagawari

Hikinuki

Bukkaeri

of a play featuring *hayagawari* is *Osome hisamatsu ukina no yomiuri*, commonly known as *Osome no nanayaku*, "The Seven Roles of Osome": written by Tsuruya Nanboku IV and premiered in 1813, the star actor must change rapidly into seven different characters.

Two specific types of onstage costume changes are called *hikinuki* and *bukkaeri*. Especially common in dances such as *Kyōganoko musume dōjōji* and *Sagi musume*, the *hikinuki* is a quick change of costume in which *kōken* stage assistants help to remove cords holding the entire garment together at the seams. The entire outer kimono is then whipped off to reveal a completely different kimono underneath. The *bukkaeri* is similar to the *hikinuki*, but the garment is secured at the waist, and the threads to be removed only hold the garment together at the shoulders. When these are pulled out it allows the torso section to fall down over the actor's waist and legs. A new design on the garment underneath is thus revealed, and the inner lining of the lowered section matches it to give the appearance of a completely different outfit. While the *hikinuki* costume change is employed mostly for visual effect and to signal the transition from one section of music to another, the *bukkaeri* symbolizes the revelation of a character's true identity. *Bukkaeri* is seen equally often in dances and in *jidaimono* plays, and is performed by Sekibei at the end of the dance-drama *Seki no to*.

MIE AND *ROPPŌ*

The glaring poses called *mie* and the fantastic exits known as *roppō* are perhaps the two most striking of Kabuki's stylized acting techniques. *Mie* are powerful poses by male characters that serve to emphasize moments of great import or tension. They have been likened to the zoom-in of the modern camera as they focus all the attention on the character performing the *mie*. All action stops, the character adopts a dramatic pose, revolves his head to one side and then back and, snapping the head into position, crosses his eyes and glares at his opponent. *Mie* are

Nakamura Kichiemon II as Kumagai performing the fierce *seisatsu no mie*, "signboard pose," in *Kumagai jinya*.

Matsumoto Kōshirō IX as Benkei about to perform the *tobi roppō* exit at the end of *Kanjinchō*.

usually accompanied by two clear beats of the *tsuke* wooden blocks. These poses almost certainly have their origins in the fearsome iconography and facial expressions seen on some Buddhist statuary. Female characters perform a softer version of the *mie* called *kimari*, which does not involve crossing the eyes.

Meaning literally "six directions," *roppō* are most commonly a kind of exit in which the hands and feet are said to move north, south, east, west, to heaven, and to earth. Occasionally they may also be performed when a character moves from one side of the stage to the other. *Roppō* express the boldness and vigor of a character, and are most often seen in *jidaimono* or *aragoto* plays. There are several different types such as the *tobi roppō*, literally "flying" or "bounding" *roppō*, executed by Benkei at the end of *Kanjinchō*, the *kitsune*, "fox," *roppō* executed by the fox Tadanobu at the end of "The Inari Fox Shrine at Fushimi" act from *Yoshitsune senbon zakura* and the *keisei*, "courtesan," *roppō* from *Miyajima no danmari*.

TACHIMAWARI

Realism is not always appreciated on the traditional Kabuki stage and fight scenes, known as *tachimawari*, are stylized and beautiful, even dance-like. Commonly involving a hero taking on a group of opponents, *tachimawari* are often performed with a variety of props such as swords, branches of cherry blossom, or even small ladders and buckets. The blows are mimed, and the movements are given aural emphasis by the beating of the *tsuke* wooden blocks. Usually the hero defeats his enemies with effortless grace. There is a variety of set patterns of movement in *tachimawari*. Two of the most common are seen when, for example, a group of assailants charges at a single hero and each of the enemy passes to either side of him in a pattern called *chidori*, or "plover birds," and when a group of characters form a single line, each holding on to the character in front in a pattern known as *jakago*, or "snake basket." *Tachimawari*

are accompanied by *geza* music, which is often rather slow and languorous, and adds to the air of unreality as the protagonists adopt picturesque poses at climactic moments and the hero strikes dramatic *mie*. In dances, such fight scenes are called *shosadate*.

The action in *tachimawari* can be very acrobatic, frequently including leaps and somersaults, though this element rarely reaches the extremes seen in Peking opera. However, since the joint Japanese and Chinese production of *Ryūō* in 1989, starring both Ichikawa Ennosuke III and the Chinese star, Li Kuan, the fight scenes in Peking Opera have strongly influenced the *tachimawari* in subsequent productions of Ennosuke's Super Kabuki.

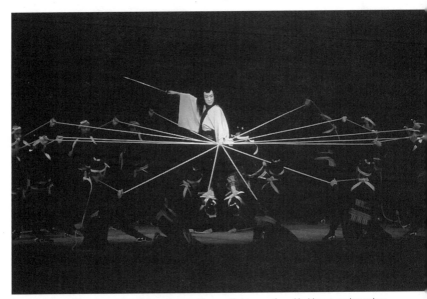

Bandō Mitsugorō X as the retainer Kokingo in a *tachimawari* fight scene from *Yoshitsune senbon zakura*.

Onoe Kikugorō VII as Lady Iwafuji performing a *chūnori*, an example of *keren* stage trickery.

KEREN

From the early days of the *wakashu* actors there has always been a tradition in Kabuki of entertaining the audience with stage tricks called *keren*. These developed in sophistication and reached their height in the nineteenth century in the works of the playwright Tsuruya Nanboku IV. Falling somewhat out of favor during the overly serious Meiji period, *keren* have enjoyed a revival in recent years through the spectacular performances of Ichikawa Ennosuke III. In his performance of the fox Tadanobu in *Yoshitsune senbon zakura*, for example, Ennosuke does a variety of appearance and disappearance tricks by means of special trapdoors, slides, and lifts.

The most spectacular of all the *keren* is the flying exit called *chūnori*. Meaning literally "riding the heavens," *chūnori* refers to the flight through the air of a character with supernatural powers. While flying (by means of a harness and winch) was originally simply across the stage, in more recent times spectacular flying over the *hanamichi* to the top floor of the theater has become very popular. In particular, Ichikawa Ennosuke III has employed this to great effect in many of his productions, such as in the fourth act of *Yoshitsune senbon zakura* for the flight of the magic fox Tadanobu, for the dramatic exit of Nikki Danjō at the end of the "Under the Floor" scene in an alternative version of *Meiboku sendai hagi*, revived by Ennosuke and called *Date no jūyaku* and often in Super Kabuki.

KUBI JIKKEN AND SEPPUKU

Both Western and Oriental societies have seen their share of violent historical periods. While the Kamakura, Muromachi, and Edo periods in Japan were by no means always brutal, the strict code of the samurai warrior known as *bushidō* is frequently depicted on the Kabuki stage.

In battle it was the custom to take the head of a defeated enemy of high rank. The exact identity of a fallen warrior could have momentous consequences for either side and so *kubi jikken*, the practice of formally identifying a severed head, became common. Famous head inspections include that by Matsuōmaru of his own son in *Terakoya*, and Yoshitsune's inspection of Atsumori/Kojirō in *Ichinotani futaba gunki*.

The practice of *hara-kiri* is one of the Japanese warrior's most notorious and misunderstood customs. The stomach, or *hara*, was regarded as the abode of the soul within the body and so cutting open (*kiri*) the stomach became the preferred method of committing suicide. The formal term for this act is *seppuku*, and its legacy has lasted into more recent times with the much-publicized suicide of the author Mishima Yukio in 1970. *Kanadehon chūshingura* features two *seppuku*, the first being the highly formal suicide of Enya Hangan, and later the more spontaneous cutting open of his own stomach by his retainer Kanpei.

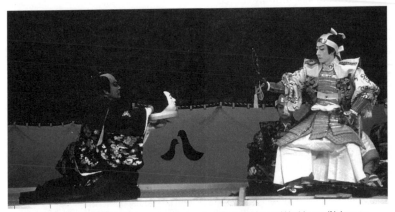

Nakamura Kichiemon II as Kumagai presents the head of his son to general Yoshitsune (Nakamura Baigyoku IV) in the *kubi jikken* scene from *Kumagai jinya*.

Nakamura Ganjirō III as the retainer Kanpei commits *seppuku* in Act VI of *Kanadehon chūshingura*. His mother Okaya (Bandō Takesaburō V) watches.

PANTOMIME, PASSION, AND PUPPETS

DANMARI

Although somewhat uncommon, one may occasionally see a wordless pantomime called a *danmari* in which several characters, supposedly in total darkness, try to gain possession of some precious object or important letter. To offstage musical accompaniment of dreamlike quality, mutual enemies move slowly in a beautifully choreographed manner, colliding with one another in the dark and, at climactic moments, forming beautiful set poses. The *danmari* may end as either the moon appears or the sun rises, and the principal hero or villain gains possession of the sought-after object. *Danmari* are divided into *jidai* (historical) and *sewa* (contemporary) *danmari*. *Jidai danmari* such as *Miyajima no danmari* are now short plays in themselves, while *sewa danmari* are set within the context of a normal play, as in the famous ghost story *Tōkaidō Yotsuya kaidan*.

Kaomise

The *kaomise*, or "face showing," performances are supposedly the most important in the Kabuki calendar. Traditionally they took place in the lunar eleventh month in Edo, and, since the mid-eighteenth century, in the lunar twelfth month in the Osaka–Kyoto region. Today they take place in November at Tokyo's Kabuki-za, and in December at Kyoto's Minami-za, where the actors' names are painted on long, vertical signboards and displayed on the front of the theater.

In the premodern period, when there were still several major theaters competing for audiences, the *kaomise* were opportunities to announce and show off all the leading actors contracted to one particular theater for the year ahead. It represented the first occasion for that group to act together. The order and type of plays were generally fixed, the first item on the program always being a *jidaimono* that probably included a reworking of *Shibaraku* and a *danmari* in its early scenes, and a dance drama such as *Seki no to* in the second act. After the *jidaimono* was completed, a shorter *sewamono* was presented.

Kaomise productions were known for the splendor of their sets and costumes, and before the Meiji period it seems that they were always the occasion for a great many of the popular woodblock prints of actors to be published.

A typical *danmari* scene from a *kaomise* play. From left, Bandō Mitsugorō III, Ichikawa Danjūrō VII, and Iwai Kumesaburō II. By Utagawa Toyokuni II, 1826. (P. Griffith Collection)

EBIZORI

A further expression of great emotion may be seen in both dances and plays when the actor performs the exaggerated pose called *ebizori*. This involves bending the body backwards from a kneeling position into a shape resembling a prawn (*ebi*). These poses are usually performed by animals and creatures of the other world at times of extraordinary stress or emotion. The heron maiden in *Sagi musume* performs an *ebizori* when describing the oppressive tortures of hell.

KUDOKI

Westerners have commented that the polite reserve of the modern Japanese appears at odds with the sometimes searing emotion that is expressed on the Kabuki stage. The *gidayū* narrators in particular can produce displays of

Bandō Tamasaburō V as Sumizome, the spirit of the cherry tree, performing the *ebizori* pose. By Paul Binnie, 1997. (P. Griffith Collection)

extreme passion, commensurate with the most melodramatic of Western theaters.

One particular form of passionate expression of sorrow or yearning by a female character is the so-called *kudoki*. In dances featuring female characters, such *kudoki* are important sections of the work where it is an expression of entreaty to an absent or imaginary lover. In plays, *kudoki* usually last around five minutes and are often a tragic lament. The woman or girl performs alternately in either her own words or in mime to those of the onstage singer. In *Shunkan*, Chidori performs a *kudoki* when she expresses her sadness at being prevented from leaving the island with her lover, Naritsune, and in *Kumagai jinya*, Kumagai's wife Sagami performs a *kudoki* expressing her anguish at the beheading of their only son Kojirō.

kudoki

NINGYŌ BURI

Kabuki's close relationship with Bunraku is rarely far from the surface in *maruhonmono* plays. In one particularly amusing technique called *ningyō buri* ("puppet style"), the actor imitates the jerky movements and gestures of a puppet. Occasionally seen in both plays and dances, the actor is "manipulated" by one or two *kōken* as though they themselves were Bunraku puppeteers. The character of Iwanaga in the *Akoya no kotozeme* scene of *Dannoura kabuto gunki* is a famous example. The technique is not always performed for amusement, however, and in one version of the *Kitsunebi*, "Foxfires," dance from *Honchō nijūshikō*, the effect is one of heightened emotion and urgency on the part of Princess Yaegaki, who is desperate to save her lover's life.

THINGS TO HEAR

Even before the curtain opens we can hear in the distance one of Kabuki's most distinctive sounds. The penetrating and high-pitched "clack" of wooden clappers being struck together warns the actors and stage hands (and the audience!) that the play is about to begin. Called *ki* or *hyōshigi*, these slightly curved rectangular wooden blocks are struck together to signal the opening and closing of a play. There are a variety of rhythmical patterns employed, the most important

ki or *hyōshigi*
A *kurogo* stage assistant
strikes the *hyōshigi*.

tsuke
The *tsuke* are struck against a
board at the side of the stage.

being the accelerating and crescendo beats that accompany the pulling open of the curtain. When the set is revealed, a dramatic pause of two or three seconds is followed by a single loud clack called the *tomegi*, which marks the start of the action. A single clack also marks the close of an act or of the play itself.

There is a further very important set of wooden blocks called *tsuke*. The two *tsuke* (one in each hand) are struck on a flat board by a special stagehand, who can be seen kneeling on the extreme right of the stage. The principal uses of *tsuke* are as an accompaniment to *mie* poses, or to provide a stylized imitation of the clashing of swords and other movements in a *tachimawari* fight, or to imitate the sound of running feet. At moments of great excitement the *tsuke* can be the loudest thing in the theater. Onomatopoeic words are usually employed to describe the beats: rapidly repeated *batabata*, for example, indicate running, and the clearly defined two principal beats around a *mie* pose are *battan*, with the *ba* beat being struck as the actor rotates his head, and the *tan* beat accompanying the snapping of the head into the glaring position.

MUSIC

Several different styles of music accompany Kabuki dances, all of which are vocal, and employ the three-stringed instrument called the shamisen. Originally imported into Japan from China through the Ryūkyū Islands in the late sixteenth century, the shamisen was first called *jamisen*, and differed from the modern instrument in that the body was smaller and covered with snakeskin, and was played with a pick. Players of the biwa started to use the *jamisen*, but changed it into a bigger instrument which they played with their biwa plectrums. The snakeskin cover was changed to catskin, because this was stronger and made a better sound, and the *jamisen* became the modern shamisen. The strings are usually made of silk. It was this instrument that was taken up by the female troupes that created Kabuki in the early seventeenth century, and to this day it remains the single most important instrument on the Kabuki stage.

Kabuki music is divided into two main categories called *katarimono* and *utaimono*. All *katarimono* is basically narrative music emphasizing the telling of a story, while *utaimono* is lyrical and emphasizes poetic imagery and mood.

KATARIMONO

Gidayū

This is named after the great narrator Takemoto Gidayū (1651–1714) and is also known as *takemoto* or *jōruri*. It is the music of Bunraku, but is also used in Kabuki for plays and dances derived from the puppet repertoire. In Bunraku, the *gidayū* narrator (the *tayū*) tells the story, describes situations, and speaks the dialogue on behalf of the puppets. The vocal style is powerful and dramatic because the *tayū* must express all the emotions for the puppet characters. For this reason the *tayū*, with his great range of voices and different characterizations, is almost as much an actor in his own right as he is a musician. In Kabuki, however, the *tayū* often shares the dialogue with human actors and so his role is somewhat diminished. There is an old tradition that forbids any Bunraku musician who defects to Kabuki from

ever returning to the puppet theater, and so the *tayū* and shamisen player for each theater are different. In Kabuki the duo are often referred to as the *chobo*. The size of shamisen used in *gidayū* is the largest, called a *futozao*, "broad neck," with a characteristically deep and resonant tone.

kendai, or "music stand" *(gidayū)*

Tokiwazu

This school was created by Tokiwazu Mojitayū (1709–81) as kabuki dance drama accompaniment in the second half of the eighteenth century. Its special characteristic is a tender, somewhat romantic vocal sound. *Tokiwazu* often accompanies historical pieces of a fantastical or mysterious nature, to which it imparts a feeling of dignified grandeur. Two good examples of *toki-*

kendai (tokiwazu)

wazu music are heard in the dances *Seki no to* and *Masakado*. The shamisen used here is smaller than that heard in *gidayū* and of the three sizes of this instrument in Kabuki, *tokiwazu* employs the medium size, called a *chūzao*, "medium neck."

Kiyomoto

This style was created by Kiyomoto Enjudayū (1777–1825) in Edo around 1814. It is also narrative music, but has a strong lyrical quality. The singer's voice is often pitched high, and a very pronounced vibrato is also a characteristic of this style. The earliest success of the Kiyomoto School was with the dance *Yasuna*. The type of shamisen used by *kiyomoto* musicians is also the *chūzao*.

kendai (kiyomoto)

UTAIMONO

Nagauta

This is the most important example of *utaimono* and, having begun in the early seventeenth century, it is the oldest form of musical accompaniment in Kabuki. It is essentially dance music, sometimes sweetly melodic but at other times highly rhythmical. Most frequently, the *nagauta* style is heard together with percussion and flute. The drums, including the stick drum (*taiko*), the hip drum (*ōtsuzumi*) and the shoulder drum (*kotsuzumi*), and the flute (*nōkan*) are taken from the early Nō theater. Such dances as *Kyōganoko musume Dōjōji* and *Fuji musume* are performed to *nagauta* music. Of the three sizes of shamisen used in Kabuki, the instrument seen in *nagauta* is the smallest, called *hosozao*, or "narrow neck," which has a lighter, higher tone.

kendai (nagauta)

BACKGROUND MUSIC

Geza

There is one further kind of music in Kabuki which is of great importance even though the audience rarely sees the musicians, who are almost always hidden from view behind a slatted wall on the left of the stage. This is Kabuki's background music called *geza*. Though these musicians play music of the *nagauta* style and use the *hosozao* shamisen, they also employ a great variety of instruments such as drums, gongs, flutes, cymbals, and bells, which are not heard in any other school. The *geza* musicians provide stylized sound effects that add immeasurably to the atmosphere and character of Kabuki performances, and learning to recognize what each of the hundreds of sound effects represent is one of the pleasures of frequent visits to the Kabuki theater. For example, with their vast array of different drum patterns, the Geza musicians can suggest the sound of waves, of flowing water, rain, or even (with a slow and steady throbbing of a bass drum) the stylized representation of snowfall. Other combinations of instruments can play melodies associated with floating in a river boat (*tsukuda bushi*), or can create a feeling of solemn dignity in scenes that take place in a palatial setting (*kagen*). The lively bustle associated with the opening of the pleasure houses immediately comes to mind on hearing the shamisen tune *sugagaki*, while the distant clamor of battle (*tōyose*) often provides a fitting background to

scenes of warfare. There is even a fast, irregular pattern of shoulder drum and flute that represents the distraught mind of a mad character (*kakeri*).

STYLES OF SPEECH

WARIZERIFU AND *WATARIZERIFU*

While the Japanese language itself may be a barrier to a total appreciation of Kabuki, there are certain special speeches and ways of speaking that possess a musicality and rhythm and can thus be enjoyed by all Kabuki fans. The most common of these are two types of antiphonal dialogue known as *warizerifu* and *watarizerifu*.

Warizerifu, "divided speech," is antiphonal dialogue shared by two characters who unite to speak the final words together. The characters may be discussing some past or future event and, at the close, come together to decide on a plan of action. Similar to *warizerifu* but spoken by a whole line of perhaps five to ten characters is the technique of *watarizerifu*, "passed speech." These characters can be a line of daimyo as in *Soga no taimen*, or ladies-in-waiting setting the scene or bringing a story up to date. Each character speaks in turn, either completing the unfinished sentence of the previous speaker, or continuing the flow with a fresh idea. All unite to speak the closing phrase in unison. Both of these forms may be spoken rhythmically, particularly towards the unified close.

The *geza* musicians are in a small offstage room to the left of the stage.

KESHŌGOE

One of the most striking aural events, frequently heard in plays in the *aragoto* style, is *keshōgoe*, which literally means "makeup voice." *Keshōgoe* is the repeated rhythmical chanting by less important onstage characters of the literally meaningless phrase "*Aa-rya, kō-rya*" to provide an imposing aural curtain of sound that complements the actions of the hero. In the play *Shibaraku*, for example, this is chanted as Kamakura Gongorō leaves the *hanamichi* and takes up his position in the center of the main stage for the major part of the play. When he arrives and strikes a grand *mie* pose, the chanting is concluded with *dekkei!*, "big!" or "impressive!," after which the action of the play continues.

MONOGATARI AND NORI

In a more serious vein is the convention called *monogatari*, which means simply "story-telling." In the *Kumagai jinya* scene from *Ichinotani futaba gunki*, for example, Kumagai has to tell his wife and Lady Fuji the story of how he was forced to take the head of Lady Fuji's son Atsumori on the battlefield. These important sections in a play are told in both the character's own words and in mime to *gidayū* narration, and climactic moments in the tale are highlighted by dramatic *mie* poses.

Monogatari often incorporate the rhythmical form of speech called *nori*.

Nori, or more correctly, *ito ni noru*, means "to ride the strings," and refers to rhythmical speaking in time to the *gidayū* shamisen. *Nori* requires perfect ensemble between the actor and musician.

AKUTAI AND TSURANE

There are two further types of speech that, while actually quite rare, occur in some of Kabuki's most famous plays. An *akutai* is a speech of abuse, and the most famous example is that of the courtesan Agemaki, directed at the hated Ikyū in the play *Sukeroku yukari no Edo zakura*. She compares Ikyū with her lover, the dashing Sukeroku, and at the end, amused by her own wit, bursts into malicious laughter.

A further very old convention is the so-called *tsurane*, which can still be heard delivered by Kamakura Gongorō, the superhero of the *kabuki jūhachiban* play *Shibaraku*. In a *tsurane*, an *aragoto* character delivers a lengthy speech of self-introduction. The speech is delivered in a poetic but rather grandiloquent manner, containing much wordplay, as well as references to both the actor playing the role and the history and traditions of his acting family. The *tsurane* of *Shibaraku* is traditionally rewritten for each performance. Both a *tsurane* and an *akutai* are also found in the play *Yanone*.

Ma and *Kata*

Most newcomers to Kabuki will be so overwhelmed by the sights and sounds of the theater that they will not have much chance to take in such esoteric concepts as *ma* and *kata*. However, experience brings with it an enhanced appreciation of the subtleties that go into the making of a Kabuki play. Hopefully it will not be too long before the newcomer is joining the real fans on the third floor of the theater discussing one actor's poor *ma* or another's use of an old *kata*.

Ma is literally a "pause" and is applicable to music, acting movements, dance, or speech. The internal psychology of a moment is expressed by the actor, who holds the attention of the audience in a pregnant pause that creates tension and emphasis. *Ma* may be expressed as tension *between* the seven and five syllable lines of poetry in *shichi go chō*. In English one could imagine, for example, "To be or not to be? (Insert dramatic pause, or *ma*.) That is the question." The winding up and final snap of the head in a *mie* is an example of a *ma* of action.

Ma is vital to a good Kabuki performance, and the sense of creating and maintaining tension is the mark of a great Kabuki actor. The *kakegoe* callers at the top of the theater interject their calls in the spaces created by *ma*, so if an actor does not allow enough of a pause the callers will complain among themselves that they are not being given enough time to be effective!

Another subtle but important Kabuki concept is *kata*. *Kata* are conventional methods or patterns of performing a certain role. Set by history and tradition, *kata* can include almost any aspect of the performance, but acting and costumes are the most immediately noticeable.

Kata usually belong to one particular line of actors or acting families and it is common to talk about the "Danjūrō *kata*" or the "Kikugorō *kata*" for a particular role. The role of Sukeroku, for example, belongs principally to the Danjūrō line, but may occasionally be performed by a member of the Onoe family. In that case, however, the *katō bushi* style of music that usually accompanies Sukeroku's entry dance must be replaced by different music because *katō bushi* is strictly for the Danjūrō *kata*.

Similarly, the most common design for Matsuōmaru's robe in *Terakoya* employed by most acting families is black with a snow-covered pine tree design. The Onoe family *kata*, however, uses a grey robe. In the head inspection (*kubi jikken*) scene from the same play, the Danjūrō *kata* dictates that Matsu-ōmaru hold his sword out towards Genzō when making the inspection, something that no other actor does.

In the play *Naozamurai*, the main character enters a soba shop in the depths of winter and drinks some saké. He spots a fleck of dust in the saké cup and flicks it out with a chopstick. This seemingly unimportant action is a *kata* that was created by Ichimura Uzaemon XV (1874–1945), and some actors choose to perform it, while others prefer not to, feeling that it trivial-izes the action of the scene.

During Benkei's famous *ennen no mai*, or "dance of longevity," at the end of *Kanjinchō*, Matsumoto Kōshirō IX has performed an old *kata* that extended his dance from the main stage onto the *hanamichi*. By far the most usual *kata* is to dance only on the main stage.

The number and variety of *kata* are enormous, and provide the Kabuki fan with interesting insights into Kabuki's history and the cre-ativity and personalities of actors past and present.

STAGE

HANAMICHI

Early Kabuki performances took place on a stage based on that of the much older Nō theater. As Kabuki developed through *onna* and *wakashu kabuki* towards the more mature *yarō kabuki*, so, too, came developments in the performance space, moving gradually away from the Nō model.

Although it was certainly added before this date, in 1687 we have the first picture of the *hanamichi*, the "flower path" walkway, set at ninety degrees to the main stage. While there is a theory that this developed from the three small steps leading from the audience floor up to the front of the

Nō stage, in fact the *hanamichi* fulfills a very similar function to the *hashi-gakari* of the Nō theater.

The *hanamichi* came to be used for entrances and exits, and as the place for such important moments in the play as a character's self-introduction or a dramatic *roppō* exit. This very close proximity to the audience pro-duced a real sense of interaction. The earlier theaters also employed another narrower, so-called *kari hanamichi* to the right of the auditorium, which enabled actors actually to walk around the main body of the audience. Today a *kari hanamichi* may be especially erected for those few plays that call for one, such as the *Yoshinogawa* act

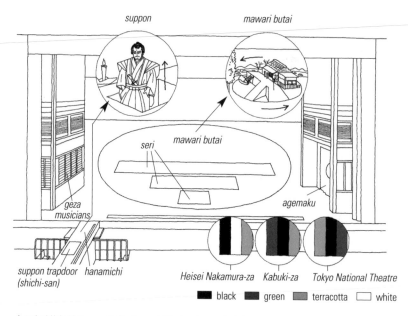

suppon

mawari butai

mawari butai

seri

geza musicians

agemaku

suppon trapdoor (shichi-san) hanamichi

Heisei Nakamura-za   Kabuki-za   Tokyo National Theatre

■ black ■ green ■ terracotta □ white

A typical Kabuki stage with the *hanamichi* extension on the left.

from *Imoseyama onna teikin.*

Important acting on the *hanamichi* usually takes place at a point called the *shichi-san*, "seven-three," which is seven-tenths from the curtain (*agemaku*) at the *hanamichi's* far end, and three-tenths from the main stage. Edo period theaters were rectangular and the *shichi-san* point was originally the opposite way round, closer to the curtain. With the building of Western-style tiered theaters, however, the position three-tenths from the curtain became invisible to all but the ground floor audience. Perhaps as a gesture to earlier times, Sukeroku in the play of the same name still poses for the audience at the original *shichi-san* position

when he makes his famous entrance.

From the backstage area actors reach the small room at the far end of the *hanamichi* by way of a basement passage called the *naraku*—literally, "hell"—which runs its whole length. A full-time stagehand is permanently stationed in this room and it is his job, on a cue given by the actor, to pull back the curtain for an entrance.

MAKU

The introduction of the draw curtain, the *hiki maku*, "pulled curtain," was another important development that enabled quicker, more dramatic revelations of the stage set and characters. From around the middle of the seventeenth century, plays developed from single to multi-act dramas, and varied stage sets (unlike the unchanging painted pine tree of the Nō) came into use. This brought about the necessity of a curtain to shield the stage while changes were being made.

The main curtain is called the *jōshiki maku*, and is of thin, billowy material. Its colors are based on the striped curtains formerly used in the three great theaters of Edo, the Nakamura-za (from left to right, black, white, and terracotta), the Morita-za (green, black, and terracotta), and the Ichimura-za (terracotta, black, and green). The present Kabuki-za curtain is the same as the Morita-za, while the National Theatre employs that of the Ichimura-za. To celebrate an actor's name-taking ceremony (*shūmei*), special curtains are usually made to display the actor's name and personal crest or *mon*.

At the start of a play the *jōshiki maku* is usually opened swiftly, pulled from left to right, accompanied by the accelerating beats of the wooden *ki* clappers. It is similarly closed (from right to left) at the end of a play, but occasionally the far left corner will be held back to allow the *geza* musicians or sometimes a lone shamisen player to accompany a *maku soto* "outside the curtain" exit, such as Benkei's at the end of *Kanjinchō*, and Kumagai's at the end of *Kumagai jinya*.

There is also a curtain at the far end

of the *hanamichi* called the *agemaku*—literally, "lift-up curtain." Despite its name, this curtain hangs on metal rings and the "swish" of these rings signals to the audience that a character is entering along the *hanamichi*. In the special category of plays derived from either Nō or Kyōgen (*matsubamemono*), this curtain is changed and is indeed lifted up on poles from the bottom corners. For these plays, the left side of the stage set incorporates a similar lifted curtain.

Occasionally the *jōshiki maku* is pulled open to reveal another billowy curtain behind it, called the *asagi maku*, or "light-blue curtain." Typically some characters enter in front of this curtain, give an explanatory prologue, and leave. To a sharp "clack" of the *ki*, this is then released by a drop mechanism from above, after which stage assistants remove it from the stage. This is done both to increase expectancy and to reveal a spectacular scene very quickly. Several other curtains of varying designs are used in a similar way to hide a scene from view temporarily, such as the *ajiro maku*, "wickerwork curtain," suggesting the outside of a garden or palace enclosed by a wicker fence. Once this curtain is dropped, we suddenly find ourselves inside, where the action continues.

Occasionally a raised curtain, similar to those used in some Western theaters, can also be seen. This curtain is called a *donchō* and is only used for dances, for *matsubamemono*, or for twentieth-century plays.

MAWARI BUTAI

The *mawari butai,* or "revolving stage," enables very rapid changes of set, as well as more dramatic scenes in which actors or even boats can appear to move from one place to the next. Initially operated manually, revolving stages are now electrically powered. The revolving stage is said to have been used in Japan before any other country, and its invention is credited to the playwright Namiki Shōzō I (1730–73) in 1758.

SERI

The most important of the lifts and traps (*seri*) found in the stage is the one at the *shichi-san* point in the *hanamichi* known as the *suppon,* "snapping turtle." This was first used at Osaka's *Ōnishi Shibai* in 1759, but is now a standard feature of all Kabuki theaters. Though in the Osaka–Kyoto region this lift is used for a variety of characters, in Tokyo it is usually employed for supernatural appearances. An especially well-known use is for the reappearance of the evil magician Nikki Danjō (nowadays in clouds of dry ice), after having disappeared down the lift's hole in the form of a giant rat in *Meiboku sendai hagi.*

Of the many lifts found in the main stage, the largest (*ōzeri*) is in the center where it can even raise or lower entire buildings. This is especially effective when the action of a fight moves from the lower floors onto the roof. At the conclusion of such a fight scene, the roof sometimes flips backwards at a ninety degree angle, allowing for a different scene to be lifted into view in its place. This stage mechanism was first seen at Osaka's *Naka no shibai* in 1761 and is called *gandō gaeshi.* It is used, for example, after the suicide of Benten Kozō in *Aoto zōshi hana no nishiki-e,* as well as in the rooftop struggle at the Hōryūkaku temple in *Hakkenden.* Today the many lifts and traps in the main stage of the National Theatre in Tokyo enable a huge variety of both scenic and acting possibilities.

GEZA AND YUKA

While the stage sets themselves vary, there are two principal unchanging features of the main stage that are usually visible. To the audience's left is a black lattice that conceals the small room where the *geza* musicians perform and, on the audience's right, are two similar positions for the *gidayū* musicians. When performing an important scene, the principal *gidayū* narrator and shamisen player kneel on a small revolving platform (*yuka*) in full view of the audience. This platform can be turned quickly so that the musicians will appear onstage or disappear almost instantly. When less important scenes are being accompanied, they play through another lattice one story up above the platform.

Chapter 2

BUNRAKU

BUNRAKU
GIDAYŪ, SHAMISEN, AND PUPPETS

Taking our seats in the auditorium, we can feel the air of expectancy in the theater. The play is about to begin. Dressed totally in black, a figure steps out from the wings on the right-hand side of the stage. To gain our attention he strikes the *hyōshigi* wooden clappers, and with the sharp "clack" the audience falls silent. He then formally calls to both sides of the theater:

"*Tōzai! Tōzai!*"—"East–West! East–West!"

This man is a junior puppeteer and, in a chanting voice, he announces the title of the act about to be performed, and the names of the narrator and the shamisen player who will provide the musical accompaniment. His announcement completed, he goes back into the wings. In a few seconds the play begins and we enter the world of Bunraku puppet theater.

Puppet theaters can be found in many world cultures, but few have reached the level of sophistication that we see in Bunraku. Four to five feet tall, Bunraku puppets are manipulated by three puppeteers, who perform together with a narrator and musical accompaniment to bring their puppets to life. They may laugh or weep, be compassionate or aloof, show hatred or love. The puppets enact for us the great tragedies and heroic tales from the more distant past, as well as from the eigh-

Sonezaki Shinjū, the lovers Ohatsu and Tokubei prepare to commit suicide in the Tenjin Forest. Ohatsu (left): Yoshida Minosuke; Tokubei: Yoshida Tamao.

teenth and nineteenth centuries when the townspeople of feudal Japan flocked to competing theaters to see the puppets one day and Kabuki actors the next.

The history of Bunraku goes back nearly four hundred years, developing from one-man operated puppets into the three-man teams we see now. But the puppets were only part of the entertainment. Even today, when we as foreigners see Bunraku for the first time, we quickly become equally entranced by the *gidayū* narrator and the three-stringed shamisen player who provides the musical accompaniment. In fact the narrator's performance is so breathtaking he seems more of an actor than a narrator or singer. The puppeteers give the puppets their movements, the *gidayū* gives them their voices. Men and women, young and old—the *gidayū* speaks for all the characters and tells us what they are doing and what they are thinking in a mixture of speech, chanting, and pure song.

In Bunraku we see amazingly skilful puppeteers working in perfect harmony with the powerful and dynamic narrator and shamisen accompanist.

HISTORY

EARLY YEARS

The history of Bunraku begins with *kugutsu*, the first recorded Japanese word for "puppet," and leads from the earliest beginnings of one-man operated puppets, their integration with the narrated stories called *jōruri*, and their development into the complex three-man puppeteer system we see in Bunraku today.

Long before the large and complex puppets that are used now, small one-man operated puppets were employed in Japanese storytelling for many hundreds of years. Traveling street puppeteers were documented as early as the Heian period (794–1185).

Unrelated to the puppets, chanted storytelling accompanied by the four- or five-stringed biwa, a lute-like instrument, was already popular by the eleventh century. The performers appear to have been mainly traveling blind minstrels. Originally the stories were of a religious nature, but gradually more secular themes were adopted and such classics as the great twelfth-century *Heike monogatari* ("The Tale of the Heike"), which dealt with the historical Genji–Heike civil wars, became popular.

These narrated stories came to be called *jōruri*. Princess Jōruri was the lover of Ushiwakamaru, who later became the great general of the Genji clan, Minamoto no Yoshitsune. The popularity of narrated tales about Princess Jōruri and Ushiwakamaru led to her name becoming synonymous with all accompanied narrations.

The addition of puppets to act out the narrated stories was a major development, as was the use of the three-stringed shamisen, which was introduced from China via the Ryūkyū Islands around the year 1560. It is unclear exactly when professional narrators abandoned the biwa for the new shamisen, but this instrument quickly became the principal form of accompaniment.

Although the name Bunraku is now most commonly used in the West, the older term is *ningyō jōruri*, or "puppet Jōruri." *Ningyō jōruri* referred to the combination of storytelling, music, and puppetry that developed toward the end of the sixteenth century some ten years before the recognized birth of Kabuki in 1603.

The creation of *ningyō jōruri* is attributed to Menukiya Chōzaburō (a sword-hilt craftsman by profession) and his partnership with a puppeteer from the island of Awaji, traditionally the home of Japanese puppetry.

While Bunraku was and remains a strictly male profession, some of the early narrators were women. Their disappearance may be a direct result of the banning of women from the stage by the shogunate in 1629, which also brought about the end of the early *onna kabuki*.

The art of storytelling was always considered more important than the puppets, and so the narrators were the influential figures in the early years of the puppet theater's history. The most important of these was Uji Kaganojō (1635–1711), who was greatly influenced by Nō. Not only was Kaganojō's chanting influenced by the Nō *utai* style, he was also a prolific playwright who borrowed extensively from the Nō repertoire. He influenced the structure of the plays themselves (even providing performance instructions for the narrator) and also made an earnest attempt to elevate the standards of his *jōruri* to equal that of Nō.

THE GOLDEN AGE

While *ningyō jōruri* was a popular entertainment, it was the chance coming together of two giants of Japanese culture that propelled it towards great art and eventually gave us the Bunraku we see today.

One of Kaganojō's young students was a boy called Gorōbei. Taking the name Takemoto Gidayū (1651–1714), this boy eventually became the performer responsible for taking accompanied narration to its artistic pinnacle. Takemoto worked most closely with the playwright Chikamatsu

Monzaemon (1653–1724) and this fortunate collaboration was to transform the narrated puppet entertainments.

Chikamatsu Monzaemon was born Sugimori Nobumori, the second son of a samurai family from the province of Echizen. His family moved to Kyoto when he was a boy, and it seems likely that he received a fine literary education, becoming familiar with both Nō *utai* chanting and classics such as the *Heike monogatari* and *Ise monogatari* ("Tales of Ise"). We know that he worked for several families connected with the imperial family and so would have had the chance to observe the cultural life of the court.

Chikamatsu entered the service of Ōgimachi Kinmichi (1653–1733), a nobleman who became a renowned Shinto philosopher and who himself wrote plays for Uji Kaganojō. Chikamatsu, too, showed talent in this direction and also began to write *jōruri*. Moving in some of the highest social and literary circles, he gained in knowledge and learning. Early in his career Chikamatsu also began to write for Kabuki and in particular, between 1693 and 1702, for the great actor of the Kansai region, Sakata Tōjūrō.

Chikamatsu's writing is most celebrated for its psychological penetration and depiction of the human condition. The conflicts between *giri*, which refers to one's social obligations and sense of duty, and *ninjō*, which refers to one's human feelings and desires, found some of their most poignant expressions in his plays.

Sometime in the early 1700s Chikamatsu began writing for the Takemoto-za puppet theater in the Dōtonbori district of Osaka. This theater was founded by the narrator Takemoto Gidayū in 1684, and it was here that Chikamatsu wrote his best known works, many of which were also immediately adapted for Kabuki. The fortuitous creative collaboration between Chikamatsu, Takemoto, and the puppeteer Tatsumatsu Hachirōbei led to the extraordinary artistic flowering of the Japanese puppet theater.

The role of narrator was often combined with that of playwright, but Takemoto, perhaps realizing Chikamatsu's genius, established a clear distinction between the two roles. By leaving the writing to a master like Chikamatsu, Takemoto could put all his efforts into perfecting his performance as narrator.

The Takemoto-za was not without competition. One of the Takemoto narrators, Toyotake Wakatayū (1681–1764) left in 1703 and, together with the playwright Ki no Kaion (1663–1742), founded his own puppet theater, the Toyotake-za. It was in part the competition between these two theaters that led to a rising of artistic standards.

By 1703 the Takemoto-za was in financial distress, and in response Chikamatsu introduced a new genre of plays to the puppet theater called *sewamono*, or "domestic play," based on the real lives of the people of the day. The first of these also portrayed a lovers' double-suicide called *shinjū*. *Sonezaki shinjū*, itself based on a true story, was so great a success that it encouraged a new boom in lovers' suicides in real life. A new level of realism and pathos was reached with this play, and Chikamatsu's words found their finest mode of expression in the musical narration of Takemoto Gidayū.

Developments were also made in the puppets themselves which, in the early days of the Takemoto-za, were small and operated by one puppeteer. In 1734 (after the deaths of both Chikamatsu and Takemoto), at the suggestion of an inventive puppeteer called Yoshida Bunzaburō, three puppeteers were used to manipulate one puppet for the first time. A three-man team enabled more fluid and complex manipulation techniques, which quickly became very popular.

Two years later, at the rival Toyotake-za, yet another innovation was made when a puppet was used that was twice the size of the puppets seen up to that time. By around the middle of the eighteenth century the puppets had reached their present dimensions—about four to five feet tall. Around this time, other intricate additions were also added with the introduction of movable fingers, mouths, eyebrows, and eyes.

Playwrights also flourished and the practice of collaborative writing became common. In particular Takeda Izumo II (1691–1756), Miyoshi Shōraku (1696–1772) and Namiki

Senryū (1695–1751) coauthored the three major *tōshi kyōgen* "full-length" plays that became the mainstays of both the Bunraku and Kabuki repertoires: *Kanadehon chūshingura*, *Sugawara denju tenarai kagami*, and *Yoshitsune senbon zakura*.

DECLINE

While both Nō and Kabuki flourished at least until the Meiji restoration in 1868, the fortunes of Bunraku entered a period of decline in the mid-eighteenth century. Throughout the golden age of Bunraku, there was an almost immediate adoption of the puppet masterpieces by the increasingly popular Kabuki. Both theaters relied on an enthusiastic public for their economic survival, and a slow but steady trend in public tastes away from the puppets towards the actors of the Kabuki theater brought about a decline in Bunraku. By the end of the eighteenth century all the dedicated puppet theaters had closed. The great age in Bunraku's history came to an end in 1765 with the closure of the Toyotake-za. Finally the Takemoto-za shut its doors for the last time in 1767.

One man, however, made a determined attempt to maintain the *jōruri* tradition, and in the process gave his name to the Japanese puppet theater. Masai Kahei (1737–1810) was from the island of Awaji and, as was common with actors and other entertainers, he adopted a stage name, Uemura Bunrakuken. He carried out a plan to revive the art of the puppet theater in Osaka and in 1871 a new theater, the Bunraku-za was named after him. While the term *ningyō jōruri* is still used, the name Bunraku has been synonymous with the puppet theater ever since.

While the traditions of Bunraku continued in Osaka, the Edo audience could not be wooed away from Kabuki, and Bunraku's reputation in the great city became that of the countrified relation.

THE MEIJI RESTORATION AND MODERN BUNRAKU

Bunraku continued in Osaka throughout the Meiji period (1868–1912). In 1909 the entertainment company called Shochiku, which still manages Kabuki, brought all the elements of Bunraku under its umbrella. However, the great fire of 1926 in Osaka destroyed all the venues at which Bunraku was usually seen, along with many invaluable heads, costumes, and other related material. While this was undoubtedly a disaster, it did have the positive outcome of forcing the Bunraku troupe to tour in order to make a living, thereby introducing Bunraku to a much wider audience.

Bunraku was still performed by fine narrators such as Toyotake Yamashiro no Shōjō (1878–1967) and puppeteers such as the very long-lived Yoshida Bungorō (1869–1962), both of whom made great impressions. A new theater was built in Osaka in 1929, and in 1933 the Japanese parliament passed legislation to give Bunraku some financial support, officially recognizing it as a National Cultural Treasure.

Bunraku was once again devastated during the air raids over Osaka during World War II, but in 1956 a new theater was built in the Dōtonbori district which had been the traditional home of the puppets during the Edo period.

There had been union factions within the Bunraku world since 1947 and their disharmony finally led to Shochiku's decision to abandon its management role. Due to this, the Japanese government and several other bodies such as Osaka Prefecture and the national broadcasting company NHK formed the *Bunraku Kyōkai* ("Bunraku Association") in 1963. Its role was to manage the puppet theater on a national basis. Osaka, however, continued to be the home of Bunraku, and the splendidly appointed National Bunraku Theatre opened there in 1984. In Tokyo, Bunraku performances usually take place on an approximately bimonthly basis in the National Theatre.

Bunraku is an art that requires years of harsh, intensive training in an atmosphere of almost feudal subservience to one's master. In the modern era, when young men regularly receive university educations and are continually subjected to the temptations of the modern world in both work and play, one of the greatest difficulties for the traditional performing arts is that of recruitment. In order to train young men and tempt them into the profession, the National Theatre in Tokyo founded a college course at the end of the 1970s both for aspiring young Kabuki actors and for those interested in Bunraku. Today, the Bunraku course is based in Osaka.

Although Bunraku audiences are still smaller than those of Kabuki, its national support and high artistic standards have ensured its survival. Bunraku continues to draw appreciative audiences both at home and on tours abroad.

PLAYS

Bunraku and Kabuki in great part share the same repertoire. Many famous Kabuki plays were originally written for the puppets and adapted almost immediately. In particular, the categorization of plays into *jidaimono* (history plays) and *sewamono* (con- temporary, domestic plays) are identical. Dances called *keigoto* or *keiji* are also occasionally performed in Bunraku. Requiring superb coordination between the puppeteers, most puppet dancing occurs in either auspicious celebratory dances such as the tradi-

Sugawara denju tenarai kagami: Lord Kan Shōjō (Sugawara Michizane) shields his eyes from his daughter (concealed beneath the robe) as he bids farewell to his aunt Kakuju. Kan Shōjō (left): Yoshida Tamao; Kakuju: Yoshida Bunjaku.

tional *Sanbasō* ("Felicitous Sambasō), or in *michiyuki* "travel-dances."

Bunraku plays were given a structure that was found, over many years, to be aesthetically pleasing. In the earliest years of *ningyō jōruri*, plays were divided into six so-called *dan* or "acts," the length of one *dan* being approximately the same as that of a Nō play —around forty-five minutes to an hour. Uji Kaganojō changed this structure, adapting his plays to five *dan*, influenced by the traditional Nō programing of five plays. One *dan* itself was also divided into three parts—the opening, the middle, and the close.

Kaganojō also adopted the *jo ha kyū* structure employed in both Gagaku court music and in Nō plays. *Jo* is the prelude or introduction to the drama, *ha* is the dramatic development (which can last for several acts), and *kyū* is the ending or coda. The three-part structure of both the *dan* divisions and the *jo ha kyū* were praised by Zeami, the man responsible for taking Nō to its pinnacle of development.

In practice, the division of a full-length five-*dan jidaimono* would be as follows:

Jo—the prelude	1st *dan*—the prelude and introduction to the drama.
Ha—the development	2nd *dan*—the beginning of the development.
	3rd *dan*—the central climatic section of the development.
	4th *dan*—the pivotal point in the dramatic development.
Kyū—the ending	5th *dan*—the conclusion to the drama.

The structural divisions for a *sewamono* play were simpler and confined to just three main sections: the first *dan*—the *jo*, the middle *dan*—the *ha*, and the closing *dan*—the *kyū*.

While these structural divisions are important, their effect is reduced by the modern practice of performing just one act of a full-length play and so the gradual development from act to act is difficult to appreciate.

STAGE

Bunraku performances usually take place either in the small hall of the National Theatre in Tokyo or in the purpose-built National Bunraku Theatre in Osaka. These theaters are typically air-conditioned, with comfortable seating. It is the working part of the stage—invisible to the audience—that is completely different, and means that when touring, stages must be specially adapted. We see on page 109 that the working stage area is divided into clear sections, separated by railings. The main working area called the *funazoko* (literally, "the ship's bottom") is lower than the stage to provide a space for the puppeteers' legs, and to allow general unhindered movement.

The first railing from the front serves to separate the audience in the auditorium from the working stage. This barrier (*tesuri*) needs to be about three feet in height to hide the legs of the puppeteers. When held, a puppet's head is roughly the same height as that of the chief puppeteer, and this first barrier therefore creates the illusion

that the puppet is walking on a floor, although it is actually being held in mid-air.

Scenes in Bunraku often display cut-away house interiors and the area (perhaps a garden) in front of it. In this case a further railing, now painted to suit the set, divides the performing area into two. Puppets on the first level are outside the house, while puppets on the second level are inside.

Finally, at the rear of the stage is the painted backdrop. This is often similar to that seen in Kabuki, although the Bunraku stage is, of course, much smaller. Sets are changed by simply moving backdrops and side screens into place by hand. Occasionally, to give the impression that a puppet is traveling a long distance, the backdrops are on a moving roller. The puppet makes the actions of walking and the countryside rolls past behind him.

There is one further extremely important adjunct to the right side of the stage. This is an auxiliary stage known as the *yuka*, which incorporates a revolving platform (*bon*) on which the *gidayū* narrator and shamisen player kneel on large cushions. As Bunraku narration is extremely strenuous, it is common for a play to be divided up among perhaps three different narrators and their partner shamisen players. This revolving platform enables seamless changes of performers for the various parts of the play. The climax of the play is invariably performed by the most famous narrator and shamisen player.

Above the visible platform (or built into the right-hand side of the set) is another area of the same size, which is partially screened from the audience by a hanging bamboo blind called a *misu*. The same combination of narrator and shamisen player performs from this area, but they are less revered players employed for the less significant parts of the play.

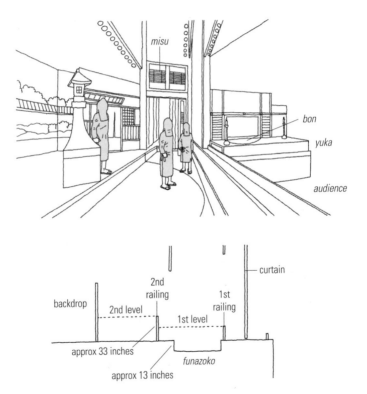

The Bunraku stage viewed from the side, and in cross section.

PUPPETS

Possibly the first thing one notices about Bunraku puppets is their sheer size, many requiring three puppeteers to operate them. In fact, while Bunraku is famous for this trio of puppeteers, they only operate the major characters. Subservient roles such as servants, bystanders, and other crowd members, and animals are operated by one puppeteer.

To bring life to a puppet is, of course, a universal requirement of all puppet theaters. What makes Bunraku so special is that these large and often beautifully attired puppets come to life through the superb coordination of all the puppeteers and the narrator.

KASHIRA

The *kashira*, or head, is the most important and most expressive part of the puppet. They are finely carved, and while most have few, if any moving parts, some do have moving eyes, eyebrows, and mouths. *Kashira* are produced by dedicated craftsmen who also maintain all the strings and toggles on the inside of the head that operate any moving parts. The making and attaching of wigs to the heads, and all hairdressing matters, are carried out by an artisan known as the wig master.

There are about seventy different types of *kashira* and, as a general rule, the heads of puppets in *jidaimono* plays

■ *Kashira* in *Terakoya* act of *Sugawara denju tenarai kagami*

Roles: ① Genzō (the schoolmaster): *kenbishi* (intelligent man) ② Tonami (his wife): *fukeoyama* (married woman) ③ Matsuōmaru (Shihei's retainer): Bunshichi (name of character) ④ Chiyo (Matsuōmaru's wife): *fukeoyama* ⑤ Midaidokoro (Kan Shūsai's mother): *fukeoyama* ⑥ Kan Shūsai (Kan Shōjō's son): male child (larger size). Others: Kotarō (son of Matsuōmaru and Chiyo): male child, Genba (Shihei's retainer): Kintoki (name of character), Pupils at the school: *tsume* (child), Village men: *tsume* (male adult)

are rather larger and more imposing than those used in *sewamono*. Many aspects of a puppet's character may be revealed by the overall facial expression, hairstyle, or headgear, as well as small details such as the shape and bushiness of the eyebrows, the eyes, and the mouth. As in Kabuki, facial color and complexion is indicative of age, character, or social status. Generally, white stands for aristocracy, youth, and goodness.

Kashira may be specific to a particular role, such as the blind warrior Kagekiyo, but are commonly role-interchangeable. They are usually classified into general categories of age, sex, and social class.

The female head known as *musume*, for example, can be employed for any unmarried girl, while married women would have the head known as *fukeoyama*. All female *kashira* have a small, upward pointing pin at one side of their mouths. At moments of great dramatic tension, women in classical Japanese dramas often bite on a piece of cloth in order to suppress their emotions and hold back their tears, and this small pin is to catch a piece of cloth to simulate this.

In some roles it is traditional for the head of the puppet to be changed to one that reflects the developments in the character as the drama progresses.

THE BODIES

The inner skeleton of a Bunraku puppet is quite simple. The *kashira* is attached to a hand grip (*dogushi*), which is placed through the shoulder board. Fabric hangs from the front and back of this shoulder board, and to this is attached the bamboo hoop that forms the puppet's hips. The arms and legs are tied to the shoulder board. As there is almost no substance to the body, it is the costume that gives bulk to the puppet, and it is sewn on to cover the entire skeleton. The costume has a hole in the back to give the chief puppeteer access to the hand grip that controls the *kashira*.

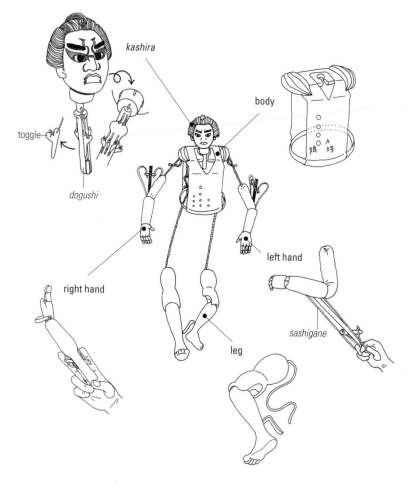

kashira

body

toggle

dogushi

left hand

right hand

sashigane

leg

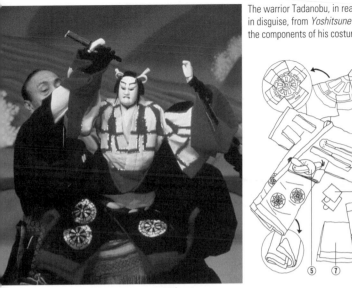

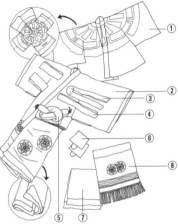

The warrior Tadanobu, in reality the fox Genkurō in disguise, from *Yoshitsune senbon zakura* and the components of his costume.

① *Juban* (under kimono) ② *Kitsuke* (outer kimono) ③ *Bōeri* (stuffed outer collar) ④ *Nakaeri* (inner collar) ⑤ *Maruguke obi* (sash tied around the waist) ⑥ *Tekkō* (covering for the back of the hands) ⑦ *Kyahan* (leggings) ⑧ *Sagari* (tasseled frontpiece)
The collars are the most important part of the costume, and indicate the puppet's role: a white collar, for example, in never used for an evil character. The wide colorful sash is part of fashionable dress. The hand coverings and leggings were traditionally worn when traveling in order to protect the hands and legs from injury and cold.

Puppets are put together anew for each run of a play. The head, costume, and all the other component parts are prepared by the backstage artisans and presented to the puppeteer. The puppeteer himself puts his puppet together, and makes any adjustments that may become necessary after the run begins. The reasons for this are twofold. Firstly, from a purely practical point of view, the puppeteer can thereby ensure that all aspects of the puppet's clothing, working mechanisms, and props are perfect. Secondly, while assembling the puppet, in much the same way that a Nō actor will contemplate his mask before the performance, the puppeteer has the chance to absorb fully all the elements of its character and to contemplate his role.

Props such as swords, fans or letters used by the puppets are similar to those used by Kabuki actors except that they are scaled down in size to suit the dimensions of the puppets.

PUPPETEERS

In most puppet theaters the puppeteers try to make themselves as inconspicuous as possible. In Bunraku, however, appreciation of the technical aspects of puppet manipulation may be an equal part of one's enjoyment. Even the simplest task, such as the entrance of a character, requires perfect coordination. It is the job of the puppeteer to make his puppet as persuasive as a living actor would be in expressing the subtleties, the depth, and the whole gamut of human emotions.

Three-man operation

The three-man operation of most puppets is divided into that of the chief handler (*omozukai*), the left handler (*hidarizukai*), and the leg handler (*ashizukai*). Of these three it is the *omozukai* who is the most important and always the most famous and venerable. Traditionally the path to chief puppeteer takes ten years of training as an *ashizukai*, followed by another ten years as the *hidarizukai*. Only then may one take on the role of *omozukai*. With a further ten years experience one may then be considered a master puppeteer. On a more practical level, however, the speed at which one moves through the ranks is determined by the skill of the individual puppeteer.

Like the *kurogo* stage assistants in Kabuki, the *ashizukai* and *hidarizukai* are normally dressed completely in black with black hoods. (They can see out from behind the hood, but their faces are invisible from the front.) In Japanese theater this black costume traditionally symbolizes invisibility. The *omozukai*, in contrast, dresses in formal costume and is in full view of the audience from the structurally important second act onwards. He wears high clogs (six to twelve inches) in order to increase his height above that of his assistants. The clogs are wrapped with straw around the soles so they will not make a sound when he

6–12 inches

High clogs

moves. Some roles have traditionally called for all three puppeteers to either show their faces or to be hooded, but these are quite rare.

A puppet may weigh from ten to thirty kilos depending on its costume, head, and wig, and the *omozukai* must carry this weight with his left hand. While holding the *dogushi*, the fingers of his left hand also operate the toggles (made of whalebone) that pull the levers to move the eyes, mouth, or eyebrows.

The other principal job of the *omozukai* is to operate the puppet's right arm by inserting his right hand through a hole in the puppets costume and grasping a rod connected to the puppet's right arm. He also manipulates the mechanism that moves the puppet's fingers.

The role of the *hidarizukai* is principally the operation of the puppet's left arm. This he does with his right hand, while keeping his left arm straight and unnoticeable, close against his left side. He may also help to support particularly large male puppets for especially intricate maneuvers. He operates the left arm by holding a twelve-inch rod called a *sashigane*, which also incorporates a mechanism to open and close the puppet's hand. While the work of the *hidarizukai* may appear relatively simple, in fact considerable practice is required to achieve perfect coordination between the chief puppeteer and the left puppeteer.

The role of the *ashizukai* is the most strenuous of all. As the most junior in the hierarchy of puppeteers, he spends his working hours in a semi-crouching position. For male puppets he holds rings on the heels, and for female puppets, which rarely have legs as they would normally be hidden by the kimono, he holds the kimono with his hands in such a way as to imitate feet. Puppet characters occasionally stamp, and it is also the *ashizukai*'s job to stamp his own feet to produce the required sound. As a member of a perfectly coordinated three-man team, the *ashizukai*'s job is a vital one.

The skill of the three-man team comes most noticeably to the fore in complex movements such as dramatic poses. As well as the posing and glaring of the puppet's head, the pose sometimes requires dramatic wide-spaced placing of the feet and stretching out of the arms. When the three men cast their puppet into such a pose, sometimes in a short spurt of feverish activity, the audience frequently bursts into applause. Puppets and puppeteers are as one.

The more profound aspects of their work can be particularly noticeable in the faces of some famous puppeteers. The standard mode of performance is for the *omozukai* to work with an expressionless "stone face." In certain roles, however, some puppeteers make tiny and subtle movements of their faces and appear to be heavily empathizing with the role, almost as though they were acting. The appreciation of such subtleties are all part of the Bunraku experience.

THE GIDAYŪ NARRATOR

Gidayū narrating is a truly amazing performance even for people who do not understand any Japanese. It requires many years of intense training, and is extraordinarily virtuosic, drawing on a huge vocal range, dynamics, and power. The pitch range is almost as extreme as is humanly possible, and the voice is at times nearly torn apart as the narrator strives to express the most searing passions.

Unlike the emotionally detached appearance of the puppeteer from his puppet, the narrator appears to be totally empathizing with the character and infusing the puppets with feelings. In the most passionate of sections he will immerse himself totally in the drama as he grasps his text stand (*kendai*), sometimes even striking it in the heat of emotion. The articulation and expressive intensity of vocal range make *gidayū* narrators as much actors as musicians. The *gidayū* narrator is regarded as the most important person in a Bunraku play, while only the most venerable of puppeteers may perhaps be considered his equal.

Both the *gidayū* narrator (also called the *tayū*) and his accompanying shamisen player appear to the right of the stage in full *kamishimo*, the formal costume of the Edo period. The narrator commonly sings from a text

Gidayū

which, in a gesture of respect to the playwrights and narrators of the past, he lifts up to his forehead before and after the performance. Despite the reassuring presence of this text, which he knows from memory anyway, the ultimate success of the play rests on the narrator's vocal performance.

The narrated chanting of the *gidayū* is divided into three broad styles known as *kotoba*, *ji* (or *jiai*), and *fushi*.

Kotoba refers to the non-melodic speech the narrator employs when he speaks dialogue for the onstage puppet characters.

Ji refers to those sections in which the shamisen joins in and which are usually semi-sung or chanted in rhythm to the instrument. Very often the shamisen plays short motifs, sometimes just a few notes, or even just a single one, which serve to punctuate the narrator's words, rather like punctuation in a sentence. These sections are usually comments on the thoughts and emotions of the characters and onstage actions.

Fushi are melodic. The narrator tends to sing rather than chant, and the shamisen plays pure melody rather than punctuating motifs. This style of delivery is usually employed at special moments of great pathos, such as the death of the boy Kotarō in the famous *Iroha okuri* section from *Terakoya*, and in *kudoki*, the emotional expressions, usually of love, by a female character.

As in any art, rules may sometimes be broken and it is not uncommon for the shamisen to join in *kotoba* sections. In essence, *gidayū* narration is the continual alternation and juxtaposition of speech and some form of song, either chant-like or more lyrical. To take a simple phrase as an example:

"I shall return home," he said, and walked sadly towards the gate.

"I shall return home" is *kotoba*, the words actually spoken by the character. These the narrator speaks dramatically exactly as though he were onstage. "He said, and walked sadly towards the gate," or any similar comment on the thoughts or emotions of the characters or the onstage action, however, is *ji* and will be rhythmically sung or chanted by the narrator to an accom-

panying shamisen motif or phrase. The elaborately and beautifully written texts that the narrators follow contain small markings in red ink which indicate *kotoba*, *jiai*, or *fushi*. In addition, there are indications as to the low, middle, or high pitching of the voice.

While the narrator may appear to be kneeling, he is actually seated on a *shirihiki*, a very low stool that lifts his body just enough to free his stomach

Shirihiki

and ribcage. He also curls his toes under his feet, as though he were about to spring forward. As the narrator's vocal production cannot be from the throat alone, he needs to employ as much of his abdomen as possible in order to achieve a wide dynamic range and great power. This position leaves the narrator's body as unconstrained as possible. To give further assistance to his abdomen muscles, he ties a belt tightly around his stomach and places a bag of either sand or beans weighing five to seven hundred grams (approx. 1–1½ pounds) at the front of his torso, under the outer garment. This supports his stomach and helps to achieve resonance in the lower body.

There are many subtly varying

The *gidayū* narrator Takemoto Tsunatayū and the shamisen player Tsuruzawa Seijirō V performing the *Terakoya* act of *Sugawara Denju Tenarai Kagami*.

styles of narration and these are passed on through imitation to successive generations learning the narrator's art. Students are expected to copy their master's vocal production exactly until they are good enough to perform the play themselves. The way in which a specific play, and even a specific character within the play, is performed is set by tradition and must be learned precisely. When changes are made, they tend to be very slight and are only made by the most respected of musicians.

Students stay close to the *gidayū* narrator in order to learn from them. As *kurogo* during the performance, one of their tasks is to bring tea to the *gidayū*, placing it beside his *kendai*.

THE SHAMISEN

Gidayū narration could not exist without the accompaniment of the three-stringed shamisen. This combination is the closest of artistic collaborations, requiring many years to achieve a harmonious working relationship. A Bunraku performance is always the result of much rehearsal and teamwork, and there is a true feeling of ensemble between the three main parties: the narrator, the shamisen player, and the puppeteers.

The music of the shamisen creates atmosphere and gives tempo to the stage action. The motifs may punctuate the speech of a character (a sharp twang, for example, could function as an exclamation), provide small bridges between one speech and the next, or link one section of the drama to what follows.

Within about one hundred years after its introduction from China (c. 1560), the shamisen had firmly established itself in Japanese culture.

Shamisen

It became the preferred instrument of both the puppet theater and Kabuki, and was also the popular instrument of entertainment in the "floating world" (*ukiyo*) of the pleasure quarters.

There are three principal sizes of shamisen and the one employed in Bunraku (and in Kabuki plays adapted from the puppets) is the largest and most sonorous, called the *futozao*, or "broad-neck" shamisen.

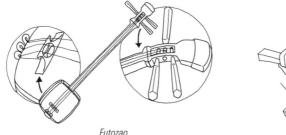

Futozao   Plectrum

Unlike the narrator, the shamisen player does not have any text or score in front of him and plays his entire part from memory. The accompaniment for each *gidayū* text is set by tradition and each consists of complex mixtures of musical styles. Some generally more lengthy pieces are original to a particular section of a play and are specifically intended to add atmosphere, accompany a special dance, or highlight a specific moment of tragedy or lamentation.

Another major style consists of many set patterns of single notes, short motifs, or longer phrases. These patterns not only punctuate the narrator's recitation but may also give aural clues to the mood of a certain section in the play. A pattern of alternating notes one tone apart called *naki*, for example, is always associated with weeping. It may be deep for a male and an octave higher for a woman.

OFFSTAGE MUSIC

Offstage background music, much like the *geza* music of Kabuki, can also be heard in Bunraku and provides stylized sound effects that add to the atmosphere and character of Bunraku performances.

Akoya kotozeme: as part of her interrogation the courtesan Akoya is forced to play musical instruments. From left, Iwanaga: Yoshida Tamame; Shigetada: Yoshida Bungo; Akoya: Yoshida Minosuke.

SYNOPSES

KABUKI

The following synopses are famous examples of Kabuki plays that are not derived from the puppet theater. They are either works originally written for Kabuki or plays of the *matsubamemono* category, originating either in Nō or Kyōgen. (For *maruhonmono*, see page 141)

Benten musume meo no shiranami ("Benten the Male–Female Bandit")

Sewamono, shiranamimono.
Alternative titles: *Aoto zōshi hana no nishiki-e* ("The Glorious Picture Book of Aoto's Exploits"); *Shiranami gonin otoko* ("The *Shiranami* Five Thieves").
Written by Kawatake Mokuami.
First performed in 1862 at the Ichimura-za, Edo.
Acts III and IV are performed regularly today.

ACT III: *Hamamatsuya* ("The Hamamatsu Textile Shop")
A wealthy young girl and her samurai servant arrive at the Hamamatsuya kimono shop to make purchases for her wedding trousseau. While looking at material, the shop assistants witness the girl steal a piece of crepe and the pair is accused of theft. There is a scuffle and she is hit on the forehead with an abacus.

The servant, however, proves that the crepe was actually bought elsewhere and that it belongs to them. Appalled by the mistake, the master of the shop is about to hand over some money in compensation when a mysterious gentleman disguised as a samurai enters. This is actually Nippon Daemon, the leader of the *Shiranami* "White Wave" gang of thieves.

He exposes the girl and her servant as the thieves Benten Kozō and Nangō Rikimaru. The actor who plays the leading role of Benten Kozō must also be an accomplished *onnagata* as his change from demure young maiden to a brash thief is the highlight of this play. He lowers the sleeve of his kimono to reveal his brightly tat-tooed arm and delivers his famous speech of introduction full of self-importance, beginning with *Shirazā itte kikase yashō* ("If you don't know me, then listen well"). This is one of Kabuki's most famous speeches, and is delivered mainly in *shichi go chō*, or seven–five meter.

In reality, all three are members of the same gang. Daemon's plan is to ingratiate himself with the shop by exposing this petty theft, and then attempt a much grander scam. To avoid a scandal, however, the master gives Benten and Nangō some money after all and they leave.

ACT IV: *Inasegawa seizoroi* ("The Gathering along the Inase River Bank")
This short riverbank scene is famous for its spectacular costumes and beautiful cherry trees in full bloom, as well as for the speeches and dramatic *mie* poses of the five thieves as they name themselves before fighting with the police.

The thieves are making their escape and enter along the *hanamichi* in splendid kimono, holding open umbrellas decorated with the characters for *shiranami*, the name of the gang. Surrounded by the police, one by one they introduce themselves with tales of their upbringing and lives of crime. The scene closes in a spectacular tableau, as the police attempt to make their arrests.

Occasionally two further short scenes are performed in which Benten, atop a temple roof, commits *seppuku* (suicide); and Nippon Daemon, perched high on a temple gate, proudly surrenders.

Fuji musume ("The Wisteria Maiden")

Shosagoto.
Nagauta music by Kineya Rokusaburō IV.
Lyrics by Katsui Genpachi.
First performed in 1826 at the Nakamura-za, Edo.
Originally one section of a five-part *hengemono* dance called *Kaesu gaesu onagori Ōtsu-e* ("Pictures from Ōtsu as Farewell Keepsakes"), but now performed independently.

In its earliest version this dance was part of a farewell performance by the actor Seki Sanjūrō II to mark his return to his native Osaka after a twenty-year sojourn in Edo. For this special occasion a dance was devised featuring characters from folk paintings sold as souvenirs in the town of Ōtsu, near Kyoto. One of these characters was the "Wisteria Maiden," and the dance portrayed a pleasure-seeking young girl dressed in all her finery out on a trip in the countryside.

In 1937, however, Onoe Kikugorō VI substantially altered the nature of the dance by changing the human Wisteria Maiden into the spirit of the wisteria vine and by adding a new section of lyrics by Oka Kitarō called *Fuji ondo* ("Wisteria Song"). It is this version that is most often performed today, although the more traditional interpretation is still seen occasionally.

The auditorium lights are turned off and the curtain lifts in total darkness. The opening lyrics are sung softly, inviting us to imagine a peaceful scene in late spring where, by the lapping waters of Lake Biwa, cascades of wisteria blossom hang from the branches of a great pine tree. Suddenly the lights are switched on and we see the tree and flowers before us. Standing at the base of the tree with a branch of wisteria over one shoulder is a charming young woman—the Wisteria Maiden.

In her black lacquered hat, she dances with the flowers as the musicians sing of the deep purple wisteria, a color associated with the city of Edo. We hear that the union of the flowers (from the west) and Edo (in the east) is a happy one. This is a reference to the Osaka actor Sanjūrō, who had spent a successful period working in Edo. The maiden retreats briefly behind the massive tree trunk.

The next section is the *kudoki*, in which the maiden expresses her love for a man and her bitterness at his fickle heart. Such sections are often highlights in dances featuring female characters, but the *kudoki* in *Fuji musume* stands out because it contains a series of puns alluding to the "Eight Sights of Ōmi Province." Famous from classical literature and art, the allusion to these beautiful views adds great poignancy. We're told, for example, that the man promised not to meet other women, the word for "not to meet," *awazu*, suggesting also the place of that name and a view of clearing skies after a storm. The word for "promise," *kanegoto*, suggests the sound of the evening bell at Mii Temple, another famous beauty spot.

A musical interlude is then followed by the *Fuji ondo* section, although very occasionally a passage called *Itako*, composed in 1854, is heard instead. *Fuji ondo* is more popular because the spirit of the wisteria is portrayed humorously as a bashful and innocent girl in love. Though the first time she accepts a cup of saké she pours it away, the second time she drinks it up and immediately becomes tipsy. For the dancer, this is the most demanding section because he must appear off beat, without actually being so.

There is a final quick section playing on the idea of pine trees called *matsu zukushi*, or "a catalogue of pines," where the pledges of courtesans at Arima are said to last forever just like the pine, a symbol of eternity. Entwined in the branches is the wisteria vine, and beneath the flowers, we're told, is a good place to sleep.

Finally, a temple bell signals the end of day. The lyrics refer poetically to the spring murmurs speaking of the eternal bond between the pine and wisteria. The maiden takes up her branch of flowers once more and fades into the deepening twilight.

Funa Benkei ("Benkei Aboard Ship")

Matsubamemono, shin kabuki jūhachiban.
Nagauta music by Kineya Shōjirō III.
Choreography by Hanayagi Jusuke I.
Written by Kawatake Mokuami.
First performed in 1885 by Ichikawa Danjūrō IX at

the Shintomi-za, Tokyo. A Nō play of the same name exists, on which the Kabuki version is based.

The year is 1185. Minamoto Yoshitsune, a young commander of the Genji clan, is forced to escape from the forces of his elder brother, the shogun Yoritomo, because the latter has become jealous of Yoshitsune's brilliance. Accompanied by his right-hand man Benkei, four faithful retainers, and his lover Shizuka Gozen, Yoshitsune travels westward from Kyoto to the Bay of Daimotsu.

Before setting sail they decide that Shizuka's presence may cause rumors to spread, and she should therefore return alone to the capital. Shizuka is reluctant to part from Yoshitsune but is finally persuaded and accepts a farewell cup of saké. As a professional *shirabyōshi* dancer she agrees to dance for them one last time and performs the *Miyako meisho*, "Famous Places of the Capital," a dance illustrating Kyoto's beauty spots through the four seasons. This is the first great highlight of the work.

With arms opening upwards to indicate the dawn of a new day and her fan fluttering to indicate the snow, Shizuka illustrates the beautiful opening lyrics:

At daybreak in spring the skies
grow pale as snowfall . . .
pale as blossoms in Omuro,
Jishu and Hatsuse.

As we hear of people gathered beneath the cherry blossoms to drink and be merry, she mimes pouring and drinking saké, and shades her eyes to view the scene at Mt. Arashi where the storm winds blow the petals from the trees. A series of equally poetic images take us through summer with the dense forests of Mt. Kurama, and autumn with the brilliant foliage of Mt. Takao. In winter the snow weighs down the bamboo in Fushimi, while in Uji fishing nets line the cold river. Finally, the dance ends with the image of another sunrise over the slopes of Mt. Asahi, symbolizing Shizuka's hopes for a better time to come. For now she must depart and she does so in tears.

The ship's captain comes to report that the vessel is prepared and Yoshitsune and his men board. The captain and sailors celebrate the

favorable weather with an auspicious dance describing the people who dwell harmoniously in the country of Japan. As they row out into the bay, however, conditions quickly change. The skies blacken with clouds and a sudden storm causes waves to surge about their craft. In the distance they see the ghost warriors of the enemy Heike clan whom Yoshitsune had defeated on these very waters a short time before. Their leader is the Heike general Tomomori, who has appeared to seek revenge. (This role is taken by the same actor who played Shizuka.) Brandishing his halberd above the waves, Tomomori's ghost charges repeatedly at the boat, but is finally defeated by Benkei's fervent prayers and is sucked back down into the ocean depths by a violent whirlpool.

Kagami jishi ("The Mirror Lion")

Shosagoto, shin kabuki jūhachiban.
Nagauta music by Kineya Shōjirō III.
Choreography by Ichikawa Danjūrō IX and Fujima Kan'emon II.
Lyrics by Fukuchi Ōchi.
First performed in 1893 by Danjūrō IX at the Kabuki-za, Tokyo. Certain sections are based on the Nō play *Shakkyō* and this dance was adapted from *Makura jishi* ("The Pillow Lion," 1742). The word *shishi* (*jishi*) refers to a mythical lion-like beast considered holy and associated with the Buddhist deity Monju.

The setting is Chiyoda Castle, the shogun's residence in Edo, where a young maid, Yayoi, is ordered to dance with a wooden *shishi* head as part of the New Year festivities. Her performance will take place in a spacious room, at the side of which is an altar set with a pair of such *shishi* heads, saké, and offerings of *kagami mochi* (rice cakes shaped like ancient circular mirrors). It is from these *kagami* rice cakes that the dance gets its name.

Two ladies-in-waiting briefly explain the proceedings to two retainers before going to fetch Yayoi so that she can rehearse. The men retire to watch from the side. When she is brought in Yayoi is bashful and reluctant to perform, but the ladies push her into the middle of the room and leave quickly. Now alone, Yayoi nervously begins.

The introductory lyrics suggest Yayoi's innocent adolescence, her life spent closeted in the women's quarters of the castle where men are forbidden and where she entertains herself with girlish dreams of romance. The topic of love reminds her of courtesans' dances at Ise where the *Kawasaki* folk songs are famous. Known as *Kawasaki ondo*, this is the first musical highlight.

Yayoi's own character is described in a section punning on hairstyles and ornaments, her sleek tresses typical of a "headstrong" young woman frustrated by living under the watchful gaze of older serving ladies.

Only rarely is she allowed on outings to view the spring blossoms. Yayoi dances with a small ladies' fan as the lyrics evoke beautifully a landscape of mountain hamlets, valleys, and rushing streams. She recalls the *Hinda* folk dances performed in the countryside where young maidens plant rice-seedlings in the fifth month. Yayoi sees a bush warbler suddenly taking to the air and she follows its upward path with her eyes.

She imagines blossoming peonies, their large petals tumbling softly to the ground, and dances with a pair of weighted fans, spinning them or flipping them one over the other in a section famous for its demanding technique. At last, the idea of peonies leads to the mention of the *shishi* lion that always gambols among peony flowers. The *shishi* is the "king of beasts," the peony, the "king of flowers".

With the appearance of the *shishi*, the lyrics transport us to a divine landscape high on a sacred mountain where a stone bridge spans a deep ravine. This bridge is not man-made and cannot be crossed by ordinary mortals, for on its far side lies the Buddhist Pure Land.

Yayoi now goes to the small altar and takes one of the carved *shishi* heads in her hand. Mysteriously, two butterflies appear in the room and as she glances up at one of them, she does not notice that the *shishi* head comes alive. The head becomes violent as it darts at the other butterfly and Yayoi is quickly overcome, dragged against her will down the *hanamichi*.

There is an interlude featuring the two butterfly spirits transformed into a pair of young girls who dance with small drums and tambourines

as the lyrics bemoan the fleeting nature of time and the brevity of a butterfly's life.

Finally, the spirit of the *shishi* itself enters on the *hanamichi* danced by the same actor who performed Yayoi. In a costume based on that seen in Nō but with a longer trailing wig, the *shishi* is teased into a frenzy by the butterflies, eventually swinging the wig around its head repeatedly in the spectacular finale of the dance.

Kagotsurube satō no eizame ("The Sword Kagotsurube")

Sewamono, enkirimono.
Written by Kawatake Shinshichi III.
First performed in 1888 at the Meiji-za, Tokyo.
Kagotsurube is the name of a famous sword which, according to legend, cannot be resheathed without drawing blood.

The wealthy farmer Jirōzaemon has a face disfigured by smallpox. Coming from the country, he has never been to the big city before and today he is visiting the "New Yoshiwara" pleasure quarters to see the blossoming cherries and bright lights just once before returning home. Soon, he is treated to one of the great spectacles of the quarter, a high-ranking courtesan's parade through the streets. He is impressed, but another parade then comes past that seals his fate. This second parade features the star attraction of the Yoshiwara, the fabulous courtesan Yatsuhashi. For her part, Yatsuhashi has never seen such a pock-marked and countrified man before, and she cannot help but smile to herself. Performed on the *hanamichi*, this is one of the most famous moments in Kabuki, for with this single smile Jirōzaemon falls in love.

Time has elapsed, and Jirōzaemon is now a regular customer at the teahouse where Yatsuhashi works. Inexperienced in the ways of love, he believes that she returns his affections and he has even begun lengthy negotiations to buy her out of her contract so that she can become his wife. In fact, she has no intention of accepting this offer but it is part of professional etiquette to act compassionately towards good patrons and she allows him to indulge himself.

Yatsuhashi's foster father is the evil Tsurigane Gonpachi, responsible for selling her into prostitution and constantly asking for money on her credit. Hearing that Jirōzaemon is to ransom her, he comes along to the teahouse to borrow yet more cash but is summarily refused by the proprietor. Jirōzaemon appears with two colleagues whom he is showing around town. Entering the teahouse, they are duly impressed with Yatsuhashi's beauty and all look forward to a pleasurable evening.

Yatsuhashi's childhood sweetheart is Shigeyama Einojō, a handsome but masterless samurai to whom she is faithful in spirit even though she must work as a courtesan. Hoping to cause trouble, Gonpachi arrives at his house to inform him that Yatsuhashi will be redeemed and that she no longer loves him. Einojō flies into a rage and decides to go to the teahouse at once to break off their relations.

At the teahouse, Einojō calls Yatsuhashi from the party and berates her for being unfaithful, demanding that she break off with Jirōzaemon publicly and at once. Though this is unpardonable behavior for a courtesan, Yatsuhashi has no choice. The following scene of rejection, known as *aiso zukashi*, is the heart-rending climax of the play.

When Yatsuhashi returns to the party she seems out of sorts. Telling Jirōzaemon to be silent, she shocks and embarrasses everyone gathered there by saying that both his voice and his face are making her ill. The idea of being redeemed by him was repugnant to her from the start. Now she firmly rejects his offer and will thank him not to bother her again. Shamed in front of his colleagues, Jirōzaemon's reply is as magnanimous as Yatsuhashi's rejection was cruel. In a moving and beautiful speech he explains that a courtesan's life is as uncertain as a reed adrift on a stream. It was to save her from this that he wanted to redeem her. But now Jirōzaemon renounces all claims on her and Yatsuhashi leaves the room.

The final scene takes place four months later. Jirōzaemon returns to the teahouse ostensibly to bury the past. Ashamed of herself, Yatsuhashi begs his forgiveness and is overjoyed when he proposes that they forget what happened and share a cup of saké. Making sure that no one else is in the room, however, he announces that the drink is to be her farewell to the world. Drawing his sword, Kagotsurube, he kills her with a single slash.

Kanjinchō ("The Subscription Scroll")

Matsubamemono, kabuki jūhachiban.
Nagauta music by Kineya Rokusaburō IV, choreography by Nishikawa Senzō IV.
Lyrics by Namiki Gohei III.
First performed in 1840 by Ichikawa Danjūrō VII at the Kawarasaki-za, Edo. The story is based on the Nō play *Ataka*, and the early play, *Hoshijūnidan*, performed by Danjūrō I in 1702.

Set in the late twelfth century, the play depicts an episode from the life of general Minamoto Yoshitsune. Accompanied by a small group of trusted retainers, he is escaping from the jealous wrath of his older brother, the shogun Yoritomo. Yoshitsune's right-hand man is the warrior priest Benkei, and it is he who suggests the retainers disguise themselves as mountain ascetics called *yamabushi*, with Yoshitsune as their porter. Hearing rumors of this, Yoritomo orders new road barriers set up in order to stop and interrogate all such *yamabushi*.

On their way north, they reach the Ataka barrier where they must confront the barrier guard Togashi. Benkei speaks for his group, declaring that they are sent on a fund-raising mission for the rebuilding of the famous Tōdaiji temple. He is challenged by Togashi to produce and read out the list of subscribers (the *kanjinchō* of the play's title) that all fund-raisers were bound to possess. Not having such a *kanjinchō*, Benkei is forced to bluff by improvising the contents from an empty scroll. He ends with the impressive *Fudō mie*, a pose copying the iconography of the Buddhist deity Fudō, guardian protector of the *yamabushi*.

Still dubious, Togashi interrogates Benkei about the complicated symbolism of the *yamabushi* costume and this fierce verbal exchange, called *yamabushi mondō*, is famous for its escalating pace and tension. Benkei concludes with the defiant *Genroku mie* pose.

Benkei's knowledge is impressive and Togashi allows them to pass. One of his soldiers then points out the figure of the porter who resembles Yoshitsune. To allay their suspicions, Benkei is forced to beat Yoshitsune with his staff as though punishing the porter. Togashi is now certain that this group is indeed Yoshitsune and his men but, deeply moved by Benkei's loyalty, he decides to allow them through the barrier, even though he knows he must pay for this later with his own life.

Having passed safely and now a short distance from the barrier, Yoshitsune resumes his rightful position as lord of his group. As beating one's lord was an act of grave disloyalty, Benkei sheds tears for the first time in his life, but Yoshitsune forgives him in a moving display of affection between lord and retainer.

Suddenly Togashi reappears. Claiming to feel sorry that he treated them so badly at the barrier, he offers Benkei some saké, which is eagerly accepted. After drinking copious amounts, Benkei entertains with the *ennen no mai* "dance of longevity," beginning with slow, circular movements and gradually increasing in speed and excitement. The lyrics tell of an ideal landscape where the power of nature reigns eternally.

Seeing that Togashi is momentarily off guard while he watches the dance, Benkei signals for his group to leave at once and they hasten on their way. Benkei bids Togashi a moving farewell and the curtain is closed. Alone on the *hanamichi*, Benkei feels relieved and elated. He performs his famous bounding *tobi roppō* exit as he rushes to catch up with his lord.

Kirare Yosa ("Scarface Yosaburō")

Sewamono.
Alternative titles: the full title of the play is *Yowa nasake ukina no yokogushi*. It is also known by the location of the second scene, *Genjidana* or *Genyadana*.
Written by Segawa Jokō III.
First performed in 1853 at the Nakamura-za, Edo.
Of the original nine acts, only Acts II and IV are regularly performed today.

Yosaburō is the adopted son of a household called Izuya in the Motoyama district of Kamakura. This story concerns his love affair with Otomi, the mistress of a powerful gangster, Akama Genzaemon. The play is replete with the realistic atmosphere and customs of its time.

ACT II: *Kisarazu hama* ("The Beach at Kisarazu")
Yosaburō has been sent to the house of a relative in the seaside town of Kisarazu. While walking on the beach he sees Otomi and falls in love with her at first sight. Dazed at her beauty, his *haori* jacket slips from his shoulders. The act closes with a romantic and somewhat comic touch as he absentmindedly picks up the jacket and, still gazing after her, puts it on inside out. Act III, entitled Akama Bessō, is rarely performed nowadays. It takes place at the country cottage of the gangster Akama Genzaemon. Yosaburō and Otomi become lovers and one night their affair is discovered. Furious, Akama has Yosaburō's body and face slashed with a sword and, covered in cuts, he is thrown into the sea and left for dead. Otomi also tries to drown herself but is rescued by the clerk Izumiya Tazaemon, who takes her back to Edo and establishes her in a house of her own.

ACT IV: *Genjidana* ("The Genjidana Concubine's House")
The playwright moved the action to *Genyadana* street in Kamakura as it was forbidden to use the names of real Edo locations, *Genjidana*, on the stage. Three years have passed and both Yosaburō and Otomi believe the other to be dead. Yosa, as he is now known, is disfigured by scars and has become a petty criminal who tries to extort money with the help of his friend, Kōmori Yasu or "Bat Yasu," so called because he bears the tattoo of a bat on his cheek.

Yosa enters Otomi's house with the intention of getting his hands on some money and is amazed to see her again. She does not recognize him but he suddenly sits himself cross-legged on the floor, removes the scarf covering his scarred face and drapes it elegantly around his shoulders. Lighting a pipe, he begins a famous speech which opens with *Otomi . . . hisashiburi da nā!* ("Otomi . . . been a long time, hasn't it?"). He regrets having met her in the first place and the dire straits to which the meeting ultimately brought him.

Otomi in turn tells of her rescue and of how she has thought of him every day since their last meeting. She also explains that, although he rescued her, she has never made love with Tazaemon. Yosa, however, does not believe her and, while trying to extort some money from her, is interrupted by Tazaemon's return. Otomi pretends that Yosa is her brother and Tazaemon gives him fifteen *ryō* (pieces of gold). Yosa is not satisfied with this but is persuaded by Yasu that they should take the money and leave.

In the following scenes, no longer performed, Yosa returns to find Otomi. It transpires that Tazaemon is actually Otomi's real brother and Yosa's scars are healed by a magical potion. The couple are happily reunited.

Kyōganoko musume Dōjōji ("The Maiden at Dōjōji")

Shosagoto, dōjōjimono.
Nagauta music by Kineya Sakujūrō and Kineya Yajūrō I.
Choreography by Nakamura Tomijūrō I and Ichikawa Dangorō I.
Lyrics by Fujimoto Tobun.
First performed in 1753 by Nakamura Tomijūrō I at the Nakamura-za, Edo. Inspired by the Nō play *Dōjōji*, this work is considered perhaps the greatest single dance in the Kabuki repertoire and the severest test of an *onnagata*'s skill.

Based on the legend of Dōjōji temple in present day Wakayama Prefecture, the dance tells of the maiden Kiyohime who, believing herself promised in marriage to a traveling priest, pursued him to the temple where he hid under a large bronze bell. At this, her bitterness and anger transformed her into a fiery serpent, which coiled itself around the bell, melting both the bell and the unfortunate priest beneath.

Now some time later, a new bell is to be consecrated and fearing that Kiyohime may reappear, the chief priest decrees that women are forbidden to enter the temple. Nevertheless,

disguised as a beautiful *shirabyōshi* dancer, the spirit of Kiyohime returns to trick the foolish acolytes and destroy the new bell.

The entire dance is very long. The first section is the *michiyuki* where Kiyohime is seen traveling to the temple. Performed on the *hanamichi*, it portrays a young maiden's romantic imaginings. Upon reaching Dōjōji, there is a *mondō* "question and answer" section with the temple acolytes, who are easily won over by this woman's beauty and wit. She offers to entertain them by dancing. Sometimes the first section is omitted and the performance starts at this point.

Heavily influenced by the Nō play *Dōjōji*, Kiyohime's dance begins with the slow *ranbyōshi*, "mad rhythm," as she puts out her right foot and lifts it slightly. She proceeds into the *kyū-no-mai*, "fast dance," during which she frequently glances up at the bell that is a hateful reminder of her suffering. Following this is the solemn "bell section" in which the singers relate the times when the bell is rung, tolling out life's impermanence and promising salvation in Buddha.

With a sudden change in mood and tempo, the dancer depicts the charms of a city girl in love. There is a *hikinuki* costume change and a *kuruwa zukushi* or "catalog of pleasure districts" as the lyrics bring together the names of real pleasure quarters in old Japan. The dancer portrays the different types and ages of women found there. She goes on to perform with flower-like hats, and the acolytes themselves join in as the lyrics compare the beauty of different kinds of blossoms. The highlight of the dance is the *kudoki*, in which the dancer imagines being in her lover's company, berating him for his inconstancy. The section is famous for its sensuality and the portrayal of a woman's tender emotions.

Next is the rhythmical *yama zukushi*, or "catalog of mountains," wherein the singers list the names of real mountains in Japan while also making a series of clever puns referring to the maiden's love affair.

Other costume changes follow and the dance increases in tempo until, at last, the spirit of Kiyohime sees her chance to destroy the bell.

Defeating the acolytes with ease, Kiyohime causes the bell to crash to the ground and climbs on top to strike the final defiant pose.

Though rarely performed, a longer, alternate ending exists in which the bell descends on top of Kiyohime. After prayers by the priests, it rises again to reveal the malevolent spirit in its true form. A fight ensues with a warrior played as an *aragoto* hero, and the demon is finally vanquished.

Migawari zazen ("The Zen Substitute")

Matsubamemono.
Tokiwazu and *nagauta* music by Kishizawa Shikisa VII and Kineya Mitarō V.
Written by Okamura Shikō.
First performed in 1910 at the Ichimura-za, Tokyo.
This comic dance-drama is an adaptation of the Kyōgen play *Hanago*.

As usual for such Kyōgen-derived works, the plot concerns a rather amusing daimyo called Yamakage Ukyō and his comical servant, Tarōkaja. Ukyō has a shrewish wife called Tamanoi and a beautiful mistress called Hanago. As he has not been able to see Hanago recently, Ukyō decides that he must find an excuse to get out of the house.

He calls his wife and, claiming that he has recently had several bad dreams, says that he wishes to make a pilgrimage to various temples. Tamanoi is suspicious of her husband and refuses his request outright.

Ukyō then tries another idea, saying that he will lock himself away here at home for seven days and seven nights to perform *zazen* meditation. This idea is better received, but Tamanoi insists that seven nights are too many. He may perform his meditation for one night only. Ukyō is satisfied with this but only on condition that she on no account disturb him. Tamanoi agrees.

Ukyō then calls in his servant Tarōkaja, telling him that he is to take his place in the meditation, covering himself (especially his face) with a robe so that he will not be recognized. Tarōkaja is petrified of the formidable Tamanoi but has no option but to agree. He must just sit

in the room and await his master's return in the morning. Ukyō goes happily off.

As Tarōkaja settles down, Tamanoi, despite having promised not to, does indeed appear. She says she will bring him some saké and, when the covered face fails to say anything, she grows suspicious. The cover is removed and she finds the petrified Tarōkaja, who soon confesses everything, including the fact that Ukyō has gone to visit Hanago. Tamanoi decides to catch her husband out and orders Tarōkaja to put the robe over her head. She will sit and await his return.

Ukyō finally wanders home down the *hanamichi*. He is the worse for drink and his appearance is made even more comical by the fact that he is wearing one of Hanago's robes. Very pleased with himself, he proceeds to tell the covered figure whom he supposes is Tarōkaja all about his night out. This description is performed as dance and is considered the highlight of the work. Tamanoi maintains her silence, her fury indicated by the occasional stamping of her foot.

Having roundly abused his ugly, shrewish wife, Ukyō finally removes the robe from the figure's head, only to discover to his horror that it was Tamanoi all along. The furious Tamanoi chases the hapless Ukyō off the stage as the curtain descends.

Momijigari ("Maple Viewing")

Shosagoto, shin kabuki jūhachiban, matsubamemono.
Tokiwazu, nagauta, and *gidayū* music by Tsuruzawa Yasutarō, Kishizawa Shikisa VI, and Kineya Shōjirō III.
Choreography by Ichikawa Danjūrō IX.
Lyrics by Kawatake Mokuami.
First performed in 1887 by Danjūrō at the Shintomi-za, Tokyo. Based on a Nō play of the same name.

Set in the mid-Heian period (794–1185), the action unfolds before scenery of breathtaking beauty at Mt. Togakushi in Shinano Prefecture. It is autumn, and the brave general Taira no Koremochi has come with his men to view the brilliant colors. Arriving at a good spot, they notice some bright curtains nearby behind which there seems to be a party of picnickers. Koremochi discovers that a lady of rank has come to enjoy the autumn leaves. Not wishing to interrupt, he is about to withdraw when the lady's voice calls him back.

Princess Sarashina, her beautiful fragrance carried on the breeze, invites Koremochi to join her party. Though he is reluctant, eventually Sarashina's attendants and his own men persuade him to stay. Politely, Koremochi accepts a cup of saké while, referring to man's weakness, the musicians sing of how unlike the rocks and trees are human hearts, so easily swayed like reeds blown in the wind.

In fact, Sarashina is not all that she appears. For some time there has been a demon terrorizing travelers in these hills and that demon is none other than the beautiful princess, here transformed in order to entice and then devour the warrior.

As entertainment for the party, a shy young maid named Nogiku is pressed to dance. The saké, meanwhile, is so delicious that Koremochi becomes tipsy, and when he professes to have had too much, it is offered to his two retainers. Once they, too, have had their fill it is their turn to entertain and, one after the other, each man takes to the stage. More saké is offered and, at last, it is time for Sarashina to dance.

The lyrics feature a description of three of the most beautiful sights in Japan, each chosen to illustrate the themes of flower, snow, and moon. Starting with Mt. Yoshino, famous for its countless cherry trees in spring, we move to a view of Koshiji covered in snow. Finally, Sarashina's senior attendant Tagoto joins her as the musicians sing of the village of Sarashina beyond the Kiso mountains where the many flooded rice fields each reflect the full moon.

The topic returns to the present and we hear how quickly autumn passes. Leaves scatter from the trees and mountain paths become sleek and treacherous. The princess suddenly darts a sinister glance in Koremochi's direction to check if he is now asleep. Seeing him awake, she continues with her dance.

In a highlight of the work, Sarashina now performs with two dance fans, which she flips and spins in a display of great technical virtuosity. The lyrics go on to list places in Kyoto famous for their autumn maples.

Soon, however, Sarashina notices that Koremochi is indeed sound asleep and she finally reveals her true nature. Her femininity vanishes as she stands, legs apart, over the sleeping retainers and, with a deep-throated cry, she stalks off with her retinue.

As Koremochi and his men continue sleeping, a mountain god appears to warn him of his danger. During this comical dance, we're told that falling asleep here is more dangerous than holding a candle to the wind. He mimes the demon eating unwary travelers as the singers describe bones crushed by the demon's teeth. Koremochi still sleeps, however, and the mountain god decides to stamp loudly in time to music. A form of Shinto festival music plays as he mimes religious rites and prayers. When this also fails, the god finally gives up and leaves Koremochi in his deep slumber.

Only then does the cold wind of approaching night stir the warrior. Remembering the god's warning in his dream, he realizes Sarashina's real identity and goes to investigate the truth of his vision. The retainers also wake up and run away in fright.

Finally, both Koremochi and the demon of Mt. Togakushi reenter to do battle. She sees that he brandishes a famous sword blessed by the gods and containing enough virtuous power to crush her evil, but still she will try her hand. The demon reveals its true shape, and the actor shows his face now painted with spectacular brown lines of *kumadori* makeup. The characters proceed into a choreographed fight.

With the help of his sword Koremochi will eventually defeat the demon, but in order to end on a visually beautiful scene, the demon climbs a great pine tree and strikes a defiant pose as the dance draws to a close.

Narukami ("The Thunder God")

Jidaimono, kabuki jūhachiban.

First staged as part of a long play, *Narukami Fudō kitayama zakura*, in 1742 by Danjūrō II at Sadoshima Chōgorō-za, Osaka. Based on an earlier work by Ichikawa Danjūrō I of 1684. The story comes from the Nō play *Ikkaku sennin*. The character of Narukami after his final transformation is performed in the *aragoto* style.

Angered at the emperor's failure to keep a promise, high priest Narukami uses his special powers to trap the dragon gods of rain in a rock pool beneath the waterfall close to his mountain retreat. A great drought spreads throughout the land and, growing desperate, the emperor sends the most beautiful woman at court to seduce Narukami and set the dragon gods free.

Arriving at the retreat, Princess Taema pretends to be a woman recently bereaved. Her unexpected appearance here so deep in the mountains causes consternation among the two comical acolytes named White Cloud and Black Cloud. Narukami himself appears and, sympathizing with Taema's loss, asks her to tell of her deceased lover. Taema's speech is the first great highlight of the play. In all apparent innocence, she relates the story of her romance but, by including much suggestive and amusing innuendo, she manages to entice and trick the priests. She gradually sheds her aristocratic bearing.

As Taema's storytelling becomes more graphic Narukami himself is engrossed, at last tumbling from his rocky altar and losing consciousness. This is an important indication of what is to come. There being no convenient cup to hand, Taema revives him by passing water from her own mouth directly into his, an action that constitutes serious defilement since women were not usually permitted even to approach so great a priest. Upon regaining consciousness Narukami is angered and suspicious, but finally relents when Taema offers to throw herself into the falls in atonement. She is to live, but she must become a nun.

Taema feigns pain in the pit of her stomach and Narukami offers to massage it for her. This section is erotic and amusing but also very serious at the same time, for as Narukami inserts his hand further and further into Taema's robes while massaging her, so his own corruption deepens. Eventually he can bear it no longer. Never before has he felt this physical longing and he decides to abandon his religious vows. She is to give herself to him and they will marry. Taema insists that they seal their marriage by sharing the customary cup of saké. With Narukami's first sip, however, the painting of the deity Fudō hanging behind his altar bursts into flames, a sign of the priest's final fall from grace. Soon he is intoxicated and, informing Taema of how to release the dragon gods, he leads her off to his private room.

Shortly thereafter, Taema reappears alone. The priest is now sound asleep and she takes this chance to climb the slippery rocks to reach the sacred rope across the falls. Cutting the rope, the dragon gods are free at last. A sudden downpour ensues, through which Taema makes her brave and victorious exit.

Finally, Narukami is awoken from his drunken stupor by the two acolytes. Realizing that he has been tricked, he is consumed with bitter rage, and the actor's wig and make-up are altered to reflect this transformation. His robes turn into a mass of orange flames by means of a *bukkaeri* costume change and, fighting off the other acolytes, he vows to transform into a bolt of lightning to pursue Taema to the ends of the earth. There is a *tachimawari* fight between Narukami and the acolytes, during which the actor performs several famous *mie* poses, including the important *hashira-maki* "pillar-winding pose," once the special reserve of the troupe's leading actor, in which he wraps an arm and a leg around a pillar. Defeating the acolytes with ease, Narukami makes his bounding *roppō* exit down the *hanamichi*.

Renjishi ("Linked Lions")

Shosagoto, matsubamemono.
Nagauta music—two different versions, the first by Kineya Katsusaburō II and the second by Kineya Shōjirō III.

Choreography by Hanayagi Jusuke I.
Lyrics by Kawatake Mokuami.
First performed as Kabuki in 1872 at the Murayama-za, Tokyo. First staged as a *matsubamemono* in 1901 at the Tōkyō-za, since which time it has remained in that form. Like *Kagami jishi*, the theme is based on the Nō play *Shakkyō*. The central comic interlude is taken from the Kyōgen play *Shūron*.

The dance begins solemnly as two itinerant actors enter, the elder named Ukon leading and holding a small white-haired lion head, and the younger Sakon following with a red-haired lion head. The musicians describe the holy landscape of Mt. Seiryō in China, dwelling place of the Buddhist deity Monju, among the towering peaks of which is a natural stone bridge. Appearing like an arching rainbow, the bridge is a miracle, and on the other side lies the Buddhist Pure Land. The dancers mime as we hear of the mountain summit ten thousand feet high and the threadlike cascade that tumbles out of the clouds. The bridge spans a deep ravine and at the bottom there is a gushing river.

The white-haired lion is the parent and the red-haired lion its cub, as the two performers begin to act out the story of the cub's strict upbringing. In order to ensure its survival by making it strong, the parent kicks its child over the edge of the precipice as a test of its strength and courage. At first, the cub scrambles back to the top but he is kicked down again and eventually falls to the bottom of the ravine. Exhausted, the cub comes to rest in the shade of some trees. What follows is the highlight of the dance. The parent lion exhibits great love and anxiety for its offspring as it peers down into the mist-obscured valley, but it can see nothing and can hear only the pounding torrent below. At last, the cub sees a reflection of his parent on the river surface and is inspired. With a sudden burst of energy, he scales the rocky cliff and, reunited at the top, both parent and cub dance for joy. Butterflies then appear and tease the lions into a frenzy, eventually enticing them onto the *hanamichi* along which they make their exit.

There follows a comic interlude featuring two priests from different Buddhist sects who are on a pilgrimage to Mt. Seiryō. The first,

called Rennen, is a follower of the Nichiren sect; the second is Hennen, a priest of the Pure Land sect. Unaware of their differences, they happily decide to accompany each other on the journey, but upon further questioning they immediately fall to arguing. They decide to settle their fight with a theological debate right there and then. In dance form, first Rennen, and then Hennen, tries to convince the other of the merits of their respective Buddhist sects, but both are stubborn. Rennen, with a small drum, starts reciting the prayer of his Nichiren sect, while Hennen, with a small brass bell and mallet, also chants the prayer of the Pure Land sect. They repeat their words with such fervor that in the end they forget themselves and begin chanting the wrong prayers. Just then, the wind rises and they hear the mountain rumbling. Convinced that the fierce *shishi* lions are about to appear, both quiver with fear and make their escape back down the mountain.

After an impressive musical passage sung in the grand *ōzatsuma* style, in which the lyrics describe once more the miraculous stone bridge and its surrounding landscape, the spirits of the two lions enter along the *hanamichi* with the white-haired parent again taking the lead. Both are now dressed in the magnificent brocade costume taken from Nō, but wear much longer wigs that trail behind. The lions dance to auspicious lyrics taken directly from the Nō play *Shakkyō*, eventually swinging their wigs around in great circles in the final spectacular highlight.

Rokkasen ("The Six Poet Immortals")

Shosagoto, hengemono.
Nagauta and *Kiyomoto* music by Kineya Rokuzaemon and Kiyomoto Saibei, choreography by Nishikawa Senzō IV, Fujima Kanjūrō, and Nakamura Katsugorō
Lyrics by Matsui Kōji
First performed in 1831 by Nakamura Shikan II at the Nakamura-za, Edo. Based on an earlier work performed by Arashi Hinasuke I in 1789.

Rokkasen is a *hengemono* composed of five different parts, although today the sections *Bunya* and *Kisen* are more often seen as independent dances. Set in the ninth century, it shows five poets who each come to woo or, in the case of Kuronushi, to challenge the poetess Ono no Komachi. Komachi is legendary for her talent, beauty, and indifference towards her many male suitors.

Henjō: The elderly abbot Sōjō Henjō struggles to maintain dignity in the face of emotional turmoil. He comes to woo Komachi at the palace only to be rejected.

Bunya: In a more lighthearted mood, the courtier Bunya Yasuhide also comes to try his hand, but is prevented even from seeing Komachi by a group of ugly court ladies (always played by actors specializing in male roles). He is reminded of another courtier, Fukakusa no Shō-shō, who was told to visit Komachi every night for one hundred nights before she would agree to his request. This he undertook, but tragically died on the ninety-ninth night. Bunya sympathizes for he, too, has come to visit Komachi.

The ladies ask Bunya a series of riddles ostensibly on the theme of romance. This highly rhythmical question-and-answer section is called *koi zukushi*, "the catalog of love." Finally, Bunya is unable to answer and his frustration is likened to a tobacco pipe stuffed up with tar. The mention of tobacco leads into a beautiful section of lyrics playing on the idea of smoke: just as smoke rises from volcanoes and bonfires, so Bunya's passion smoulders and burns. At last, he has had enough and rushes away.

Narihira: Famous as one of Japan's most handsome poets, Ariwara no Narihira begs Komachi to requite his love. Both appear in Heian-period costume and are portrayed as icons of ancient courtly romance. Sadly he, too, is rejected and departs alone.

Kisen: The cherry blossoms are at their height as Kisen Hōshi makes his way toward the pleasure quarters for an evening of fun. This character is a contemporary parody of a poet priest, and here Komachi herself becomes the smart tea waitress Okaji. Kisen is infatuated with Okaji but she, hearing of his bad reputation, is diffident. During her *kudoki* she berates him for his inconstancy, and the lyrics play on her identity as a tea waitress with a series of puns

on the real names of tea brands.

Kisen performs a rhythmical storytelling section called *chobokure*, an amusing and irreverent parody on what was originally the chanting of Buddhist scriptures. Kisen's subject, however, is secular love. At last, the priests from Kisen's temple come in search of him. Kisen puts on a red apron and an oversized headscarf as, for fun, he pretends to be a lowly maidservant trying to entice customers at a roadside inn. The priests dance in a group around the large umbrella and all prepare to make their return.

Kuronushi: For the final section we return to the ninth century as the evil courtier Ōtomo no Kuronushi challenges Komachi in a poetry contest. He accuses her of plagiarism but she successfully defends herself, and exposes him as a villain with designs on the imperial throne. A lively fight scene brings the dance to a close.

Sagi musume ("The Heron Maiden")

Shosagoto, hengemono.
Nagauta music by Kineya Chūjirō.
Lyrics by Fujita Yoshiji.
First performed in 1762 by Segawa Kikunojō II at the Ichimura-za, Edo. The current version is based on a revival of 1892 by Ichikawa Danjūrō IX when the *hikinuki* costume changes were first introduced. Originally one of a five dance *hengemono* called collectively *Yanagi ni hina shochō no saezuri*. The idea of a young maiden transforming into a heron came from the repertory of trick dolls known as *Takeda karakuri*.

The dance portrays the anguish of a maiden's love, illustrating the Buddhist doctrine that emotional craving and attachment to this world will keep one from salvation. The introductory musical passage is especially beautiful and expresses the essence of the whole work:

> A mind's delusions
> like leaden clouds, will not clear…
> Here there lies my heart
> lost on this moon-obscured night…
> led astray by love.

By the frozen edge of a lake appears a beautiful woman dressed in a pure white kimono and hood, but with a black sash. Her dance includes strange birdlike movements resembling those of a white heron as the lyrics describe her alone and drenched by the snowfall. She expresses the misery and bitterness of one whose love has been betrayed.

A sudden *hikinuki* onstage costume change begins the *kudoki* section and the character transforms into a young city girl obsessed by romance. She prays to the god that unites man and woman, and is overjoyed when her wishes are granted. Briefly leaving the stage, she re-enters in a different kimono for the *teodori*, or "hand dance" section, performed to popular songs of the mid-eighteenth century that describe the difficulty of capturing a loved one's heart. Another onstage costume change signals the start of the *kasa zukushi*, or "catalog of umbrellas" section, in which the pretty maiden shades herself with a parasol as she views the blossoms of Mt. Yoshino. The lyrics liken the spinning umbrella to the wheel of karma.

The stage darkens and snow begins to fall again. Behind the umbrella the maiden changes costumes twice, firstly into the color red to express her hatred for the man, and then back into the silver feathers of a heron by means of the *bukkaeri* quick-change technique. The religious implications are that, due to the maiden's clinging resentment, she has been reborn a white heron after experiencing the tortures of hell. In the final highlight, the lyrics describe Enma, the King of Hell, with his iron stave, assisted by hell's demons. We hear of the different chambers of hell, the Chamber of Striking and Crushing and the Chamber of Revival, in which sinners are hacked to pieces only to be revived and torn apart once more, and the Chambers of Wailing and Great Wailing. The creature's hair becomes disheveled expressing her distraction as she recalls her suffering and acts out her final death throes.

Two alternative endings exist for the dance today. In the older and more traditional version, stage assistants bring on a cloth-covered box with two steps, on top of which the actor poses as the stage lights suddenly come on. In the second, more modern version, the character

visibly weakens and the dance ends with the heron collapsed onto the stage.

Sannin Kichisa kuruwa no hatsugai ("The Three Kichisas")

Sewamono, shiranamimono.
Written by Kawatake Mokuami.
First performed in 1860 at the Ichimura-za, Edo.
Only four scenes of the original seven acts and fourteen scenes are regularly performed.

The story concerns three thieves who, by chance, all have the same name of "Kichisa": Ojō Kichisa, who disguises himself as a woman; Obō Kichisa, who was once a samurai; and Oshō Kichisa, a former priest. The subplots are many and interwoven, but the main scenario is as follows.

ACT I, SCENE II: *Ōkawabata Kōshinzuka* ("The Kōshin Shrine by the Sumida River")
Otose, a low-ranking courtesan, meets and falls in love with Jūzaburō, a timber merchant's clerk. He visits her and carelessly leaves one hundred *ryō* (pieces of gold) at her lodging. By chance, Otose finds the money and the next day she follows him in order to return it. On the banks of the Sumida river, another woman approaches, actually Ojō Kichisa, who robs her and throws her unconscious body into the river. Ojō delivers a famous speech at this point which begins, *Tsuki mo oboroni* ("The shadowed moon floating in the spring sky"). It is one of the most popular in the play and known as the *yakubarai*, or "exorcism."

Ojō is watched by Obō who, in turn, tries to rob him. He is surprised by the fight which Ojō puts up, not realising that he is a man. Oshō then appears and breaks up the fight. The three thieves realise that they all bear the same name of "Kichisa" and agree to become bloodbrothers. Oshō keeps the money for them.

ACT II, SCENE III: *Warigesui Denkichi uchi* ("The House of Denkichi")
Otose has been rescued and is living at the house of Denkichi, the father of Oshō. It turns out that she is actually Denkichi's daughter, who had been given away for adoption. Oshō is, therefore, her brother. Jūzaburō, in despair

at losing his master's money, tries to drown himself but is stopped by the passing Denkichi who takes him to his house. Jūzaburō and Otose meet again and marry.

Oshō comes to his father's house intending to give him some money—that stolen from Jūzaburō. Denkichi, however, realizing that it is probably the money Oshō stole, refuses to take it and throws it out the door. The money is then stolen by another apprentice called Kamaya Buhei, and Denkichi chases after him. He gets the money back but is robbed and killed by Obō, who does not know that Denkichi is the father of his comrade.

ACT IV: *Sugamo Kichijōin* ("Kichijō Temple at Sugamo")

Obō and Ojō are being sought by the police and Oshō hides them at the Kichijō temple. Otose and Jūzaburō come to find their brother Oshō to ask him to help find their father's murderer. Obō discovers that he is the murderer of Oshō's father, and Ojō is distraught because it was his theft that originally caused the tragedy. They decide to kill themselves.

Meanwhile in the graveyard behind the temple, Oshō tells Otose and Jūzaburō that he must kill them because he knows that Jūzaburō is in fact Otose's brother, given away for adoption at birth. The couple have committed incest and so their only redemption is for him to kill them. He also decides to use their heads as substitutes for those of Obō and Ojō.

ACT V: *Hongō hinomi yagura* ("The Fire Watchtower in Hongō")

The three thieves meet again and Oshō tells the other two to make their escape while he tries to trick the police by saying that the two heads he has taken are those of Obō and Ojō. The police, however, are not fooled by this ploy and the city gates are closed in an effort to catch them. In one of Kabuki's most beautiful and impressive closing scenes, Ojō climbs a fire watchtower in the snow in front of the temple. To create a diversion, he strikes the drum used to signal the capture of the fugitives and the opening of all the city gates. This fails, however, and so the three Kichisas decide to take their own lives.

Shibaraku ("Wait A Moment!")

Jidaimono, kabuki jūhachiban

Written and first performed in 1697 by Ichikawa Danjūrō I at the Nakamura-za, Edo. This play is the epitome of the *aragoto* style founded by its author. The script used today is based on a revival by Danjūrō IX of 1895 with revisions by Fukuchi Ōchi. It was at this time that the name of the hero was fixed permanently as Kamakura Gongorō Kagemasa.

The villain of the play, Takehira, has come to the Hachiman shrine at Kamakura to give thanks for being appointed to high office. In fact, he has plans to take over the country, and presents a famous sword to the shine as part of his offerings.

Takehira is an archvillain of the *kugeaku* type, his wig and blue makeup all contributing to his aura of total evil. Among his retainers, Narita Gorō and the other red-faced *haradashi* are typical comic villains. Shinsai, the so-called "catfish" priest with his bald head and very long sidelocks, is another exotic member of his retinue.

Meanwhile, a young lord called Yoshitsuna has lost both a precious sword and some valuable imperial seals. To atone for this, he and his retinue have also come to the shrine to present a merchant's ledger, a symbol of wealth. For these losses, however, Takehira, who is aware that Yoshitsuna is loyal to the emperor and is therefore his enemy, has them arrested and orders their execution.

However, the executioners' hands are stayed by mighty shouts of "*Shibaraku*," "Wait a moment!" The young hero of the play, Kamakura Gongorō Kagemasa, enters along the *hanamichi*. Gongorō's costume is one of the most spectacular in theater history, made up of several layers of clothing and an armor breastplate. Underneath the long, trailing *nagabakama* trousers the actor is standing on nearly one foot-high clogs to increase his presence. His gigantic sleeves are stretched out on bamboo struts in order to display the actor's *mon*, or personal crest, normally the *mimasu*, the "three rice measures" of the Danjūrō line of actors. Gongorō's great seven- or eight-foot sword is the longest

in use on the Kabuki stage. His wig is characterized by the long pieces of stiffened paper
called *chikara gami*, symbolizing strength, and
the sidelocks are waxed into the shape of wheel
spokes (*kuruma bin*). The fact that he still possesses his forelock of hair (parted in the middle)
indicates that, for all his strength and bravado,
he is still a youth. Gongorō's makeup is the
sujiguma style of *kumadori* and signifies his
strength and righteous indignation when con-
fronting a villain.

On the *hanamichi* Gongorō delivers a lengthy
speech of introduction known as a *tsurane*,
traditionally rewritten for each performance.
This grandiloquent speech contains much wordplay and references to both the actor playing
the role, and the history and traditions of the
Ichikawa Danjūrō line of actors, *aragoto* in
particular. One by one, members of Takehira's
retinue confront him, but he frightens them off.

At last, Kamakura Gongorō leaves the
hanamichi and takes up his position in the center of the main stage and, as he does so, the
minor characters begin a rhythmical *keshōgoe*
chant of "*Aa-rya, kō-rya.*" Once he has reached
the center of the stage, the actor strikes the
famous pose called *Genroku mie*, expressing the
character's strength and defiance in the face of
the enemy.

Gongorō argues with Takehira, and then
cuts off the heads of several of his men with a
huge sweep of his sword. It turns out that the
lost seals and the famous sword were stolen
by Takehira. They are returned to Yoshitsuna,
and Gongorō's presence renders Takehira powerless to stop Yoshitsuna and his retinue from
leaving.

Having saved the day, Gongorō poses at the
end of the *hanamichi* in another furious *mie*.
The curtain then closes on the other characters
and Gongorō prepares for his spectacular *roppō*
exit. As he progresses, moving with great difficulty in his enormous costume, he repeatedly
shouts the nonsense syllables, "*Yattoko totchā
un toko nā!*" This phrase is occasionally heard
in other *aragoto* plays and provides an imposing vocal accompaniment to his fantastic stylized departure.

Sukeroku yukari no Edo zakura
("Sukeroku, Flower of Edo")

Sewamono, sogamono, kabuki jūhachiban.
Commonly known simply as "Sukeroku."
Katō bushi music replaced the original *itchū bushi*
in 1761.
Written by Tsuuchi Jihei II and Tsuuchi Hanemon.
First performed in 1713 by Ichikawa Danjūrō II at
the Yamamura-za, Edo. The play is set in the world
of the Soga brothers, who are seeking revenge for
their father's murder. When performed by actors
other than those of the Danjūrō line, the title
changes and *kiyomoto* music replaces the *katō
bushi*.

Agemaki, the most prized courtesan of the
Miura-ya teahouse in the Yoshiwara pleasure
quarters of Edo, enters. She is a courtesan of
the highest rank, dressed in resplendent robes
and the magnificent *date hyōgo* hairstyle. Her
lover is the dashing and gallant Sukeroku, an
otokodate, or "chivalrous commoner," who
always defeats his samurai betters.

Agemaki is followed by a wealthy but
unwanted admirer, an old man with a great
white beard by the name of Ikyū. Agemaki hates
Ikyū and, when he speaks ill of Sukeroku, she
insults him in a famous speech of abuse known
as an *akutai*. This is the highlight of her role
beginning with the words, *Moshi, Ikyū san,
omae to Sukeroku san o, kō narabete miru toki
wa* ("Well, Ikyū, if I were to compare you with
Sukeroku . . ."). Having roundly berated him,
Agemaki and her retinue enter the Miura-ya.

Just then the sound of the *shakuhachi*
bamboo flute is heard. It is Sukeroku—or rather,
Soga no Gorō in disguise—who enters on the
hanamichi. This entrance is a highpoint of
Sukeroku's role, known as the *deha*. With a
magnificent umbrella, both character and actor
display themselves to the audience in a series
of poses linked by dance.

Sukeroku's role is basically an *aragoto* one
but with a softer more *wagoto* human side. His
kumadori makeup is the subtle *mukimi guma*
with highlights only around the eyes and the lips.
He wears a stylish black kimono and a dashing
purple headband that pleases the ladies of the
quarter. The present Danjūrō XII said that the

key to playing Sukeroku is to think oneself the most fantastic man in the world.

Sukeroku comes to the Yoshiwara district hoping to locate the blade that slew his father. To this end, he picks quarrels with men so that they will draw their swords and he will recognize the blade. Sukeroku continually tries to incite Ikyū to fight to check his sword too, but he refuses to be provoked. Sukeroku fights with Ikyū's retainers, however, and humiliated, they too enter the teahouse.

At this point Gorō's gentle brother Soga no Jūrō arrives to try and stop Gorō's fighting but, once he knows the reason, gets involved in the quarrels himself. The most humorous scene in the play follows, with much comic improvisation, when the brothers pick fights by forcing passersby to crawl between their legs. Their antics are halted by the arrival of their mother. She takes Jūrō home and forces Gorō (Sukeroku) to wear a paper kimono (*kamiko*) to prevent him from fighting.

Ikyū tries to woo Agemaki again but is interrupted by Sukeroku. However, remembering his promise to his mother, he is powerless. Ikyū insults and beats him, but goes on to suggest that he and the brothers could form a powerful alliance and perhaps even rule the country. Unless they act together, however, they will be like an incense stand with only two legs instead of three. Carried away by his own metaphor, Ikyū then draws his sword and cuts off the leg of an incense stand. Sukeroku recognizes the blade immediately as the one that cut down his father.

The play normally ends at this point but occasionally a final scene is performed in which Sukeroku kills Ikyū and then hides from the authorities in a huge vat of water.

Sumidagawa ("The Sumida River")

Shosagoto, matsubamemono.
Kiyomoto music by Kiyomoto Umekichi II.
Lyrics are closely based on the Nō play of the same name by Jōno Saigiku .
First composed in 1885 and first staged as a Kabuki

dance in 1919 at the Kabuki-za, Tokyo. Since that time it has been an acknowledged masterpiece of the twentieth century repertoire.

The main character is a *monogurui* or "crazed person," in this case a mother mad with grief at the loss of her son. The introductory lyrics set the theme: "Truly a parent's heart, though not in darkness, can still be lost in thoughts of her child."

It is evening, and approaching the banks of the Sumida river is a woman of elegant but disheveled appearance. Her outer robe draped over one shoulder only, and the branch of cherry blossoms she carries, are both stage conventions indicating madness. The lyrics tell us that she is burdened with some great suffering, but there is no one with whom she can speak to relieve her pain.

The actor dances on the *hanamichi* as we hear the reason for her journey from the capital in Kyoto. Her beloved son was kidnapped by a slave trader and, searching for him, she has journeyed far to the east beyond the famous Ōsaka Barrier. In her distracted state, she has pursued him all the way to the Sumida river where she now arrives. The actor goes to the main stage.

The woman sees a ferryman and begs him to take her across the river. Noticing some unfamiliar white birds, she asks what they are called and the ferryman replies that they are merely seagulls from the ocean. But he is heartless to call them common seagulls, for they must be none other than the famed *miyako dori*, or "capital birds," which she has read about in the classic poem by Ariwara no Narihira. Indeed, her situation is similar to his for he also journeyed far to the east, yearning for one who was dear to him. She adapts Narihira's lines from the mid-tenth century *Ise monogatari* asking the "capital birds" whether the one he left behind was still alive or dead. She, too, is anxious about her child.

The man agrees to ferry her across. Looking to the far bank, she asks why a group of people has gathered around a willow tree there. It is a sad tale, he replies, but he will tell it to her. The actor performing the ferryman mimes a man luring and capturing children, as we hear that in the spring of last year a slave trader passed this way from the capital with a young boy in tow. But the boy was not used to so hard a journey and, unable to take another step, he collapsed by this riverbank and was abandoned. The locals felt pity for the boy, and when they asked where he had come from and his name, he answered that he was from the capital, and that his family name was Yoshida. Just then, with the sound of the vesper bell in his ears, the boy passed away. According to Buddhist thought and as stated here in the lyrics, the vesper bell signifies the impermanence of all living things.

The woman is horrified. When she hears that it happened exactly a year ago to the day, that the boy's age was twelve and that his given name was Umewakamaru, she declares that he was her very own son. In the emotional climax of the play, she wonders if this is not all some terrible dream, and she breaks down in tears. Deeply moved by her plight, the ferryman offers to take her to the grave mound where she can pray for the deceased, and both board the boat. Once there, she agrees to join in the prayer chant, and the lyrics tell us that here on this moonlit night, the sound of the river breeze comes to accompany her.

Suddenly, she sees a vision of her son and hears his voice. In her distress, the woman loses her senses again and as she struggles with the ferryman, we are told that the vision now appears, now disappears from sight. In fact, all she sees is the slender willow above the grave, and all she hears are the calls of the "capital birds" as they dart to and fro above the river.

Tōkaidō Yotsuya kaidan ("Yotsuya Ghost Story")

Sewamono, kaidanmono.
Written by Tsuruya Nanboku IV.
First performed in 1825 at the Nakamura-za, Edo.
Of the original five acts, only Acts II and III are commonly performed today.

Considered the best Kabuki ghost story, it deals with the numerous murders by the villain Tamiya

lemon and, in particular, that of his wife, Oiwa. The macabre and dramatic part of Oiwa is a marvelous vehicle for an *onnagata* who must show Oiwa's awful disfigurement. The same actor may take on the companion roles of the young man, Kohei, and Yomoshichi, the fiancé of Oiwa's sister Osode. This work was originally alternated with *Kanadehon chūshingura* and so the plays were given a tenuous link by making lemon a disloyal retainer of Enya Hangan.

ACT II: *Tamiya lemon rōtaku* ("The House of Tamiya lemon")

lemon lives in poverty with his sick wife, Oiwa, and their baby. He ekes out a living by making umbrellas. Their neighbour, Kihei, wants lemon to divorce Oiwa and marry his granddaughter Oume, a scheme with which lemon is happy to involve himself. Kihei sends Oiwa some medicine that is actually a poison causing severe facial disfigurement. A young servant by the name of Kohei tries to prevent lemon's abuse of Oiwa, but lemon has his henchmen tie Kohei up and lock him in a cupboard. Oiwa takes the poison.

lemon has a plan to make the masseur Takuetsu rape Oiwa and thus give him grounds for divorce. He threatens to kill Takuetsu if he refuses. Left alone, Oiwa fends the masseur off with Kohei's short sword, accidentally imbedding it in a pillar. Eventually Takuetsu decides he cannot possibly rape the now disfigured Oiwa, and shows her her face in a mirror.

One of Kabuki's most riveting and awful scenes follows. As the masseur tries to comfort the crying baby, Oiwa prepares to go out and confront Kihei. One of her eyes is almost obliterated by the poison's work, and, in the custom of married women of the day, she blackens her teeth. Then, as she begins to comb her hair, great clumps dripping blood come away in her hand.

The masseur tries to stop Oiwa leaving and, by accident, she stumbles into the sword in the pillar and cuts her own throat. The terrified masseur runs off. lemon returns and finds her body. He accuses the bound and gagged Kohei of killing her, and kills him too. He has both bodies tied to either side of a door and then thrown into a canal. Their spirits, however, begin to haunt lemon.

ACT III: *Onbobori* ("The Canal Bank")

After several other murders, Iemon goes fishing for eels in a canal and manages to hook the door to which Oiwa's body is tied. Her spirit haunts Iemon. He then turns the door over and finds Kohei. (This trick door has two headless dummies lashed to it, and a hole through which the actor puts his head, enabling him to take both roles.) Kohei pathetically asks for medicine and then his body turns into a skeleton.

After the horror of this scene, characters from other parts of the play (now usually never performed) suddenly enter. The evil Gonbei, the brother of Osode, and Yomoshichi, her fiancé, join with Iemon in an eerily beautiful *danmari* as they try to gain possession of a letter connected with the *Chūshingura* vendetta.

Tsumoru koi yuki no seki no to ("Mounting Love at the Snowbound Barrier")

Shosagoto.

Tokiwazu music by Tobaya Richō I and Kishizawa Shikisa II.

Choreography by Nishikawa Senzō II.

Lyrics by Takarada Jurai.

First performed in 1784 at the Kiri-za, Edo. Originally from the play *Jūnihitoe Komachi zakura* ("The Twelve-Layered Robe and the Komachi Cherry Tree").

Soon after the death of Emperor Ninmyō in 850, his loyal courtier Yoshimine no Munesada retires to Mt. Ōsaka to pray for the repose of his soul. Nearby is the barrier gate of Ōsaka, an official security checkpoint, where the barrier guard Sekibei doubles as a local woodcutter. Also growing here is the late emperor's favorite cherry tree. Despite being winter the tree is in full bloom, although its flowers are pale as if in mourning for the emperor.

In this heavy snow a lovely woman appears, the famous court beauty and poetess Ono no Komachi. She requests permission to go through the barrier, but Sekibei will not allow it without an official pass. She does not possess one, but Sekibei agrees to let her through if she will answer some questions. There follows the first highlight, the *mondō* "question and answer" section, in which the *tokiwazu* musicians take over the dialogue leaving the actors to mime. Some of Sekibei's questions are suggestive and humorous, and eventually he is more than willing for her to pass through.

Munesada has been watching from his quarters close by, and he and Komachi recognize each other. They had previously been lovers and Sekibei asks to hear about their first meeting. Komachi recalls this in dance form, which is another highlight presented as a *kudoki*.

Sekibei will now act as go-between and congratulates them on their present reunion. Just then, two important objects fall out of his sleeves, one of which he manages to retrieve but the other is picked up by Komachi. In order to allay their suspicions Sekibei pretends not to care, and all three characters dance in celebration. This is the *teodori* section, yet another highlight, in which the character's reveal their personalities through their different manners of dancing. Sekibei offers to warm some saké to toast the happy occasion and departs eagerly to do so.

A white hawk appears bearing a message written in blood. It is a quotation from a classical poem, "Two brothers aboard the same boat." Understanding the message, Munesada knows that his own younger brother Yasusada has been attacked and killed. Komachi then brings out the object previously dropped by Sekibei and discovers that it is one half of a broken tablet. She happens to possess the other half and when she puts them together, they see that it belongs to their archenemy, Ōtomo no Kuronushi, who is plotting to usurp the throne. They now realize that the barrier guard Sekibei must in fact be Kuronushi in disguise. Komachi goes back to the capital to get help, while Munesada manages to hide the bloody message behind his koto before Sekibei returns with the saké. Sekibei is now very drunk and Munesada retreats into his house.

Left alone, Sekibei is about to drink more saké when he notices an unusual formation of stars reflected in his cup. He takes this as a sign that the time has come for him to take action in conquering the land. As an offering, he will cut down and burn the cherry tree. Taking his great axe, he lifts it to strike but is held back by some unseen force.

Mysteriously, from behind the tree appears the spirit of the cherry dressed as a courtesan from the city's pleasure quarters. This spirit had fallen in love with Munesada's brother, and now that he is slain she appears to take revenge upon Sekibei for ordering his death. The spirit declares that she is the courtesan Sumizome and pretends to be in love with Sekibei. Finding this strange, Sekibei asks her to tell of her life in the pleasure quarters and both characters begin a section of dance describing some activities seen there.

At last Sumizome finds the bloody message, and recalls her bitterness. Still pretending to be in love with Sekibei, she accuses him of inconstancy and insists that the message must be from another woman. She expresses feigned jealousy in another famous *kudoki* section.

Growing suspicious, Sekibei presses her to tell him why she is so attached to this message. Both characters then make *bukkaeri* costume changes as they reveal their true identities, she as the spirit of the cherry tree whose lover wrote the message, and he as the evil nobleman Ōtomo no Kuronushi, a *kugeaku* villain. They begin a fierce struggle and the dance comes to a close with a picture-like tableau as Sumizome poses above her defiant enemy.

Tsuri onna ("Fishing for a Wife")

Shosagoto, matsubamemono.
Tokiwazu music by Kishizawa Koshikisa VI.
Choreography by Hanayagi Jusuke I.
Written by Kawatake Mokuami.
First performed in 1901 at the Tōkyō-za, and as Bunraku in 1936 at the Bunraku-za, Yotsubashi, Osaka.
This comic dance-drama is an adaptation of the Kyōgen play *Tsuri bari*.

A daimyo and his servant Tarōkaja enter. The lord says that he has reached his present age but still has no wife. He wishes to pray for one at the Nishinomiya shrine to the god Ebisu who,

it is said, brings good luck and a good marriage. Tarōkaja is also lacking a wife, so he will go too. In the *kyōgen* tradition they walk in a circle to symbolize their journey to the shrine.

They arrive at the shrine and begin their prayers for beautiful wives. The daimyo decides to spend the night. While he sleeps, Tarōkaja is to keep watch and wake him if any thieves or robbers come along. Eventually, however, Tarōkaja also falls asleep.

The daimyo awakens from a dream. In it he was told that at the western gate of the shrine he would find someone to take home with him. Tarōkaja too has had exactly the same dream. At the gate, however, instead of a wife the daimyo finds a fishing rod and line. The deity Ebisu is always depicted with a fishing rod and a fish under his arm, so this hook will surely catch him a wife. He casts the line and draws in a young maiden, her face coyly veiled. When he sees her, she is as beautiful as the famed poetess, Ono no Komachi. Luckily, Tarōkaja has some saké so the couple can perform the traditional ceremonial toast used in Japanese weddings. They celebrate their union in dance to the auspicious lyrics.

Tarōkaja—now the worse for drink—asks if he can borrow the rod and have a go himself. He tries a few times and finally also catches himself a veiled young lady. When Tarōkaja lifts the veil, however, he finds to his horror that she is terribly ugly.

Despite the comedy of the situation, the beautiful lyrics parody a *kudoki*, in which a rejected woman pours out her grief. "Will you not turn to me?" the lyrics ask. "What do you think you are doing? Thinking about it, our love is so deep. Love as deep as the pool from which you fished me. Tied by love here at Nishinomiya."

As this bride was chosen by the god Ebisu, Tarōkaja cannot refuse her and his lord now offers to dance in celebration of his marriage. As the singers celebrate the auspicious marriages, the one happy, and the other not so happy, the couples dance. Tarōkaja tries to get away, but his wife catches him and pulls him off with the fish hook in *his* mouth.

Yanone ("The Arrow Head")

Jidaimono, kabuki jūhachiban, sogamono.
Ōzatsuma (nagauta) music.
First performed in 1729 by Ichikawa Danjūrō II at
the Nakamura-za, Edo, as part of the play *Suehiro
ebō Soga*. The role of Gorō is a model of the *aragoto*
acting style.

The story takes place at the end of the twelfth
century. It is New Year's Day, and we are at the
simple house of our hero, Soga no Gorō. He is
one of the two legendary Soga brothers, famous
in Japan for avenging the death of their father.
The vendetta took many years to carry out, and
the brothers were forced to bide their time making preparations and waiting for the right opportunity to strike. As the play opens, that is what
Gorō is doing, seated indoors and sharpening his
great arrow. It was customary in Edo to stage
a Kabuki play featuring the Soga brothers at the
New Year, and this one in particular is so full of
auspicious references that it has the flavor of
theater ritual.

Gorō mimes shooting an arrow. In ancient
times arrows were thought to possess magical
properties, and so we begin with a section
praising famous warriors of the past who
excelled at archery. He then launches into a
verbal tour-de-force known as a *tsurane*. In this
immensely difficult speech, Gorō expresses his
determination to avenge his father's death,
but at the same time makes a series of amusing puns on special New Year's food. Such elo-
quence is also an important feature of *aragoto*.

Gorō's armor is old and rusty because he is
poor. For this he blames the Seven Gods of Good
Fortune, whom he abuses in another humorous
speech called an *akutai*. The dialogue is shared
between actor and singer as, for example, the
god Ebisu is called a filthy rascal. Gorō poses as
though carrying a large fish underarm and a fishing rod over his shoulder. This is how the god
Ebisu is usually depicted, and the singer implies
that the fish must really smell bad.

Just then a visitor approaches. In fact, it is
one of the musicians who announces himself
as Ōzatsuma Shuzendayū come to wish Gorō
a Happy New Year. He brings presents of a
pair of fans and a painting of a lucky treasure
ship. The musician soon departs and Gorō
decides to take a nap, placing the painting under
his pillow in the hopes that his first dream of
the New Year will be a happy one.

However, in his dream Gorō sees a vision of
his elder brother Jūrō, now a helpless captor in
their enemy's hands. He must rush to his aid.
Upon waking, Gorō is determined to go at once,
vowing to pursue their enemy wherever he may
go. Should he scale the very skies, Gorō will
climb also. Should he descend into the earth,
Gorō, too, will follow. It is during this section
that the actor performs several powerful *mie*
poses, including the *hashira maki* or "pillar
winding" pose, once the special reserve of the
troupe's leading actor, and the *Genroku mie*,
the quintessential *aragoto* pose expressing
heroic strength and defiance.

What Gorō lacks, however, is a mode of
transport. Just then a local farmer comes along
with his horse and, though the farmer refuses
to lend the animal, Gorō is insistent. Finally,
using one of the farmer's giant radishes as a
whip, Gorō gallops away to his brother's rescue.

BUNRAKU AND KABUKI (Maruhonmono)

The following synopses are famous examples of Bunraku plays, and in the *maruhon-mono* category of Kabuki. Most were originally written for the puppet theater and adapted for Kabuki, often very shortly after their first performances. Though the stories are almost the same, the scene or act titles and the stage direction may differ between the Bunraku and Kabuki versions.

Akoya ("The Courtesan Akoya")

Jidaimono, maruhonmono.
Written by Matsuda Bunkōdō and Hasegawa Senshi. First performed in 1732 at the Takemoto-za, Osaka. First staged as Kabuki in 1733 at the Kado no Shibai, Osaka. The full title of the play is *Dannoura kabuto gunki* ("The War Chronicles at Dannoura") but only Act III is regularly seen today.

It is the late twelfth century and civil war rages between two military clans, the Heike and the Genji. Due to their recent victories in battle the Genji now have the upper hand, and in order to consolidate their position they are searching out and destroying all remaining Heike warriors. One of the greatest is the Heike commander, Kagekiyo. Kagekiyo's whereabouts are a mystery but, believing that his lover is bound to know, the Genji forces have captured the courtesan Akoya and will subject her to torture if she does not divulge this information.

ACT III: *Akoya Kotozeme* ("Akoya's Torture by Koto")
Presiding over the interrogation are two senior-ranking Genji men, the wise and benevolent governor of Chichibu, Hatakeyama Shigetada, and the vicious coward Iwanaga Saemon. The contrast between these two is important. While Shigetada is played as a gentle *sabakiyaku* type, always thoughtful and prudent, Iwanaga is a comic red-faced villain performed in the amusing *ningyō buri* technique. Seen occasionally in both plays and dances, the actor is "manipulated" by *kōken* as though he were himself a Bunraku puppet.

Akoya is led in under armed escort, her showy appearance in the magnificent robes and ornaments of a top-ranking courtesan contrasting with her sad expression. This entrance along the *hanamichi* is one of the most spectacular in Kabuki.

Iwanaga immediately objects to the fact that she is not tied up and promises that when he takes over the interrogation tomorrow his skill at torture will soon have her confessing everything. For today, however, Shigetada is in charge and they must abide by his judgment. So far, Akoya has only been subjected to quiet reasoning and, claiming that she knows nothing, has not told them Kagekiyo's place of hiding. Shigetada says regretfully that if she will not confess they must torture her. The delighted Iwanaga calls for his men to bring in the equipment at once. These are also comic roles, performed to resemble minor-role puppets that bob up and down. Akoya shudders at the sight of the equipment but remains defiant.

Shigetada orders it sent away, calling instead for his own. What is brought in, however, is not an instrument of torture at all but rather one of music. He demands that Akoya play three musical instruments in succession starting with the multi-stringed koto. After this will be the shamisen and finally the Chinese kokyū fiddle. This is the great highlight of the play, requiring many years of training for the Kabuki actor who, unlike the puppets of Bunraku, must play and sing by himself. Iwanaga is outraged at the idea of a musical recital given under the pretext of torture, but Shigetada ignores him. He knows that during her performance, Akoya will pour out her true feelings of anxiety and love for Kagekiyo and it will be by these very emotions that he will judge her.

After listening to the koto, Shigetada asks Akoya when she first met Kagekiyo and how they came to be intimate. This leads into another highlight, the *kudoki*, during which dialogue is shared between actor and chanter as Akoya describes their first meeting and how they shared a single umbrella in the late autumn showers. The passage is famous for its romantic lyricism. When Akoya plays the kokyū the music becomes increasingly emotional, with the screeching high notes expressing perfectly the feelings that tear at Akoya's heart. Finally, Shigetada is convinced that she really does not know Kagekiyo's whereabouts and declares the torture at an end. Akoya is free to go.

Honchō nijūshikō ("Japan's Twenty-Four Paragons of Filial Piety")

Jidaimono, maruhonmono.
Written by Chikamatsu Hanji, Miyoshi Shōraku, Takeda Inaba, Takemoto Saburōbei, and Takeda Hanbei.
First performed in 1766 at the Takemoto-za, Osaka. First staged as Kabuki the same year at the Naka no Shibai, Osaka. Today Acts IV and V are the most regularly performed. The character of Yaegaki is classed as one of the *sanhime*, the three most difficult 'princess roles' in Kabuki.

Set in the sixteenth century, the play depicts the power struggle between warlords Takeda Shingen and Uesugi Kenshin. The two are feuding over a sacred helmet bestowed upon the Takeda clan by the god of Suwa, but now in the hands of the Uesugi. In order to make peace, Takeda Shingen's son, Katsuyori, and Uesugi Kenshin's daughter, Yaegaki, are betrothed. However, before they can be married, Katsuyori supposedly commits suicide.

In fact, the Katsuyori who died was a substitute and the real man has now infiltrated Kenshin's mansion disguised as a humble gardener in an attempt to steal back the sacred helmet. Kenshin sees through this plan. However, without revealing that he knows, he unexpectedly promotes Katsuyori to the rank of samurai. His intention is to send him away on some mission on which he will be ambushed and killed.

ACT IV: *Jusshukō* ("Ten Types of Incense")
Dressed in samurai robes, Katsuyori enters pensively. While he wonders what to do at this unexpected turn of events, he hears the sound of a prayer bell coming from the room on his left, and realizes that it must be Yaegaki chanting sutras for the fiancé she believes dead. Though betrothed, Katsuyori and Yaegaki have not actually met, and the only way she knows his features is from the portrait hanging in her alcove. She is seated before this now, burning incense and praying.

From another room on Katsuyori's right comes the sound of weeping. When Katsuyori came to the mansion he was accompanied by a woman loyal to the Takeda House named Nureginu. She has now become Yaegaki's lady-in-waiting and it is she who weeps because the substitute who died in Katsuyori's place was none other than her husband.

Katsuyori is moved by both women's sad situations. Nureginu comes out of her room and is surprised to see him in the robes of a samurai. Meanwhile, aroused by the noise, Yaegaki also comes out and is shocked to see someone who so resembles the portrait of her late fiancé. Surely he must be Katsuyori. Wanting to keep his plan secret, Katsuyori denies his true identity, insisting that he is a gardener whom Kenshin has just now promoted.

Though at first confused, Yaegaki soon asks her lady-in-waiting to act as go-between, but Nureginu will only do so if Yaegaki steals the sacred helmet from the garden shrine. Now Yaegaki is certain that this man is her future husband to whom she owes all love and allegiance. Her *kudoki* entreaty is a major highlight of the play, as she begs Katsuyori to trust her and return her affection, even threatening to kill herself if he refuses. At last, Katsuyori is convinced and relents.

Just then, however, Kenshin himself appears and orders Katsuyori to deliver a message. Katsuyori departs at once and, soon after, Kenshin calls out two of his most able warriors, instructing them to follow after Katsuyori to kill him. Yaegaki and Nureginu are horrified but can do nothing, and the scene ends with a *mie* pose as Kenshin holds back both women and glares fiercely.

ACT V: *Oku niwa, kitsunebi* ("Fox Fires in the Inner Garden")

Later that night, Yaegaki is desperate to warn Katsuyori of his danger before her father's men get to him. She appears alone in the mansion's garden wondering how she can possibly do this. One way would be to cross Suwa Lake by boat and beat the men to him, but the lake is now frozen over. She resolves to go on foot. Despite her courage and determination, however, she has only a woman's strength and so her only recourse is to beg the gods for help. She goes to pray before the garden shrine where the sacred helmet is kept. Taking the helmet in her arms, she carries it into the garden and, as she passes over a bridge across the pond, she is shocked to see a white fox's reflection in the water. She remembers that the fox is the god of Suwa's emissary and realizes that the helmet will therefore be protected by magic foxes. Suddenly the dancing shapes of fox fires appear, flickering all about her. With supernatural assistance Yaegaki is sure to succeed and so, with joy and gratitude in her heart, she starts to cross the lake as though taking to the air.

Imoseyama onna teikin ("Exemplary Tales of Womanhood at Mt. Imo and Mt. Se")

Jidaimono, maruhonmono.

Written by Chikamatsu Hanji, Matsuda Baku, Sakai Zenpai, Chikamatsu Tōnan, and Miyoshi Shōraku. First performed in 1771 at the Takemoto-za, Osaka. First staged as Kabuki the same year at the Kogawa-za, Osaka. The following scenes and the *michiyuki* dance are regularly performed today.

The basic story concerns the seventh-century power struggle between the Soga and Fujiwara families. The evil Soga no Iruka has usurped control of the state and the emperor is in hiding. Two feuding families—the Dazai and the Daihanji—are loyal to the emperor, but to consolidate his power Iruka orders that the daughter of the deceased Dazai no Shōni become his concubine and the son of Daihanji become his retainer.

ACT III, SCENE III: in Bunraku, *Imoseyama* ("Mt. Imo and Mt. Se"); in Kabuki, *Yoshinogawa* ("The Yoshino River")

This act requires the use of two *hanamichi*. The set shows a wide river with a mansion on either side: one mansion is at the foot of Mt. Imo, the other at the foot of Mt. Se—the *Imose* of the play's title. *Imose* can mean "man and wife," and is therefore appropriate for the plight of the two young lovers. The river flows as if into the audience and the two *hanamichi* are the river banks.

Sadaka, the widow of Dazai, enters on the main *hanamichi* and Daihanji on the *kari* (temporary) *hanamichi*. They are both deep in thought and each carries a sprig of cherry blossom, which they have been ordered to cast into the river once their children agree to Iruka's demands. The two children, however, are unwilling to comply since they are in love with each other and each decides to die. Koganosuke, Daihanji's son, commits *seppuku*, and Hinadori, Sadaka's daughter, agrees to be decapitated by her mother.

In the climax of the act, to symbolize the couple's posthumous wedding and the reconciliation of the two families, Sadaka floats her daughter's head and items from the "Dolls' Festival" set over to Daihanji. These items of dolls' furniture serve as the girl's mock trousseau.

ACT IV (SPECIAL SCENE): *Michiyuki koi no odamaki* ("The Journey of Love's Spindle")

Another man loyal to the emperor is a young nobleman named Fujiwara no Tankai, who has been in hiding for several months disguised as a commoner called Motome. This dance takes up his story, as well as that of the two women with whom he has become romantically involved. The first of these, Princess Tachibana, has been visiting Motome secretly after dark but has not disclosed her identity to him. In fact, she is the younger sister of his archenemy, Iruka. On the night of the Tanabata Festival, Motome resolves to follow Tachibana home in order to find out who she is, but, catching up with her close to the Kasuga Shrine, he finds her still reluctant to tell him. Nevertheless, the pair exchange promises of love.

Following after the young couple is yet another girl who is in love with Motome and who, having found out about the affair, is mad with jealousy. This character is Omiwa, daughter of a saké salesman living next door to Motome. Omiwa had previously given Motome a spindle of red thread and kept a similar spindle of white thread for herself, believing in the custom that by winding the two colors of thread together, she and Motome would never be parted. Now, confronted by both women, Motome is at a loss what to do. The hour grows late and Tachibana must leave. In order not to lose track of her, Motome attaches the end of his red thread to Tachibana's kimono and, with the same idea in mind, Omiwa attaches the end of her white thread to Motome. But as the other two rush off, Omiwa's thread snaps, leaving her alone again and consumed with bitter frustration.

ACT IV, SCENE IV: in Bunraku, *Kinden* ("The Palace"); in Kabuki, *Mikasayama goten* ("The Mikasayama Palace")

Iruka has magical powers and can only be harmed by the sound of a magical flute through which is poured the mixed blood of a jealous woman and a black-footed doe. He appears seated in opulent splendor enjoying a magnificent banquet.

Motome's father is Fujiwara no Kamatari, a loyal follower of the emperor and Iruka's chief opponent. One of Kamatari's retainers now enters disguised as a fisherman called Fukashichi. He comes bearing a message of congratulations from his master as well as some saké and a letter of surrender. Iruka is highly suspicious at this sudden turn of events, and decides to keep Fukashichi hostage while they investigate whether Kamatari's words are true.

Fukashichi is then left alone and becomes the object of an attempted assassination. In a famous moment, he deftly avoids spears that are thrust up at him through the floor. Poisoned saké is then served, which he pours onto some flowers that immediately wither. Finally he is arrested and taken off to be interrogated in another room.

Princess Tachibana also lives at her brother Iruka's palace and it is to this place she now returns, pursued by Motome. Now realizing who she is, Motome demands that she retrieve an imperial sword stolen by Iruka in order to prove herself to him before they can wed. This she promises to do, and the couple retires.

The stage is now deserted as the unfortunate Omiwa enters. Discovering that her precious Motome is now betrothed to Princess Tachibana, Omiwa is outraged. Before she can take action, however, she is accosted by a group of ladies-in-waiting, played by actors who usually specialize in male roles to make them both comical and sinister. Cruelly, they make fun of Omiwa, beating her and forcing her to sing and dance for them. Finally they attack her and leave her unconscious.

Regaining consciousness, she hears the ladies congratulating the lovers on their marriage. Omiwa is overcome with jealousy and is about to confront the party when Fukashichi reappears and stabs her. Fukashichi reveals that he is one of Kamatari's retainers, and he explains that, having already obtained the blood of the black-footed doe, he now needs the blood of a jealous woman, Omiwa, in order to defeat Iruka. He bids Omiwa rejoice at her part in Iruka's forthcoming downfall and collects her blood in the magical flute.

Kanadehon chūshingura ("The Treasury of Loyal Retainers")

Jidaimono, maruhonmono.
Written by Takeda Izumo II, Miyoshi Shōraku, and Namiki Senryū.
First performed in 1748 at the Takemoto-za, Osaka. First staged as Kabuki the same year at the Arashi-za, Osaka. All eleven acts of *Kanadehon chūshingura* are occasionally performed as a *tōshi kyōgen*, particularly in December when the actual vendetta took place. The acts described here are also some of the most frequently performed of all Bunraku and Kabuki plays.

Chūshingura is based on a true incident that took place between 1701 and 1703. To avoid shogunate censorship, the authors set the play in the earlier Muromachi period (1333–1568) and the names of the characters were altered.

The central story concerns the daimyo Enya Hangan, who is goaded into drawing his sword and striking a senior lord, Kō no Moronō. Drawing one's sword in the shogun's palace was a capital offense and so Hangan is ordered to commit *seppuku*, or ritual suicide by disembowelment. The ceremony is carried out with great formality and, with his dying breath, he makes clear to his chief retainer, Ōboshi Yuranosuke, that he wishes to be avenged upon Moronō.

Forty-seven of Hangan's now masterless samurai, or *rōnin*, bide their time. Yuranosuke in particular appears to give himself over to a life of debauchery in Kyoto's Gion pleasure quarters in order to put the enemy off their guard. In fact, they are making stealthy but meticulous preparations and, in the depths of winter, storm Moronō's Edo mansion and kill him. Aware, however, that this deed is itself an offense, the retainers then carry Moronō's head to the grave of their lord at Sengaku-ji temple in Edo, where they all commit *seppuku*.

ACT I: *Tsurugaoka kabuto aratame* ("The Helmet Selection at Hachiman Shrine")

This play has a unique opening, in which the curtain is pulled open slowly over several minutes, accompanied by forty-seven individual beats of the *ki*, one for each of the heroic *rōnin*. Gradually the actors are revealed in front of the Hachiman Shrine in Kamakura, slumped over like lifeless puppets. As the *gidayū* narrator speaks the name of each character he comes to life. Lord Moronō's evil nature is immediately demonstrated by his black robes and the furious *mie* pose that he strikes when his name is announced. He is hostile to the younger, inexperienced lords. They have all gathered to find and present a special helmet at the shrine and it is Hangan's wife, Kaoyo, who is the one to identify it. When the ceremony is over and he is eventually left alone with Kaoyo, Moronō propositions her but she rejects his amorous advances.

ACT III, SCENE II: in Bunraku, *Denchū ninjō* ("Bloodshed within the Palace"); in Kabuki, *Matsu no ma ninjō* ("The Pine Room in the Shogun's Palace")

This is the scene that seals Hangan's fate. Offended by Kaoyo's rebuff, Moronō hurls insults

at Hangan, accusing him of incompetence and of being late for his duties. Hangan, he says, is like a little fish: he is adequate within the safe confines of a well (his own little domain), but put him in the great river (the shogun's mansion in the capital) and he soon hits his nose against the pillar of a bridge and dies. Unable to bear the insults any longer, Hangan strikes Moronō but, to his eternal chagrin, is restrained from killing him by his retainer, Kakogawa Honzō.

ACT IV, SCENE I: *Enya Hangan seppuku* ("Enya Hangan's Seppuku")

Hangan is ordered to commit *seppuku* and his castle is confiscated. The emotional highlight of this scene is Hangan's death. The preparations for the ceremony are elaborate and formal. He must kill himself on two upturned *tatami* mats that are covered with a white cloth and have small vases of anise placed at the four corners. The details of the *seppuku* were strictly prescribed: the initial cut is under the left ribcage, the blade is then drawn to the right and, finally, a small upward cut is made before withdrawing the blade. Hangan delays as long as he can, however, for he is anxious to have one last word with his chief retainer, Yuranosuke. At the last moment, Yuranosuke rushes in to hear his lord's dying wish to be avenged on Moronō. Hangan is left to despatch himself by cutting his own jugular vein.

ACT IV, SCENE II: in Bunraku, *Shiro akewatashi* ("The Hand-Over of the Castle"); in Kabuki, *Uramon* ("The Rear Gate of the Mansion")

Night has fallen and Yuranosuke, left alone, bids a sad farewell to their mansion. He holds the bloody dagger with which his lord killed himself and licks it as an oath to carry out his lord's dying wish. The curtain closes and a lone shamisen player enters at the side of the stage, accompanying Yuranosuke's desolate exit along the *hanamichi*.

INTERACT, *Michiyuki tabiji no hanamuko* ("The Bridegroom's Journey"), also called *Ochiudo* ("The Fugitives") in Kabuki

This *michiyuki*, or "travel-dance," was added to the play in 1833 and is very often performed separately. The dance depicts the lovers Okaru and Kanpei journeying to the home of Okaru's parents in the country after Hangan's death. Kanpei was the retainer who accompanied Hangan to the shogun's mansion and he is now guilt-ridden at his failure to protect his lord. He would take his own life to atone for his sin, but Okaru persuades him to wait. The couple are waylaid by the comical Sagisaki Bannai and his foolish men. They are working for Lord Moronō, but Kanpei easily defeats them and they continue on their way.

ACT V: *Yamazaki kaidō teppō watashi* ("The Musket Shots on the Yamazaki Highway")

While only a peripheral part of the story, these two scenes are very popular because of their fine staging and dramatic action. Kanpei is now living with Okaru's parents and is desperate to join the vendetta. On a dark, rainy night we see him out hunting wild boar.

Meanwhile, Okaru has agreed that her father, Yoichibei, sell her into prostitution in Kyoto to raise money for the vendetta. On his way home from the Gion pleasure quarter with half the cash as a down payment, however, Yoichibei is murdered and robbed by Sadakurō, the wicked son of Kudayū, one of Moronō's retainers. Sadakurō is dressed in a stark black kimono and, though brief, this role is famous for its sinister and bloodcurdling appeal.

Kanpei shoots at a wild boar, but misses. Instead, the shot hits Sadakurō and, as he dies, the blood drips from Sadakurō's mouth onto his exposed white thigh. Kanpei finds the body but cannot see who it is in the darkness. Hardly believing his luck, he discovers the money on the body and decides to take it to give to the vendetta.

ACT VI: *Kanpei harakiri* ("Kanpei's Suicide")

Yoichibei's murder is discovered and Kanpei, believing mistakenly that he is responsible, commits *seppuku*. The truth, however, is revealed before he draws his last breath and, in his own blood, Kanpei is permitted to add his name to the vendetta list.

ACT VII: *Gion Ichirikijaya* ("The Ichiriki Teahouse at Gion")

This act gives a taste of the bustling atmosphere of the Gion pleasure quarter in Kyoto. Yuranosuke is feigning a life of debauchery at the same teahouse to which Okaru has been indentured. Kudayū, the father of Sadakurō, arrives. He is now working for Moronō and his purpose is to discover whether Yuranosuke still plans revenge or not. He tests Yuranosuke's resolve by offering him food on the anniversary of their lord's death, when he should be fasting. Yuranosuke is forced to accept. Yuranosuke's sword—the revered symbol of a samurai—is also found to be covered in rust. It would appear that Yuranosuke has no thoughts of revenge. But still unsure, Kudayū hides under the veranda.

Now believing himself alone, Yuranosuke begins to read a secret letter scroll about preparations for the vendetta. On a higher balcony Okaru comes out to cool herself in the evening breeze and, noticing Yuranosuke close by, she also reads the letter reflected in her mirror. As Yuranosuke unrolls the scroll, Kudayū, too, examines the end, which trails below the veranda. Suddenly one of Okaru's hairpins drops to the floor and a shocked Yuranosuke quickly rolls up the scroll. Finding the end of the letter torn off, he realizes that yet another person knows his secret and he must silence them both. Feigning merriment, he calls Okaru to come down and offers to buy out her contract. He goes off supposedly to fix the deal. Then Okaru's brother Heiemon enters and, hearing what has just happened, realizes that Yuranosuke actually intends to keep her quiet by killing her. He persuades Okaru to let him kill her instead so as to save their honor and she agrees. Overhearing everything, Yuranosuke is now convinced of the pair's loyalty and stops them. He gives Okaru a sword and, guiding her hand, thrusts it through the floorboards to kill Kudayū.

ACT VIII: *Michiyuki tabiji no yomeiri* ("The Bride's Journey")

When Enya Hangan drew his sword against the evil Moronō within the shogun's palace, it was Kakogawa Honzō who held him back, preventing him from killing the older lord. Honzō's daughter, Konami, is betrothed to Yuranosuke's son, Rikiya, but since that fateful event the marriage arrangements have been stalled, causing much embarrassment to the girl. Not prepared to leave things as they are, Honzō's wife, Tonase, resolves to deliver Konami to Yuranosuke's home in order to force the marriage.

This act takes the form of a *michiyuki* dance in which Tonase leads her stepdaughter along the great Tōkaidō Highway, the main thoroughfare linking Edo in the east with Kyoto in the west. On the way, they pass a number of famous sites such as Mt. Fuji and, as a marriage procession passes by, Konami watches enviously, thinking that in better times she herself would have ridden in just such a grand palanquin. Tonase encourages her daughter, telling her of the happiness to come once she is wed.

ACT IX: *Yamashina kankyo* ("The Retreat at Yamashina")

Set in the depths of winter, Kakogawa Honzō's wife Tonase, and daughter Konami, arrive at Yuranosuke's home in Yamashina near Kyoto. Yuranosuke's wife is adamant that after all that has happened there can be no possibility of marriage between Konami and Rikiya. In despair, Tonase and Konami decide to take their own lives. Just then, Honzō arrives disguised as a wandering priest. To atone for his part in restraining Hangan from killing Moronō, he deliberately pulls Rikiya's spear into his own stomach and, dying, gives Yuranosuke and Rikiya a plan of Moronō's mansion in Edo.

ACT XI: in Bunraku, *Hanamizu hikiage* ("Withdrawal over Hanamizu Bridge"); in Kabuki, *Moronō yakata uchiiri* ("The Attack on Moronō's Mansion")

The final act takes place at Moronō's mansion on a snowy night. The attack is presented in a series of *tachimawari* fight scenes before Moronō is finally captured and killed.

Kumagai jinya ("Kumagai's Battle Camp")

Jidaimono, maruhonmono.
Written by Namiki Sōsuke, Asada Itchō, Namioka Geiji, and Namiki Shōzō I.
First performed in 1751 at the Toyotake-za, Osaka.
First staged as Kabuki in 1752 at the Nakamura-za and the Morita-za, Edo. The full title of the play is

Ichinotani futaba gunki ("Chronicle of the Battle of Ichinotani"). Act III is the most commonly performed act.

The country is in a state of civil war between the Genji and Heike clans. In a previous act, the Genji warrior Kumagai supposedly beheaded Atsumori, a young Heike lord and son of an emperor. The time approaches for the official *kubi jikken* to verify the identity of Atsumori's head.

ACT III: *Kumagai jinya* ("Kumagai's Battle Camp")

Kumagai returns to his battle camp where, by order of his lord Yoshitsune, a signboard has been placed by a cherry tree. The sign bears the cryptic message, "He who fells one branch of this tree must also shed a finger." Kumagai is unsure of the meaning behind this message.

His wife, Sagami, arrives at the camp to enquire about their own son Kojirō, who also fought in the battle. As women are usually forbidden at the camp, Kumagai gruffly tells her that Kojirō fought well, and that he, Kumagai, killed Atsumori. Hearing this, Atsumori's mother Fuji-no-kata rushes in to attack him. Sixteen years before, when Sagami (a member of the Heike clan) became pregnant by Kumagai (from the Genji clan), Sagami had been in Fuji-no-kata's service. It was Fuji-no-kata who enabled the couple to flee from the authorities when their illicit union was discovered. Kumagai is still conscious of the debt they owe her. He easily fends her off and, realizing who she is, bows humbly. In the first great highlight of the play, called the *monogatari*, or "storytelling" section, he tells them how Atsumori died. He did not wish to kill the boy but when he hesitated, another general accused him of betrayal and so it was impossible not to take the boy's head.

Lord Yoshitsune enters. Kumagai presents the head in a box for the formal identification known as the *kubi jikken*. As he lifts the lid, however, Sagami sees not Atsumori's head, but rather that of their own son, Kojirō. Kumagai quickly orders her to be silent until Yoshitsune has spoken. In another highlight, he holds back the grieving women and then performs the famous *seisatsu no mie*, the "signboard" pose, to express the heightened tension of this moment. Kumagai is unsure whether his interpretation of the signboard's message has been correct. Yoshitsune inspects the head, but deliberately identifies it as that of Atsumori. Kumagai has indeed understood correctly, for the meaning of the sign was that he who would spare the cherry branch (Atsumori) must sacrifice his own finger (Kojirō) in its place.

Sagami is now permitted to show the head to Fuji-no-kata. This is the celebrated *kudoki* in which, obliged to keep up the pretense that it is Atsumori's head, Sagami must suppress unbearable pain as she looks upon her own son's face, now so changed in death.

Suddenly a spy named Kajiwara appears, saying he will report these traitorous deeds to their commander. However, he is immediately killed by a chisel thrown by an old stonemason called Midaroku, in reality the Heike general Munekiyo in disguise. Yoshitsune recognizes him by a mole between his eyes as many years ago Munekiyo helped protect him, his brother, and their mother. By ordering that Atsumori's life be spared, Yoshitsune has paid the debt he owes Munekiyo, and Kumagai has paid the debt he and his wife owe to Fuji-no-kata. Yoshitsune orders a box of armor to be given to Fuji-no-kata. Inside the box is the boy Atsumori, alive and well.

They all mourn the death of Kojirō, and Kumagai laments the impermanence of life. He requests permission to renounce his status as a warrior and enter the priesthood. In the closing moments Kumagai comments on his son's short life. *Jūroku nen wa hito mukashi . . . yume da, yume da!* ("Sixteen years have passed . . . like a dream . . . like a dream!"). A lone shamisen player enters to accompany the actor as, with great sorrow, Kumagai says farewell to his life as a warrior and departs along the *hanamichi*.

Kuruwa bunshō
("Love Letters from the Licensed Quarter")

Sewamono, maruhonmono.
The original play about the famous Osaka courtesan Yūgiri was entitled *Yūgiri nagori no shōgatsu*

("Yugiri's New Year Farewell"), and written by Chikamatsu Monzaemon in 1678 for Sakata Tōjūrō I. The version commonly seen today was first staged in 1808 at the Nakamura-za, Edo. This play is also known as *Yoshida-ya*, the name of the teahouse in which it is set, and is performed today in one act.

Kuruwa bunshō is one of the most celebrated examples still surviving of the *wagoto* acting style made famous by Sakata Tōjūrō. Many plays were written about the love of Yūgiri and Izaemon, which was Tōjūrō's most famous role.

The curtain opens on the exterior of the Yoshida-ya teahouse in the Shinmachi pleasure quarter in Osaka. Some men are pounding rice flour to make *mochi* rice cakes, and we see from the decorations by the door that it is the New Year. A delicate young man enters on the *hanamichi*. He is Izaemon, son of the wealthy Fujiya family, but his appearance suggests that he has fallen on hard times. His head and face are covered by a straw hat and he is wearing a *kamiko*, supposedly a thin paper kimono stitched together from love letters. The actor is accompanied by two *kurogo*, who hold candles on the ends of long poles called *sashigane* to light his way, a charming reminder of the times before electric lighting.

As he arrives at the Yoshida-ya, the men make to drive him off, but the teahouse master recognizes this once-honored customer and welcomes him into the establishment. Izaemon has, in fact, been disinherited because of his philandering in the pleasure district and now has no money. Pathetic in his downfall, his reason for coming here is to meet his former lover, the beautiful courtesan Yūgiri who, he has heard, was gravely ill but is now recovering. She is busy with another customer. Having been shown into a spacious room close by, Izaemon displays agonies of jealousy at Yūgiri's apparent inconstancy, and shame at his own strained circumstances.

In a style typical of *wagoto*, Izaemon's character, manners, and body language are refined and gentle, almost feminine. In this play he expresses himself a great deal in short dance-like interludes to the words of the singers. The comic side to Izaemon's character is best displayed in his nervousness as he tries out different poses and attitudes, even attempting to sit on top of a *kotatsu* foot-warmer, while he awaits the arrival of Yūgiri.

Yūgiri finally enters. She is a courtesan of the highest rank, and her robes and wig are resplendent. When she enters it appears that she is walking through many different rooms. This is achieved by a series of doors being drawn aside, each smaller than the other, to give the impression of perspective. Around her head she wears a purple headband of the sort called *yamai hachimaki*, knotted on the left, which is a Kabuki convention indicating illness.

The jealous Izaemon is at first cool towards her. She has always loved him, however, and pours out her emotions in a famous *kudoki*. It was because she could not see him for so long that she became ill. Gradually the lovers are reconciled. As their hearts are reunited, many servants suddenly rush in bearing money. Izaemon's family has relented and he is rich once more. With the couple in the center, all pose together in a scene of general rejoicing.

Kuzunoha kowakare ("The Parting of Kuzunoha from her Child")

Jidaimono, maruhonmono.
Written by Takeda Izumo II.
First performed in 1734 at the Takemoto-za, Osaka. First staged as Kabuki in 1735 at the Nakamura Tomijūrō-za, Kyoto. The full title of the play is *Ashiya Dōman ōuchi kagami* ("A Courtly Mirror of Ashiya Dōman").
Only scenes from Act IV are regularly performed today. This act is famous for its pathos as well as the use of *keren* stage trickery. It features two female characters, both named Kuzunoha. In Bunraku, it was in this play that a puppet operated by three men was first used.

Abe no Yasuna, a young astrologer at the imperial court, goes mad with grief after his lover commits suicide. Wandering through Shinoda forest, he happens upon a woman who is the spitting image of his deceased lover. She is Kuzunoha-hime, the daughter of Shinoda no Shōji. Yasuna regains his senses and before parting, he and Kuzunoha-hime are betrothed.

Some time later, he rescues a white fox that is being hunted in the forest. Yasuna is injured, and Kuzunoha appears mysteriously to dress his wounds. The two are married and live happily together for six years, during which time she gives birth to a son. However, unknown to Yasuna, this Kuzunoha is actually the fox that he saved now transformed into human shape.

ACT IV, SCENE I: in Kabuki, *Abeno hataya* ("The Weaving Room at Abeno")
Yasuna and his family live in a humble dwelling at Abeno, where Kuzunoha helps to make ends meet by weaving cloth. One day their domestic bliss is shattered when an elderly couple and their daughter appear. It is none other than Shōji, his wife, and their daughter Kuzunoha-hime. Having heard nothing from Yasuna for so long, Shōji has come to give his daughter to Yasuna in marriage.

Calling on the house, Shōji is shocked to see another Kuzunoha inside. Yasuna himself returns and after greeting Shōji fondly he, too, is amazed that there are two seemingly identical Kuzunohas. During this scene, a single actor plays both young women and must quick-change between the roles using the *hayagawari* technique. Special attention is paid to the difference in characterization: Kuzunoha-hime's role type is the refined and sheltered *akahime*, while the fox Kuzunoha is performed as a loyal, hard-working, and practical *sewa nyōbo*, or "domestic wife."

ACT IV, SCENE II: in Bunraku, *Kuzunoha kowakare* ("The Parting of Kuzunoha from her Child"); in Kabuki, *Oku zashiki* ("The Inner Room")
Realizing the impossible situation, the fox Kuzunoha feels she must return to the forest and leave her dear husband and child in the care of the real Kuzunoha-hime. Though it causes her anguish to leave, she cannot face her husband now that he knows the truth. Kuzunoha's *kudoki* is the climax of the play, and what follows requires great skill and practice. Resolving to leave a farewell poem on the sliding paper doors, Kuzunoha begins to write when her sleeping child awakens. She comforts the boy with her right hand and so must hold the brush in her left, writing characters that are in fact back to front.

When he will not stop crying she holds him with both arms and bites the brush in her mouth to finish her poem. These abilities reveal her supernatural powers as a fox. The poem reads:

If you should miss me,
Come seek me in Izumi's
Shinoda Forest,
Where kuzu vine leaves upturned
Will mark my bitter dwelling.

(The name Kuzunoha means "*kuzu* vine leaves.") With this, she makes her sad departure, leaving behind her beloved son. This is a famous example of a scene of separation between a parent and child known as *kowakare*, "parting from one's child."

Soon after, Yasuna hurries in. He has heard all and desperately calls her back. Noticing the poem, he realizes where the fox Kuzunoha has gone and, taking their child up in his arms, he rushes after her.

Meiboku sendai hagi ("Precious Incense and the Bush Clover of Sendai")

Jidaimono, maruhonmono, oie sōdōmono.
Written for Kabuki by Nagawa Kamesuke.
First performed as Kabuki in 1777 at the Naka no Shibai, Osaka. First staged as Bunraku in 1785 at the Yuki-za, Edo, adapted by Matsu Kanshi, Takahashi Buhei, and Yoshida Sumimaru. The following scenes are the most frequently performed.

The part of the wet-nurse, Masaoka, is considered one of the greatest *onnagata* roles and is of the type called *katahazushi*, referring to samurai women who serve at a daimyo's mansion. Masaoka's sacrifice of her own son is an example of the conflict between *giri* and *ninjō*.

Ashikaga Yorikane, daimyo of the northern province of Ōshū, has become infatuated with the courtesan Takao and, as a result, has neglected affairs of state. There is a plot to usurp his power. Yorikane is forced to withdraw and he is succeeded by his small son, Tsurukiyo, but those loyal to him fear for the boy's life.

ACT II: *Goten* ("The Ashikaga Mansion")
Masaoka looks after Tsurukiyo together with her own son, Senmatsu. Fearing poison, she makes

the boys wait for their food, scolding Senmatsu when he shows impatience. The boy replies, "Though my stomach be empty, yet I will feel no hunger," a famous line that has come to typify the samurai ideal of loyalty and self-sacrifice. Meanwhile, Masaoka cooks their rice herself using the implements of the tea ceremony. This cooking scene as performed by some actors may take some twenty minutes as the tension builds.

The wife of one of the conspirators, Lady Sakae, arrives with a message and a gift of cakes from the shogun, but her real intention is to poison Tsurukiyo. Senmatsu, instructed by his mother to test all food, rushes past Tsurukiyo and eats a cake. He immediately shows signs of poison and, fearful that their plot is discovered, the evil lady-in-waiting Yashio stabs the boy. Chastising him for his insolence, she cruelly tortures Senmatsu by twisting the knife in the boy's throat. This role is usually taken by a *tachiyaku* actor in order to make her as unattractive and sinister as possible.

Masaoka is appalled, but her first duty is to protect her young lord from danger and so stands shielding him as she looks on. During this highlight, the chanter praises her behavior as a mirror of heroism. Sakae cannot believe that the boy was really Masaoka's son for a mother would be incapable of merely standing by while her child was murdered. She is therefore convinced that Masaoka has switched the boys and that it is Tsurukiyo, not her son, who dies. Believing mistakenly that Masaoka is loyal to their cause, Sakae gives her a scroll on which are written the names of all the conspirators before she leaves.

Left alone, Masaoka pours out her emotions over Senmatsu's body. She is observed by Yashio who comes out to confront her. Masaoka stabs Yashio but, as they strike the final pose, a large rat appears and runs off with the incriminating scroll.

ACT IV: *Yukashita* ("Beneath the floorboards")
In the cellar, the loyal retainer Otokonosuke stands guard. The role is played in the *aragoto* style. He fights with the giant rat and wounds it on the forehead before it disappears down the *suppon* trap-door in the *hanamichi*. Seconds later, in a cloud of smoke, the archvillain and sorcerer

Nikki Danjō appears through the floor dressed in rat-grey clothes with the scroll in his mouth and an identical wound on his forehead. Otokonosuke is powerless against his magic and the curtain closes. Left alone on the *hanamichi*, Danjō takes the scroll from his mouth, laughs silently to himself and slowly walks away.

Meido no hikyaku ("The Courier from Hell")

Sewamono, maruhonmono.
Written by Chikamatsu Monzaemon.
First performed in 1711 at the Takemoto-za, Osaka. First staged as Kabuki in 1796 at the Kado no Shibai, Osaka. Adaptations: *Keisei koi bikyaku* ("The Courtesan and Love's Courier"); *Koi bikyaku Yamato ōrai* ("Love's Courier on the Yamato Highway"). The Kabuki play was adapted from a later puppet version by Suga Sensuke and Wakatake Fuemi. In Kabuki the character of Chūbei is performed in the *wagoto* acting style. *Fūingiri* and *Ninokuchi mura* are the only acts regularly performed today.

Kameya Chūbei works as a courier, delivering money for clients. He has fallen in love with a courtesan named Umegawa and has already paid off part of her contract. However, he is having difficulty raising the rest of the money.

IN BUNRAKU, ACT II; IN KABUKI ACT I: *Fūingiri* ("Breaking the Seal")
Chūbei's so-called friend Hachiemon is a rival for Umegawa's affections and is intending to buy out her contract that evening. Chūbei, eavesdropping from an upper room, overhears Hachiemon severely maligning him. Unable to stand it any longer, Chūbei bursts into the room insisting that he has the money for the contract after all.

The highlight of the play follows. Hachiemon doubts that someone like Chūbei could have so much cash and asks to see it. In fact, Chūbei does have a large sum of money with him, but it is cash that he is supposed to be delivering and it is officially sealed in a paper packet. Pretending that it is his own, Chūbei taps the packet on the charcoal brazier to prove that it contains hard gold pieces. With the teahouse employees all looking, they argue back and forth, Hachiemon doubting that the package is real

money and Chūbei insisting it is genuine. This famous section contains much ad-libbing by the actors. As the tension increases, Chūbei is goaded beyond endurance. He stands, breaks the seal, and the money clatters to the floor.

Chūbei realizes immediately the implications of what he has done. Although he had no intention of stealing the money, merely breaking the seal is a capital offense. Chūbei buys out Umegawa's contract, but he knows that their future is bleak. They decide to be together for just three days and then take their own lives.

IN KABUKI, ACT II: *Ninokuchi mura* ("Ninokuchi Village")
With the police chasing them, Chūbei and Umegawa return to his home in Ninokuchi village to pay his last respects at his mother's graveside. They spot his father, Magoemon, walking in the snow, but Chūbei does not wish to see him because his father will then be obliged to report his whereabouts. Magoemon slips, however, breaking the strap of one of his clogs and Umegawa rushes to help him.

Although Magoemon wishes to talk with his son, seeing him would put him in a difficult position because he would feel honor-bound to hand him over to the police. Umegawa, therefore, hits upon the idea of blindfolding the old man so that he can talk to Chūbei and truthfully say that he has not seen him. As the police close in, Magoemon tells them the best route for their escape, and they bid their final farewells.

Natsu matsuri Naniwa kagami ("Summer Festival: Mirror of Osaka")

Sewamono, maruhonmono.
Written by Namiki Sōsuke, Miyoshi Shōraku, and Takeda Koizumi (later Izumo II).
First performed in 1745 at the Takemoto-za, Osaka. First staged as Kabuki the same year in both Kyoto and Osaka. Only Acts III, VI, and VII are regularly performed today.

ACT III: *Sumiyoshi torii mae* ("Before the Torii Gate at Sumiyoshi Shrine")
Danshichi is a fishmonger and an *otokodate*, a "chivalrous commoner," who looks after the welfare of ordinary townsmen against the

samurai. Danshichi has been imprisoned for wounding a samurai, but has been pardoned and is to be released. His wife, Okaji, his young son, Ichimatsu, and another *otokodate* called Sabu come to the Sumiyoshi shrine to meet him. While Okaji and the boy pray, the bound Danshichi is brought out and released. He goes to the barber and changes into the clean clothes they have brought him.

The courtesan Kotoura enters pursued by Sagaemon, an evil samurai who is in love with her. He is the enemy of Danshichi's benefactor, the samurai Hyōdayū. Danshichi emerges fresh from the barber shop, restrains Sagaemon, giving him a beating, and allows Kotoura to go on her way. Just then one of Sagaemon's hirelings, Tokubei, also an *otokodate*, arrives with some palanquin bearers to get the girl. Danshichi and Tokubei fight, but are interrupted and restrained by Okaji. It turns out that Tokubei, too, is loyal to Hyōdayū, and so he and Danshichi forget their differences and swear eternal friendship.

ACT VI: *Tsuribune Sabu no uchi* ("The House of Sabu the Boatman")
Kotoura and Hyōdayū's son Isonojō are in love. To protect the couple from their enemies, Sabu is sheltering them. Tokubei's wife, the beautiful Otatsu, enters. She has come to thank Sabu for keeping her hotheaded husband out of trouble. She says that she is soon to leave for her house in the country, and Sabu's wife Otsugi asks her to take Isonojō with her as it is too dangerous for him here in Osaka. Sabu, however, angrily says that the beautiful Otatsu cannot travel together with the rather wayward Isonojō. Otatsu is offended at this insinuation and deliberately presses a hot poker against her cheek to make herself less attractive. Sabu is pleased with her act and agrees that she and Isonojō may leave together.

Danshichi's evil father-in-law Giheiji arrives with a palanquin, saying he has a message from Danshichi to pick up Kotoura and take her to Danshichi's house for protection. Danshichi and Tokubei then arrive and they realize that Giheiji has tricked them and captured Kotoura. Danshichi runs after him.

ACT VII: *Nagamachi ura* ("The Backstreet of Nagamachi")
There is a festival in progress and Danshichi catches up with Giheiji. They argue until finally Giheiji confesses that he kidnapped Kotoura in order to sell her to Sagaemon. Danshichi begs him to let the girl go and finally offers Giheiji thirty gold pieces for her. Giheiji lets the palanquin take her back home.

Danshichi has no money, of course, and Giheiji realizes that he has been tricked. They argue again and Danshichi mistakenly gives Giheiji a slight wound. Giheiji calls for help and, trying to silence him, Danshichi fights and kills him. During the fight, Danshichi is stripped down to his loin cloth to reveal his tattooed body in an exciting series of grotesquely beautiful *mie* poses, while in the background we hear all the gaiety of the festival. Covered in mud, Danshichi desperately tries to wash himself with water from a well. Speaking his final line, "Evil though he was, a father-in-law is still a parent. Father, please forgive me!" he blends into the festival crowd.

Shinjū ten no Amijima ("Love Suicides at Amijima")

Sewamono, maruhonmono, shinjūmono.
Written by Chikamatsu Monzaemon.
First performed in 1720 at the Takemoto-za, Osaka. First performed as Kabuki in 1721 at the Morita-za, Edo. Based on a true incident. Several adaptations exist of which the most famous is Chikamatsu Hanji's *Shinjū kamiya Jihei* of 1778. In Kabuki, the role of Jihei is performed in the *wagoto* style and either of the first two scenes, *Kawashō* or *Shigure no kotatsu* may be staged independently.

ACT I: *Kawashō* ("The Kawashō Teahouse")
Despite having a loving wife and two children, the paper merchant Jihei has fallen in love with the courtesan Koharu and has spent so much money on visiting her that his business faces financial ruin. Jihei's rival Tahei, however, is wealthy and has made arrangements to redeem Koharu's contract so that she can be his wife. Now desperate, Jihei and Koharu have agreed to commit suicide together and Jihei comes

nightly to the pleasure quarter looking for an opportunity to run away with her.

One night, Koharu is called to the Kawashō teahouse to entertain a samurai customer. She cannot help but reveal her anguish and, realizing the situation, the samurai offers to lend her cash. Surprised and moved by such kindness from a stranger, Koharu admits that she has agreed to die with Jihei, but insists that this is not her true desire. She has been trapped by circumstances. This spurning of Jihei is an example of *aiso zukashi*.

At that very moment Jihei is listening outside and he becomes frantic with anger, believing that Koharu has lied to him all along. Seeing her shadow against the sliding paper doors, he thrusts his knife in at her but misses. The samurai quickly intervenes.

The samurai is, in reality, Jihei's elder brother Magoemon in disguise. He has come to buy off Koharu. Jihei promises him that he will have nothing more to do with her, demanding that Koharu return his written pledges of love. When she seems reluctant, Magoemon snatches the pledges from her. As he does so, he sees that in amongst them is a letter from Jihei's wife begging Koharu to give up her suicide for the sake of Jihei's family. Magoemon realizes that Koharu has, after all, acted honorably.

ACT II: in Bunraku, *Tenma Kamiya uchi* ("The House of Jihei"); in Kabuki, *Shigure no kotatsu* ("Beneath the kotatsu in Jihei's House")
Jihei is married to his cousin Osan. Ten days later at Jihei's house, Magoemon and Osan's mother pay a visit. Having heard rumors that a rich patron is to buy out Koharu's contract, they feel sure it can only be Jihei himself. He denies it and assures them that the patron is his rival Tahei. Once they have left, Jihei slumps down upon the *kotatsu* brazier and dissolves in tears. Thinking that he is still in love with Koharu, Osan berates him in a moving *kudoki*, but Jihei claims that, on the contrary, it is Koharu's deception that causes him pain. Koharu promised that she would take her own life rather than marry Tahei, and yet now she is allowing herself to be redeemed. At this, Osan realizes Koharu's true intentions: she does indeed

intend to die. Osan confesses that it was she who wrote to Koharu begging her to give Jihei up, but now Osan cannot bear the thought of Koharu's self-sacrifice. Jihei must go and save her by redeeming her contract first. Though they have little money, Osan is willing to sell the clothes off her own and her family's backs to raise the cash, and is even prepared to take the role of nursemaid or cook when Koharu comes to live with them. Just then, however, Osan's father appears. He is enraged, and when he sees that all her clothes are gone he forcibly drags Osan away, separating a loyal wife from her husband for the last time.

ACT III: *Michiyuki nagori no hashi zukushi* ("The Lovers' Farewell—a Catalogue of Bridges")
Later that night, Jihei returns to the pleasure quarter, and he and Koharu set off on their journey towards death across the many bridges of the district. Out of a sense of obligation to Osan and in order not to cause her further public shame, Koharu begs that they not die in the same place and Jihei agrees.

Shunkan ("Shunkan")

Jidaimono, maruhonmono.
Written by Chikamatsu Monzaemon.
First performed in 1719 at the Takemoto-za, Osaka. First staged as Kabuki in 1720 at the Naka-za, Osaka. The full title of the play is *Heike nyogo no shima* ("Shunkan on Devil Island"), but only Act II, commonly known as "Shunkan" after the name of the principal character, is regularly performed today. It is based on a story in the epic twelfth-century *Heike monogatari*, and the same story has also been adapted to Nō.

ACT II: *Kikaigashima* ("Devil's island")
Shunkan, together with lords Naritsune and Yasuyori, has been exiled to remote Kikaigashima—"Devil's Island"—for plotting to overthrow the ruling Heike clan. Life on the island is hard, particularly as Shunkan is saddened by thoughts of his wife left in the capital.

Naritsune falls in love with a fishergirl called Chidori, played as a coy young island girl. Her costume is a green kimono, decorated with an octopus design, and the *uma no shippo* wig. In a simple makeshift ceremony, the couple exchange marriage vows by drinking water from empty shells in place of saké. Just then, a ship approaches and docks close by. An envoy named Seno'o disembarks. The role is that of an *akattsura* villain and he wears the stylized costume of an envoy, known as the *ryūjin maki*, with trousers tucked up to the thighs, and one sleeve stretched out on bamboo struts in order to show off his official crest.

Seno'o reads a decree granting an official amnesty. Though Naritsune and Yasuyori are pardoned, Shunkan's name is missing. The envoy revels in Shunkan's despair, and when the latter pleads for mercy, Seno'o speaks the famous line, "Sympathy and compassion are to me unknown." At that moment, another envoy named Tansaemon disembarks with a pardon for Shunkan, too. Tansaemon's white face and pale blue costume mark him out as a more sympathetic *nimaime* role type. All of them, including Chidori, make to board the ship. Seno'o stops her, however, saying that their orders permit the return of only three persons.

When Shunkan protests, Seno'o informs him of his wife's death. She was murdered by Taira no Kiyomori, leader of the Heike, for refusing to become his mistress. Now Shunkan is permitted to return, but only as far as the mainland; if he enters the capital he will be executed. The three exiles are pushed aboard the boat and Chidori is left alone to bemoan her fate in a famous and beautiful *kudoki*. She expresses her sadness at being prevented from leaving the island with her lover, Naritsune, speaking the famous line, "It is not on Devil's Island that demons dwell, for they are all to be found in the capital."

Before they can sail, however, Shunkan reappears saying he no longer has a reason to go home. The order is for three people, so Chidori should take his place. Seno'o also disembarks to find out what is going on and, when he refuses to permit this compromise, Shunkan attacks him. About to be killed by Shunkan, Seno'o calls to Tansaemon for help, but he coolly replies with Seno'o's own words from earlier in the play, "Sympathy and compassion

are to me unknown." Realizing that for this further crime he must remain on the island after all, Shunkan grasps his beard with one hand and poses in the famous *Kan'u mie* (Kan'u is the name of a Chinese general) expressing sad resignation.

The closing minutes of the play are a tour-de-force of emotional intensity. Shunkan runs after the departing vessel to the water's edge, only to be driven back by the waves. The revolving stage turns and he climbs a rocky outcrop to watch the boat sail away. The role's psychological depth here has made this play universally popular.

Sonezaki shinjū ("Love Suicides at Sonezaki")

Sewamono, maruhonmono, shinjūmono.
Written by Chikamatsu Monzaemon.
First performed in 1703 at the Takemoto-za, Osaka. First staged as Kabuki in 1719 by Ichikawa Danjūrō II at the Nakamura-za, Edo. The current Kabuki version was adapted by Uno Nobuo in 1953.

Tokubei, a clerk at the Hirano-ya soy sauce shop, is in love with the courtesan Ohatsu. For this reason, he has refused a marriage arranged by his uncle and is obliged to return the dowry money by a certain date. Tokubei retrieves the money from his stepmother but, there still being a few days before the deadline, he is persuaded by an acquaintance called Kuheiji to lend him the cash just for a short time. This is Tokubei's fatal mistake.

ACT I: in Bunraku, *Ikudama shazen* ("Before the Ikudama Shrine"); in Kabuki, *Ikudama Jinja Keidai* ("The Precincts of the Ikudama Shrine") A few days later he chances upon Ohatsu before the precincts of the Ikudama Shrine. Kuheiji comes along, too, but when Tokubei asks him to return the money as promised, he denies all knowledge of the loan. Tokubei takes out the promissory note with Kuheiji's seal affixed, but Kuheiji accuses him of being a swindler because he, Kuheiji, had lost the seal three days before the date of the note. A crowd gathers and Tokubei is beaten and publicly humiliated.

Later that night at the Tenmaya brothel, Ohatsu sees Tokubei approaching and slips out to talk to him. Believing that his situation is now impossible, Tokubei thinks he cannot survive the night. Before their discussion can go further, however, Ohatsu is called inside and she must hide Tokubei under the hem of her long outer robe to sneak him in with her. Tokubei then conceals himself under a veranda ledge extending from the main room, and Ohatsu seats herself directly above, nonchalantly lighting a long-stemmed tobacco pipe.

Kuheiji comes in with his companions and starts to talk noisily about Tokubei, saying Tokubei must have picked up Kuheiji's seal and used it to try to cheat some money out of him. In the highlight of the scene, Ohatsu speaks in Tokubei's defense. Due to the disgrace, Tokubei will be forced to commit suicide, and if that should be the case, she too would die with him. Desiring to know if Tokubei agrees to this, Ohatsu sticks out her foot as a signal that he should indicate his own resolve to die. From his hiding place below, Tokubei drags the foot across his neck as a sign that he will indeed end his life with her. (Female puppets do not usually have legs, but the character of Ohatsu in this scene is a rare exception.) Kuheiji laughs off Ohatsu's words and retires into another room to drink.

Presently the house is locked up for the night. Ohatsu retires to her room, ostensibly to sleep, but in reality to make preparations for her death journey with Tokubei, who waits for her below. She comes down the stairs from her room and tries to put out the ceiling lamp, but in doing so she misses her footing and falls. The light goes out and the lovers grope around for each other in the dark while the maid servant sleepily tries to relight a lamp. Fearful of being discovered, the couple must time the door's opening to the sound of the tinder box, eventually slipping through the door just as the lamp is relit.

ACT III: in Bunraku, *Tenjin mori* ("The Tenjin Forest"); in Kabuki, *Sonezaki no mori* ("Sonezaki Forest")
The lovers arrive at the forest of Sonezaki. The opening lyrics of the final scene have been praised, even in Chikamatsu's own day, as being among the most beautiful ever written for the theater:

> From this world we take our leave,
> Farewell to this night.
> To what may we be compared
> On the road to death?
> To the frost on the path to
> Adashigahara
> That with each step, vanishes,
> Melting from our sight.
> How pitiful life is
> In this dream of a dream.

Tokubei stabs Ohatsu, and then kills himself.

Sugawara denju tenarai kagami ("Sugawara's Secrets of Calligraphy")

Jidaimono, maruhonmono.
Written by Takeda Izumo II, Miyoshi Shōraku, and Namiki Senryū.
First performed in 1746 at the Takemoto-za, Osaka.
First staged as Kabuki the same year at the Arashi-za, Kyoto.

The story concerns the rivalry between the great calligraphy master and "Minister of the Right" at the imperial court, Sugawara no Michizane (845–903), also known as Kan Shōjō and later deified as a god, and the evil "Minister of the Left," Fujiwara no Shihei. A subplot concerns triplet brothers, Matsuōmaru, Umeōmaru, and Sakuramaru. A further theme is that of the separation of parent and child: Kan Shōjō and Kariyahime in Act II, Shiratayū and Sakuramaru in Act III, and Matsuōmaru and Kotarō in Act IV.

ACT I, SCENE II: *Kamo zutsumi* ("The Kamo River Bank")
Kan Shōjō's adopted daughter, Kariyahime, and the emperor's younger brother Prince Tokiyo are in love, and a rendezvous is arranged for them by Sakuramaru and his wife Yae. Such a tryst between a commoner and a prince of the royal blood was strictly forbidden. One of Shihei's spies finds them and they are forced to hide. For his part in this, Sakuramaru brings disgrace both to his family and to his lord, Kan Shōjō.

ACT I, SCENE III: *Hippō denju* ("The Transmission of the Calligraphy Secrets")

Kan Shōjō's former pupil Takebe Genzō was dismissed for falling in love with a lady-in-waiting called Tonami and now runs a village school. Nevertheless, Kan Shōjō recalls Genzō and passes on his calligraphy secrets to him as his favorite student.

Kan Shōjō is summoned to attend the emperor but his hat falls off, which is considered a bad omen. Shihei accuses him of trying to usurp the throne by arranging the assignation between his daughter and Prince Tokiyo. Though innocent, Kan Shōjō is banished. With the help of Umeōmaru, Genzō escapes with Kan Shōjō's son, Kan Shūsai.

ACT II, SCENE III: in Bunraku, *Shōjō nagori* ("Shōjō's Farewell"); in Kabuki, *Dōmyōji* ("Dōmyōji Temple")

While waiting for the tide that will carry him into exile, Kan Shōjō is permitted to spend one night at the mansion of his elderly aunt, Kakuju (one of the three great *sanbaba* roles of Kabuki). Kakuju has two daughters, Tatsuta and Kariyahime (Kan Shōjō in fact adopted his own niece). Though it pains her to do so, the strict old woman beats Kariyahime for the trouble she has caused. Just then, however, from behind some sliding doors Kan Shōjō's voice tells her to stop. Kakuju explains that she beat Kariyahime so that Kan Shōjō would not have to beat her himself. Mysteriously, on opening the sliding doors they find nothing but a wooden statue in Kan Shōjō's place. Kariyahime believes she will never see her adoptive father again.

At dawn Kan Shōjō is to be escorted away. However, Kakuju's son-in-law Sukune Tarō and his father, Haji no Hyōe, are in league with Shihei and plan to assassinate Kan Shōjō. Tarō's wife, Tatsuta, overhears their scheming and is murdered. The men cause a cock to crow in the middle of the night so that those of the household will think it is daybreak. They then send a false escort to take Kan Shōjō away. He leaves with them, but miraculously turns himself back into the wooden statue and the men return to the house, believing they have been tricked. Later, when the sun does rise, the real escort Terukuni arrives and the trick is exposed. Kakuju takes Tarō's sword and mortally wounds him. Kan Shōjō bids a heartrending farewell to his beloved adopted daughter Kariyahime, and his final exit along the *hanamichi* is justly famous for its pathos.

ACT III, SCENE I: *Kuruma biki* ("Pulling the Carriage Apart")

Two of the triplet brothers, Umeōmaru and Sakuramaru, are loyal to Kan Shōjō. Matsuōmaru, however, has been in Shihei's service. Before the Yoshida Shrine, Umeōmaru and Sakuramaru halt Shihei's carriage, intending to confront him. Matsuōmaru, however, is part of his entourage and orders them to desist. The two brothers unleash the ox and begin to smash up the carriage when Shihei appears from within. They make to attack him, but he glares menacingly at them and they lose all strength before his magical powers.

This act is unique to Kabuki and was not part of the original puppet play. It is a magnificent example of the *aragoto* style of acting. The designs of the brothers' costumes reflect their names, plum for *ume*, cherry for *sakura*, and pine for *matsu*. Umeōmaru's makeup is the red *suji guma* style of an impetuous hero, while Shihei's is the blue color of an archvillain. Umeōmaru's *tobi roppō* exit, as he runs off to stop the carriage, is a magnificent and exciting example of this *aragoto* feature. The dramatic standoff between the brothers and Shihei make this short scene one of Kabuki's most celebrated.

ACT III, SCENE II: in Bunraku, *Satamura* ("The Sata Village"); in Kabuki, *Ga no iwai* ("The Birthday Celebration at Sata Village")

This act begins in a festive mood as the wives of the three brothers prepare to celebrate the seventieth birthday of Shiratayū, their father. Umeōmaru and Matsuōmaru also return to the family home for the celebration but, upon meeting, the two brothers come to blows. As they fight they break off a branch of their father's favourite *sakura* (cherry) tree. Umeōmaru and Matsuōmaru are still performed in *aragoto* style, and their fight with straw bales is a short but fine example of a *tachimawari* fight scene.

Shiratayū returns and notices the broken cherry branch immediately. It is a bad omen. The mood of this scene turns to one of great tragedy as Sakuramaru then appears from the rear of the house with the intention of committing *seppuku*. He feels responsible for the scandal of Prince Tokiyo's love affair with his lord's daughter. To atone for this, Sakuramaru takes his own life. Rather than assist his son's suicide by dispatching him with a sword, Shiratayū strikes a prayer bell as his son dies.

ACT IV, SCENE III: *Terakoya* ("The Village School") Genzō and his wife, Tonami, are hiding Kan Shōjō's son and heir, Kan Shūsai, at their school. Shihei suspects this and orders that the boy's head be cut off and presented to Matsuōmaru for inspection. He is the only one among Shihei's retainers who can verify the head. Matsuōmaru's costume is a magnificent robe decorated with a snow-covered pine design. His hair is the *gojū nichi*, or "fifty-day" wig, with a thick, bushy crown indicating that Matsuōmaru has been too ill to have it cut. After completion of his duties today, he wishes to be excused from service.

Genzō thinks of substituting one of the village boys' heads for that of Kan Shūsai, but their rustic appearances makes them unsuitable. That very morning, however, a lady brought a new, well-bred boy called Kotarō to the school. As his features are more refined, they decide to sacrifice him and to pass off his head as Kan Shūsai's. This boy was brought to the school by Matsuōmaru's wife, Chiyo, and is, in fact, their son. Once again the conflict between *giri* and *ninjō* is integral to the drama. Genzō is forced to take the life of an innocent child in order to save that of his young lord. Matsuōmaru demands that the head be presented immediately. Heard from an inner room, the sound of Genzō's blade striking off the head causes Matsuōmaru to stagger with emotion and, knowing that it is his own son who dies, he poses in the famous *Matsuō mie* to express his suppressed anguish.

The climax of Matsuōmaru's role comes when he must perform the *kubi jikken* head inspection. He purposely identifies it as that of

Kan Shūsai, all the while knowing that it is actually that of his son Kotarō. Matsuōmaru departs with his entourage. Kotarō's mother, Chiyo, then arrives to take him home. Genzō thinks he has no option but to kill her, too, when Matsuōmaru suddenly reappears. He tells the shocked Genzō that Kotarō was their son and explains that, to atone for his past disloyalty to his family, Matsuōmaru deliberately had him brought here so that his head could be used as a substitute for Kan Shūsai's. Genzō relates how bravely the boy died.

As it was considered dishonorable for a warrior to cry over his own son's demise, Matsuōmaru mourns openly for the death of his brother Sakuramaru, while inwardly he grieves for Kotarō. The act closes with the beautiful and moving musical passage known as the *Iroha okuri* performed by the *gidayū* narrator and shamisen player. *I-ro-ha* is an old-fashioned syllabary based on a famous poem in which each of the Japanese syllables is used just once. These characters are cleverly worked into the text of this passage, which functions as a kind of requiem for the repose of Kotarō's soul. The narrator remarks, "How sad the child who writes his letters, *i-ro-ha*, for his life was destined to scatter like petals in the breeze." One by one, the others offer incense to speed the dead boy's soul to the next world. (In the Bunraku version, this *Iroha okuri* becomes a passionate *kudoki* for the boy's mother as she laments the passing of her beloved child.)

Yoshitsune senbon zakura ("Yoshitsune and the Thousand Cherry Trees")

Jidaimono, maruhonmono.
Written by Takeda Izumo II, Miyoshi Shōraku, and Namiki Senryū.
First performed in 1747 at the Takemoto-za, Osaka.
First staged as Kabuki in 1748 at the Nakamura-za, Edo
Certain acts of *Yoshitsune senbon zakura* are some of the most frequently performed of all Kabuki and Bunraku plays.

This story is set during the Genji-Heike civil wars that wracked Japan throughout the twelfth century. The Heike have been defeated at several important battles and the Genji lord, Yoritomo, has established himself as shogun in Kamakura. Yoshitsune, his younger half-brother, has been greatly successful in battle but has incurred Yoritomo's jealousy. Despite the title of the play, the role of Yoshitsune is a peripheral one throughout, serving primarily as the central character around which his retainers and enemies act. In particular, the Heike generals Tomomori and Koremori and the fox Tadanobu are characters of great importance, and these roles are reserved for the most prestigious Kabuki actors.

ACT I: *Horikawa gosho* ("The Mansion of Yoshitsune at Horikawa, Kyoto")

Despite Yoshitsune's success in defeating the rival Heike clan at the battle of Ichinotani, the shogun suspects him, and has sent Yoshitsune's father-in-law to ask him three questions: He asks why Yoshitsune sent three heads to Yoritomo, claiming falsely that they were those of the Heike generals Koremori, Noritsune, and Tomomori. Yoshitsune replies that, although the three probably escaped, he hoped to stifle any further rebellion among the Heike by making everyone believe that they were dead.

Secondly, was the precious shoulder drum that was given as a gift to Yoshitsune by the retired emperor meant to persuade Yoshitsune to try to overthrow his brother? Yoshitsune replies that it was merely a gift of friendship.

Thirdly, Yoshitsune is asked why he married Kyō no Kimi, a woman of Heike birth. At this, to prove her husband's loyalty, and believing herself to be the cause of this quarrel between the brothers, Kyō no Kimi commits suicide.

Eventually some of Yoritomo's soldiers arrive to capture Yoshitsune. He is willing to submit, but his impetuous right-hand man, the warrior priest Benkei, defeats and kills the soldiers single-handed. Benkei is an *aragoto* role and, in the comical closing scene called *imo arai*, or "potato washing," he casts the severed heads into a huge bucket and stirs them around like potatoes.

ACT II, SCENE I: *Fushimi inari torii mae* ("Before the Torii Gate at the Inari Fox Shrine at Fushimi")

Yoshitsune decides to flee to Kyushu. His lover, the dancer Shizuka-gozen, however, cannot accompany him on such a dangerous journey. To console her, he leaves in her keeping the precious shoulder drum and, to prevent her from following him, Yoshitsune's men tie her to a tree.

Comical soldiers arrive from the capital to try to capture Yoshitsune. They find Shizuka and the drum, but she is saved by the timely appearance of Satō Tadanobu, one of Yoshitsune's most loyal retainers. In this scene Tadanobu is also played as an *aragoto* character and he easily defeats the men. In gratitude, Yoshitsune makes him a present of some armor and one of his own names, Genkurō. He then continues on his journey, leaving Shizuka in the protection of Tadanobu–Genkurō.

Shizuka leaves, beating the drum as she goes. Following her, Tadanobu suddenly begins to act strangely and runs after her in the famous *kitsune roppō*, "fox exit," leaping and bounding like an animal. This creature is in fact a magic fox disguised as the retainer Tadanobu.

ACT II, SCENE II: *Tokaiya* ("The House of the Boatman, Tokaiya Ginpei")

Yoshitsune and his men arrive at Daimotsu and hire a boat from Tokaiya Ginpei. They are delayed, however, by bad weather. It turns out that Ginpei is actually the Heike general Tomomori in disguise and his wife, Suke no Tsubone, is a high-ranking court lady, while their so-called "daughter" is the child-emperor Antoku.

After Yoshitsune and his men leave for the ship, Tomomori is revealed in ghostly white and silver armor, and announces that he and his men intend to attack Yoshitsune at sea.

ACT II, SCENE III: *Daimotsu no ura* ("The Beach at Daimotsu")

By the seashore Suke no Tsubone and the other ladies-in-waiting dressed in their court robes await the outcome of the battle between Tomomori and Yoshitsune. The battle is lost, however, and some of the ladies leap to their deaths in the sea. Suke no Tsubone and the child emperor are prevented from following them by the arrival of Yoshitsune's men, and she is captured. Wounded, Tomomori arrives back on shore to confront Yoshitsune. Antoku, the child emperor, however, says that today Yoshitsune has saved him and that they should make peace. In the climax to this act, Tomomori decides to take his own life by tying a great anchor around his waist and casting it into the sea.

ACT III, SCENE II: *Sushiya* ("The Sushi Shop")

The Heike general Koremori is disguised as the apprentice Yasuke and works at the sushi shop of Yazaemon and his wife. This is a famous example of the convention called *jitsu wa*, or "in reality," a subcategory of which is called *yatsushi* or "disguise." Not knowing who he really is, Yazaemon's daughter Osato has fallen in love with him.

The son of the house, the evil Gonta, arrives home and persuades his mother to give him some money. Just then his father returns and so he hastily hides the money in a sushi tub and goes off. Koremori's retainer Kokingo was killed in the previous act defending Koremori's wife, Wakaba no Naishi, and son, Rokudai, and Yazaemon had cut off his head to use as a substitute for that of Koremori. He enters and puts the head into an adjacent tub. Wakaba and Rokudai arrive and are surprised to see Koremori disguised as an apprentice. Gonta, however, realizes who he really is and rushes off to claim the reward for his capture. Wishing to take his mother's money with him, he mistakenly takes the tub with the head instead.

The Genji general Kajiwara arrives demanding to see Koremori's head. Just as Yazaemon is about to open the tub (the wrong one containing the money), Gonta returns with both the head and the captive Wakaba and Rokudai. Kajiwara accepts the head and takes away the captives.

Appalled by his treachery, Yazaemon stabs his own son. The dying Gonta, however, reveals that the captives were in fact his own wife and daughter and that he knew the head to be that of Kokingo. Koremori, his wife and child enter safe and well. Gonta's change of heart is a further subcategory of *jitsu wa*, known as *modori* or "reversal."

ACT IV, SCENE I: in Bunraku, *Michiyuki hatsune no tabi* ("The Hatsune Drum's Journey"); in Kabuki, *Yoshinoyama* ("Mt. Yoshino")

In this *michiyuki* dance, Yoshitsune's lover Shizuka-gozen and the magic fox disguised as the retainer Tadanobu are seen journeying through the beautiful blossom-filled landscape of Mt. Yoshino. They are on their way to meet Yoshitsune, who is sheltering at the mansion of an old friend. Shizuka is sad to be separated from her lover and Tadanobu consoles her. He sets up the suit of armor earlier given to him by Yoshitsune on a tree stump, and Shizuka places the shoulder drum on top. In this way, the armor and drum can represent their lord's presence and both bow before them. In the highlight of the dance, Tadanobu reenacts the story of the warrior Tsuginobu's death in battle. Tsuginobu was the real Tadanobu's brother who, when an arrow was shot at Yoshitsune by the enemy, gallantly rode his horse in front of his lord to block the arrow's path, thereby saving Yoshitsune's life. Tadanobu and Shizuka bemoan the cruel fate of so noble a man. Then they are waylaid by the comical Hayami no Tōta and his men, who work for Yoritomo and wish to capture Shizuka. With his magical powers, the fox Tadanobu easily defeats them and the pair continue on their way.

ACT IV, SCENE II: *Kawatsura Hōgen yakata* ("The Mansion of Kawatsura Hōgen"), often called *Shi-no-kiri* ("End of the Fourth Act")

Yoshitsune is being sheltered by the mountain priest Kawatsura Hōgen. The real Tadanobu arrives to see Yoshitsune, whom he has not met for many months. When Yoshitsune asks for Shizuka, who Tadanobu is supposed to be protecting, the retainer claims to know nothing. Yoshitsune is furious and suspects treachery. Just then, however, Shizuka herself arrives claiming that Tadanobu was in her company until a few moments ago. It appears that there are two men called Tadanobu, one of who must be an impostor. The real Tadanobu is led away for questioning. Shizuka remembers that whenever she lost sight of Tadanobu along the way, she only needed to strike the drum in order for him to materialize before her. They decide to strike the drum again now to see if the other Tadanobu will reappear. Employing several trap doors and other *keren* tricks, the actor transforms from Tadanobu into his real fox form. He tells how the drum is in fact made from the hides of his fox parents and it is because he yearns to be with his parents again that he is irresistibly drawn to the drum. He disguised himself as Tadanobu in order to follow it. In the highlight of the scene, praised as an excellent example of filial piety, the fox expresses his deep love and longing for his parents.

Having lost his own father at an early age and now hunted by his elder brother, Yoshitsune feels the deep irony of the situation: while in the world of men family relations fight against each other, it is left to mere animals to display such human virtues as filial love. Moved by the tale and grateful for his protection of Shizuka, Yoshitsune makes the fox a present of the drum. A group of comical priests enter with the intention of capturing Yoshitsune, but the fox defeats them with his supernatural powers and joyfully goes off with the drum.

In a short scene occasionally performed after this, in Act V, the real Tadanobu enters to confront the third of the Heike generals, Noritsune.

OTHER WELL-KNOWN KABUKI PLAYS

Futatsu chōchō kuruwa nikki ("Chōgorō and Chōkichi: A Diary of Two Butterflies in the Pleasure Quarters")

Genroku chūshingura ("The Genroku Era Treasury of Loyal Retainers")

Gensō to Yōkihi ("The T'ang Emperor Hsuan Tsung [Gensō] and his beloved Yang Kuei-fei [Yōkihi]")

Gion sairei shinkōki ("The Gion Festival Chronicle of Faith")

Godairiki koi no fūjime ("Five Great Powers That Secure Love")

Ibaraki ("The Demon of Ibaraki")

Ichinotani futaba gunki ("The Chronicle of the Battle of Ichinotani")

Kamakura sandaiki ("A Chronicle of Three Generations in Kamakura")

Kasane ("Disfigured Kasane")

Kinkakuji ("The Golden Pavilion")

Kirare Otomi ("Scar-face Otomi")

Kokusenya kassen ("The Battles of Coxinga")

Kotobuki Soga no taimen ("The Auspicious Confrontation of the Soga Brothers")

Masakado ("The Taira Warrior Masakado")

Miyajima no danmari ("*Danmari* at Miyajima")

Moritsuna jinya ("Moritsuna's Battle Camp")

Noda-ban Nezumi Kozō ("Noda's Rat Bandit Kozō")

Noda-ban Togitatsu no utare (Noda's version of "Revenge on Togitatsu")

Osome Hisamatsu ukina no yomiuri ("News of the Affair of Osome and Hisamatsu")

Osome no nanayaku ("The Seven Roles of Osome")

Satomi Hakkenden ("Legend of the Eight Dog Samurai")

Tenjiku Tokubei ("The Tale of Tokubei from India")

Toribeyama shinjū ("Love-Suicides at Toribeyama")

Tsuchigumo ("The Earth Spider")

Yamatotakeru ("Prince Yamatotakeru")

Yasuna ("Abe no Yasuna")

Chapter 3

NŌ

NŌ
SUBTLE AND PROFOUND

It is the year 1400. The courtiers enter the grounds of the Kyoto palace of the shogun Yoshimitsu, the supreme military leader of Japan. They are assembled to see a performance of the shogun's favorite entertainment, the Nō. There is a theater built in the garden featuring a square stage with a long walkway leading off to the left-hand side. This stage has its own temple-style roof and even the walkway is covered. There are no seats and the company make themselves comfortable on fine mats placed on the ground around the stage.

Before long, formally clad musicians enter and seat themselves on the stage. One of them begins an eerie wail—"*yoh!*"—followed by a sharp "clack" as he strikes his shoulder drum. The curtain at the end of the walkway rises and, very slowly, with great solemnity an actor walks toward the main stage. The Nō play has begun.

Today, we enter a modern concrete building in the heart of Tokyo's Shibuya district. It appears to be a theater much like many others. Inside it is well-lit and the seats are luxuriously comfortable. Not until we see the stage do we notice anything different. It is much smaller than those we are used to, square in shape with a long walkway leading off to the left-hand side. It also has its own roof, rather like a temple, and even the walkway is covered—unnecessary, of course, as the building has a roof of its own! The

Eguchi: the Lady of Eguchi (center), in reality the Bodhisattva Fugen, appears on a boat with her companions. *Nochijite*: Kanai Akira. Hōshō School.

stage area is surrounded by a gravel path, and the walkway is lined by small pine trees: are they real or imitation? The main stage has no curtain and we see another huge pine tree, painted this time, on the rear wall of the stage set.

Once again, one of the musicians begins with "*yoh!*" followed by a sharp "clack" from the drum. The curtain at the end of the walkway rises. Almost nothing has changed.

WHAT IS NŌ?

Nō is the medieval theater of Japan, perfected during the Muromachi period (1333–1568). It includes musical accompaniment and dance, but its plays are performed in a solemn, dignified, and measured manner. Richly symbolic and performed in beautiful costumes with some actors wearing finely carved masks, Nō plays are pared down to their barest essentials. Even the stage is magnificent in its simplicity: Nō actors perform on a bare stage in front of a permanent wall on which is painted a solitary great pine tree. With texts of profound beauty that are regarded as pinnacles of literary achievement, Nō has fascinated generations of Japanese as well as people from the West, who have marveled at its grace, its austere splendor, and the unique artistry of its actors.

HISTORY

Nō has its roots in an early form of entertainment called *sarugaku*, which was made up largely of dancing, singing, and comical amusements. *Sarugaku* may originally have come from China, but became popular in Japan in the Heian (794–1185) and Kamakura (1185–1333) periods. It was performed mostly outdoors, in makeshift enclosures set up in places such as the grounds of temples and shrines.

By around the middle of the Kamakura period, *sarugaku* performers had divided into separate troupes and the four best known of these were the Enamani-za, the Sakado-za, the Tobi-za, and the Yūzaki-za. These early troupes are important because they were to develop into four of the Nō schools still in existence today.

The *sarugaku* plays consisting of music, dance, and song came to be called Nō, while the short plays that were more dialogue-based were called Kyōgen. A clear division occurred within the *sarugaku* troupes between the performers of the sombre *sarugaku nō* plays and those of the humorous *sarugaku kyōgen.*

KAN'AMI AND ZEAMI

Kan'ami was a playwright and actor born in 1333. The court of the shogun had moved from Kamakura to Kyoto in the year of his birth and, after becoming the first leader of the Yūzaki-za, he moved the troupe to Kyoto and founded a new school that took his own stage name of "Kanze." Still in existence today, Kan'ami's connection with this troupe makes Kanze the most prestigious of all Nō schools.

At that time there was a rhythmic celebratory music for rice planting festivals, called *dengaku.* Kan'ami took elements of this rhythmic music together with the more melodic *sarugaku*, and developed and refined it toward the Nō we see today. Some of Kan'ami's plays have also survived, although they have almost certainly been rewritten over the centuries.

The third of the Muromachi-period shoguns was Ashikaga Yoshimitsu, who in 1374, when he was only seventeen, witnessed a performance by Kan'ami that so impressed him that he adopted Nō as his favorite form of entertainment. Performing often for the shogun, this gave both Nō in general, and Kan'ami in particular, great prestige. This was the beginning of hundreds of years of patronage by successive shogunates and, by extension, the whole of the ruling class.

Kan'ami died in 1384. His son, Ze-ami, born in 1363, was just twelve years old when he first performed before the shogun. Following in his father's footsteps, he became the second head of the Kanze school. Zeami appears to have enjoyed both artistic patronage and a long-lasting personal friendship with the shogun Yoshimitsu. This put him—a low-ranking commoner—in a unique position to mix with men of letters and other court nobility.

Zeami's contribution to the development of Nō was enormous. He was the finest actor of his time, as well as a theater manager, a director, a musician, a choreographer, a theatrical scholar, and also a prolific playwright. Many of his plays are still performed today. He also created the so-called *mugen nō*, or "dream Nō," in which the central characters are spirits rather than living people.

The reason that we know so much about Zeami's contribution to the development of Nō is that he was also a fine teacher and wrote a number of treatises about Nō acting, including the *Fūshi kaden*, or *Kadensho* ("Communication of Flower Acting"), the *Shikadō* ("The Path to the Flower"), and *Sarugaku dangi* ("Discourse on Sarugaku"). Zeami likened an actor on the stage to a blossoming flower and he also referred to the "flower of mystery," infusing Nō acting with almost mystical powers. His writings are among the first essays in the world to deal with the theater, and the profession and art of the actor, and he was without doubt one of the great geniuses in the history of world theater.

With the death of Yoshimitsu, however, Zeami's fortunes began a gradual but inexorable decline. Under the shogun Yoshimochi, his troupe lost their preeminent status and Zeami suffered a series of affronts as the troupe of his rival, Zōami, came to the fore. After Yoshimochi's death, the new shogun, Yoshinori, showed a clear aversion to Zeami. In 1434 he exiled the seventy-two-year-old Zeami to the remote island of Sado, where he is thought to have died around the year 1443.

Over time all the *sarugaku* troupes changed their names. As well as the Yūzaki-za, which became the Kanze school, the Enamani-za became the Konparu school, the Sakado-za became the Kongō school and the Tobi-za, the Hōshō school. Gradually the old Nō acting styles such as *sarugaku* and *dengaku* disappeared in favor of what we can now call the classic Nō, perfected by Kan'ami and Zeami. This Nō, together with the accompanying Kyōgen, came under the collective title of *nōgaku*.

After the death of Zeami, the Kanze traditions were carried on by his son Kanze Motomasa, who wrote, among other things, *Sumidagawa*, a Nō performance of which was the inspiration for the composer Benjamin Britten's cantata, "Curlew River."

This great creative period in the development of Nō came to a close with the work of Kanze Kojirō Nobumitsu (1435–1516). Nobumitsu was the actor and playwright who wrote *Ataka*, *Funa Benkei*, and *Momijigari*, all plays which are also famous in their Kabuki adaptations.

Despite the civil wars that wracked

the country towards the end of the Muromachi period, Nō continued to receive support from among the diverse fiefdoms; even Toyotomi Hideyoshi, the warlord who finally united the country in 1590, was a great supporter and, like many nobles, performed Nō himself.

THE EDO PERIOD (1603–1868)

The Tokugawa shoguns finally ushered in a long period of peace in Japan's history. During this time, the importance of careful and faithful imitation of past masters became paramount, and Nō crystallized into the refined art that today remains almost identical to that of the past. The shogunate, the daimyo feudal lords, the samurai war-rior class, and some educated common-ers all became avid supporters of Nō.

The four existing Nō schools all received official status from the shogunate, and the shogun Hidetada permitted the founding of a further school called "Kita." This brought the number up to five, all of which are still performing today. Kanze, however, has always been regarded as the most prestigious. The *iemoto* system of maintaining the head of a school as a hereditary position became the norm, and this too continues. The *iemoto* is at the top of a pyramid of students, amateur practitioners, low-ranking actors, musicians and high-ranking actors. The traditions of a particular school are handed down in the form of personal tuition from master to pupil.

Dōjōji: a Nō/Kyōgen performance in the early Edo period.

Throughout the Edo period Nō continued to be the favorite entertainment of the samurai class. Commoners, however, could only occasionally see Nō in places such as temples or shrines in special performances called *kanjin nō*, or "subscription Nō," performed to raise funds for such virtuous objectives as the rebuilding of a temple. The Nō songs called *utai* and the dances called *shimai*, were very popular and well-known to many. The hobby of singing *utai* remains a popular one.

FROM THE MEIJI PERIOD (1868–1912) TO THE PRESENT DAY

The overthrow of the Tokugawa shogunate in 1868 and the subsequent demise of the feudal system left Nō bereft of its former patrons, and many Nō actors without employment. Although politicians and scholars alike were looking principally toward Europe as a source for new culture, the historical and artistic value of Nō was not forgotten and, with the support of the imperial family, it was found worthy of protection. Some may have been influenced in their views by the appreciation Nō received from foreign diplomats, scholars, artists, and performers.

Having lost their traditional venues in the mansions of the nobility, the Nōgakusha (Nō Society) was founded in 1881 to erect a purpose-built theater in Tokyo for the first time. The Nō Society was renamed the Nōgakudō

with the intention of representing the Nō world, providing financial support, and broadening Nō's popularity.

During the lead-up to World War II, new plays were employed as imperialist propaganda. During the fire bombing, however, all the Nō theaters in Tokyo were destroyed. The prosperity of the postwar years enabled the schools to rebuild their theaters in modern styles, and Nō has since regained much of its prestige and popularity. In addition, there have also been many opportunities for Nō troupes to travel abroad, introducing their art to appreciative new audiences.

Takasago. Nochijite: Tomoeda Akiyo. Kita School.

PLAYS

There are some two hundred and forty plays in the repertoires of the five Nō schools. Plays take themes from poetry anthologies such as the *Kokin wakashū* ("Ancient and Modern Japanese Poems"), and from the great classical works of literature such as the *Ise monogatari* ("Tales of Ise") and especially the *Heike monogatari* ("The Tale of the Heike"), which deals with the lengthy Heike–Genji civil wars that wracked Japan in the twelfth century.

A traditional Nō performance took the whole day and consisted of the ceremonial *Okina* dance and five plays, interspersed with Kyōgen comedies. These five plays were each of a different category, following the set pattern called *shin-nan-jo-kyō-ki*: gods, men, women, lunatics, and demons.

OKINA

Okina is treated separately from all other plays. Officially titled *Shikisanba*, *Okina* has no plot and is an ancient ceremonial diversion made up of three auspicious dances featuring the three characters Senzai, Okina (whose mask depicts a white-bearded, smiling old man), and Sanbasō. After the Senzai dance the Okina mask is brought onto the stage for the *shite*, or principal actor. This is the only occasion when the mask is put on while the actor is on stage in view of the audience. The Senzai and Okina dances are general pieces, while the Sanbasō dance is specifically for a good harvest. Adaptations of *Okina* can be found in both Bunraku and Kabuki.

Okina. Nochijite: Hōshō Fusateru. Hōshō School

THE FIVE CATEGORIES

ICHIBANMEMONO (FIRST CATEGORY) —WAKI NŌ, KAMI NŌ

These are about gods, and the *shite* actor plays a god or godlike individual who often appears in disguise in the first half of the play and in his true form in the second. *Takasago.*

NIBANMEMONO (SECOND CATEGORY) —SHURA MONO

The actor plays the spirit of a deceased warrior. These characters are usually paying for the deeds they committed in the heat of battle. *Atsumori, Yashima.*

SANBANMEMONO (THIRD CATEGORY) —KATSURA MONO

Katsura mono, literally "wig pieces," are so-called because the actor often, although not invariably, plays a woman and must wear a wig. *Hagoromo, Izutsu, Matsukaze.*

Kantan. Shite: Asami Masakuni. Kanze School.

YONBANMEMONO (FOURTH CATE-GORY)—ZATSU MONO

Zatsu mono are really plays that do not fit into any of the other groups. Among these are *kyōran mono* which deal with madness, usually a woman driven mad with grief. There are also some modern pieces in this group. *Aoi no ue, Kantan, Sumidagawa, Sotoba Komachi, Dōjōji.*

GOBANMEMONO (FIFTH CATEGORY) —KIRI NŌ

Kiri nō means "closing piece" and plays in this category form the final group. Traditionally these are plays about demons. *Momijigari, Shakkyō, Funa Benkei.*

Izutsu. Nochijite: Kanze Hideo. Kanze School.

Funa Benkei. Nochijite: Kanze Hideo. Kanze School.

Genzai nō and *mugen nō*

Overall, Nō plays may be divided into two main types: *genzai nō*, or "realistic Nō," in which the characters are real people, and the type founded by Zeami called *mugen nō*, "dream Nō," whose characters are ghosts and spirits from the other world. The *shite's* character is supposedly a "dream" of the character played by the *waki*, or supporting actor.

Jo ha kyū

The script for a Nō play is called the *yōkyoku*. Nō adopted the *jo ha kyū* structure that had been employed in Gagaku court music. The *jo* is the prelude or introduction to the drama and covers the entrance of the *waki* and his establishment on the main stage. The *ha* is the dramatic development and this covers the appearance of the *shite*, the exchange between the *shite* and the *waki*, the tale of the *shite*, and his exit. The *kyū* is the ending. Generally the pace of the play increases with each section.

STAGE

Called the *nōgakudō*, the Nō stage as we see it today was established during the Muromachi period. At that time, however, all Nō stages were outdoors and it was not until the Edo period that indoor theaters were built.

The main stage is about six meters, or twenty feet, square. Adjoining this is the *hashigakari*, a walkway leading from the backstage area called the *kagami no ma* ("mirror room") to the stage. A lift curtain called an *agemaku* separates this room from the walkway. The *hashigakari* is very important, as the slow entrance along it toward the main stage creates tension and expectancy.

Under the main stage are large earthenware (nowadays concrete) pots which are so placed as to resonate when the actors stamp their feet.

Perhaps the most striking thing about the Nō stage is the *kagamiita*, the permanent wall painted with a large twisted pine tree. This and the painted bamboo to the sides are said to be a reminder of the days when Nō was performed outside. Both grandeur and simplicity, such important features of Nō, are symbolized by this unchanging set.

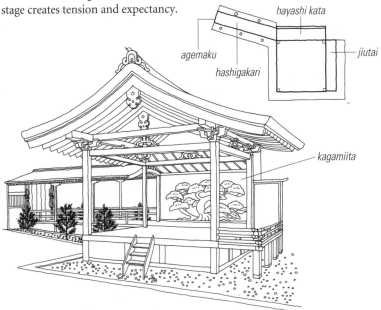

hayashi kata

agemaku

hashigakari

jiutai

kagamiita

PERFORMERS

Nō performers (both actors and musicians) are classified into four types—
shite kata (principal players), *waki kata* (supporting players), *hayashi kata*
(musicians) and *kyōgen kata* (*kyōgen* players).

SHITE KATA

The principal character and actor in a
Nō play is called the *shite kata*. The
shite are the actors who often appear
wearing masks. If a play has two acts,
then the *shite* role is referred to as the
maejite ("opening *shite*") in the first
act, and the *nochijite* ("closing shite")
in the second. These two roles may be
either the same character, such as a
demon in disguise that appears in its
real form for the second act, or
totally different characters. A famous
example of the latter type is the play
Funa Benkei, in which the *maejite* role
is that of Yoshitsune's lover, Shizuka

Gozen, whereas the *nochijite* role is
that of the ghost of the Heike general
Tomomori.

WAKI KATA

The supporting role to that of the *shite*
is the *waki kata*. *Waki* roles are always
human beings, and do not wear
masks. The *waki* actor often appears
to introduce the play and the *shite*
character, and to provide a foil to the
shite. In the play *Ataka*, for example,
the role of Benkei is taken by the *shite*
and that of Togashi, the barrier
guard, by the *waki*.

Supporting Roles

Certain supporting roles are also traditionally played by actors from *shite
kata* schools:

Tsure or companion actors, who
may accompany the main *shite* or
waki characters.

Kokata or child roles. Children
may also take on some of the more

mild-mannered adult roles such
as Yoshitsune from *Funa Benkei*.
Children do not wear masks.

Kōken are formally dressed stage
assistants who assist the actor by
handing him props and making
any adjustments to the costume
that may be necessary.

Aoi no ue: the jealous spirit of Lady Rokujō possesses Lady Aoi (represented by the robe on stage). *Shite*: Asami Masakuni. Kanze School.

KYŌGEN KATA

The role of *kyōgen* actors in Nō is discussed on page 194.

HAYASHI KATA

The musical accompaniment to Nō plays consists of a chorus and instrumentalists referred to as the *hayashi kata*. The instrumentalists are lined up at the rear of the main stage in the following order, left to right: the *taiko*

stick drum (required only for some plays); the sharp toned *ōtsuzumi* drum played at the hip; the softer toned *kotsuzumi* drum played at the shoulder; and the *fue* or *nōkan*, a wooden flute that is the only melodic instrument. The percussionists may also use vocal calls called *kakegoe*, which increase the dramatic tension by filling in the space before an actual drum beat. Perhaps once used as a rehearsal technique, they are now an integral and very noticeable part of the Nō experience.

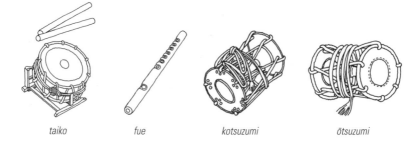

| taiko | fue | kotsuzumi | ōtsuzumi |

Jiutai—the Chorus

The chorus is referred to as the *jiutai*. Chant-like songs called *utai* are sung either by the actors or a chorus of about six to eight, who are seated along the right-hand side of the stage, facing inwards. *Utai* may be divided into music for heroic scenes called *tsuyo-gin*, "strong songs," and music for more sorrowful scenes called *yowa-gin*, "weak songs." In Nō, and indeed Bunraku and Kabuki, the Japanese poetic convention of *shichi go chō*, the seven-five meter, is very important. The syllables of the following lines from *Dōjōji* (a play also famous in Kabuki), for example, are divided into groups of first seven then five, which are matched to differing rhythmic patterns. Here the Japanese words are hyphenated to make clear the syllables.

Tsurigane from *Dōjōji*

Tsu-ki wa ho-do na-ku
I-ri-shi-o no
Tsu-ki wa ho-do na-ku
I-ri-shi-o no
Ke-mu-ri mi-chi-ku-ru
Ko-ma-tsu-ba-ra

The time is not long before
The set of the moon,
The time is not long before
The set of the moon,
And mist from the rising tide
Shrouds fields of young pine

Nō song is derived from Buddhist chanting, and embellishments and vibrato add to the overall effect of melodic solemnity. Important songs may be sung either by the actors or by the chorus, and are called *kuse*. *Kuse* are heard at significant moments such as the telling of a tale that explains why a certain character is acting the way he or she is. The climactic song often heard, for example, when a devil or mad woman reaches a major emotional climax is called the *kurui* or *kuruichi*.

COSTUMES, WIGS, AND PROPS

In its earliest years, the costumes for Nō were fairly plain, but when it was adopted by the aristocracy, the custom of wealthy patrons providing their actors with magnificent costumes became widespread. Although there are numerous types of costume (called *shōzoku*), the most noticeable are the highly-colored brocade robes such as that worn in *Hagoromo*, the long trailing *nagabakama* trousers worn by Togashi in *Ataka*, and the very wide-legged trousers called *ōguchi* worn by

many characters, including the ghost of Yoshitsune in the play *Yashima* and the *shishi* lions in the play *Shakkyō*.

Also characteristic of the Nō costume are *tabi*, the white socks that separate the big toe from the other toes.

Wigs are worn only by female characters, and by demons and spirits. Unlike the piled and twisted shapes of women's hair in Edo period Kabuki, styles in the earlier Muromachi period were much simpler. Hair is generally long, parted in the center, held back

Hagoromo: the angel in her feathered robe dances for the fisherman. *Shite*: Kanze Hideo. Kanze School.

Ataka: the barrier guard Togashi. *Waki*: Hōshō Kan. Hōshō School.

Yashima: the ghost of general Yoshitsune. *Nochijite*: Hōshō Fusateru. Hōshō School.

from the face with a headband, and allowed to hang down the back. Some roles such as madwomen employ special, extra-long hair to enhance the appearance of insanity. The spirit wigs are usually very shaggy, with long side locks hanging down by the side of the ears.

The various types of headgear such as hats, hoods, crowns, and cloths indicate social status and sometimes the vocation of the wearer, such as priests.

Like the bare stage set, props in Nō are kept to a minimum and may be mere symbols of what they are supposed to represent. The most common symbol is a simple rectangular framework large enough to hold a man.

Simply decorated in a variety of ways, this frame may represent a carriage, mountains, a boat, a bell tower, a prison cell, or a mountain hut. One particular example of realism in a Nō play is the temple bell that is hung from the roof for the play *Dōjōji*.

Props also include such items as brooms, pails, lances, halberds, and walking sticks. The most important hand prop is the fan which is usually carried by all the actors, musicians, and assistants. In contrast to the fan commonly used in Japanese dance (*mai ōgi*), the historically older *chūkei* is the one most frequently used in Nō. The slats of the *chūkei* maintain a fan-shaped curve even when the fan is closed.

MASKS

Seated in his dressing room a few minutes before the start of the performance, the actor will take out the mask for the role he is about to play and bow before it. The mask is put on with great reverence, as this action represents the actor's total empathy with the character. Masks are intimately connected with the history of Nō, and an Okina mask dating from the time of *sarugaku nō* still exists.

Masks are worn only by the *shite* and sometimes the *tsure* actors, and there are about sixty different types. With the exception of some clearly ferocious or very happy masks, their most important characteristic is the ambiguity of their expressions. It is the task of the actor to communicate a range of emotions through the unchanging expression on the mask's face. As artistic objects, Nō masks are celebrated the world over.

Some masks, such as Atsumori and Kagekiyo, are named after characters and are reserved for particular roles, while others represent role types. Some of the more important types of mask include those illustrated here.

▪Female Masks

Ko-omote
The youngest female mask.

Waka-onna
Young woman.

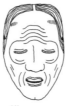

Uba
Old woman.

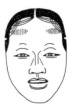

Fukai
Middle-aged woman.

▪ Male Masks

Heida
A middle-aged warrior.

Chūjō
A young aristocrat.

Kasshiki
A character who is both
worldly and religious.

▪ Okina Masks

Okina
A god, represented
as the smiling face
of an old man.

▪ Special Masks

Hannya
A demoness consumed with sorrow
and hatred.

Ko-tobide
Used for the fox spirit
and demons.

Yase-otoko and *yase-onna*
Male and female spirits undergoing the anguish of hell.

PERFORMANCE

Kamae is the basic posture in which Nō actors stand. The back is kept completely straight, with a slight forward lean from the hips. Arms curve downward, slightly forward of the body and the legs are flexed at the knee with the feet a little apart. Female characters place their feet closer together, with their hands and arms less widely spaced.

Hakobi is the name for walking and is designed to avoid up and down movements while moving along. Smooth walking, seeming to glide, is the mark of a master actor. The heels are kept in contact with the floor at all times and the feet slide along the stage (*suriashi*). Actors walk in this way even when hurrying. Male characters move energetically, taking longer strides than females, and their arm movements are also broader.

Ashibyōshi is rhythmical stamping and may have its roots in religious dances in which the stamping was to drive away devils. The large acoustic pots placed under the stage floor are intended to enhance the sound of this movement.

Sotoba Komachi: the aged figure of Ono no Komachi recounts her early days of glory. *Shite*: Umewaka Manzaburō. Kanze School.

Kamae

Hakobi (sashikomi)
Forward movement with a fan
held out in front of the body.

Hakobi (hiraki)
Three steps backward with
the arms outstretched.

Yūken
Expressing joy by mov-
ing a fan up and down
in front of the chest.

Makura no ōgi
Representing the
act of sleeping.

Shiori
Holding one hand over
the eyes to hide tears.

Morojiori
Holding both hands over
the eyes to hide tears.

Dances are a fundamental part of most Nō plays. Actors usually dance alone, and the dances are typically slow and are several minutes in length. Early Japanese dancing is called *mai*, which literally means "to circle." The center of gravity is low, and *mai* is always smooth and flowing. There is an earthbound solidity to the dancing that may stem from its very early roots in symbolic rice planting ceremonies.

Chapter 4

KYŌGEN

KYŌGEN
HUMAN COMEDY

T he actor walks onto the stage and turns to face the audience.

"*Kore wa, kono atari no mono de gozaru.*"
("I am one who comes from around here.")

With these words he begins a story which could be about anybody and
anywhere. Thieves rub shoulders with feudal lords, and servants and
masters share the common failings of humanity that usually lead one or
all of them into a series of hilarious scrapes.

There are few smiles in classical Japanese theater. Facial expressions
seem to reflect that life in medieval and feudal Japan was clearly a serious,
if not downright tragic business. But laughter can be found in abundance
in Kyōgen, the plays that were historically performed between the serious
Nō dramas. Much Japanese theater is played with a "stone-face," but
Kyōgen actors have to be masters of exaggerated facial expressions and
comic gestures.

Kyōgen are played on the same stage as Nō, but the actors do not usually use masks, and the acting style is more realistic. Today Kyōgen plays
have also become popular as independent performances.

HISTORY

THE MUROMACHI PERIOD (1333–1568)

The history of Kyōgen follows the history of Nō, both having developed from the early *sarugaku* entertainment consisting mainly of dancing, singing, and comical entertainment, including impersonation.

Gradually more serious themes were introduced into *sarugaku*, and by 1349 the singing and dancing part of the entertainment had become known as Nō. At first, dances were performed between these Nō plays, but then spoken comical entertainments were introduced, which took the name Kyōgen. Soon there was a clear distinction between the performers of the serious Nō plays and those of the comical Kyōgen. Collectively Nō and Kyōgen came to be called *nōgaku*.

Nōgaku would probably have remained in this form were it not for two actors, father and son, called Kan'ami (1333–84) and Zeami (1363–1443), who developed the musical, dance, and playwrighting aspects of Nō, turning it into one of the world's great theatrical art forms. The prestige of the two *nōgaku* entertainments was further enhanced when the leader of the Kamakura shogunate, Ashikaga Yoshimitsu, adopted Nō as his favorite theatrical diversion.

Inuyamabushi: a Nō Kyōgen performance in the early Edo period.

THE EDO PERIOD (1603–1868)

Patronage of *nōgaku* continued under the Tokugawa shoguns. Although the common people could sometimes see *nōgaku* performances in places such as temple or shrine grounds—the so-called *kanjin nō*, or "subscription Nō" —it remained chiefly the entertainment of the samurai warrior class.

One actor in particular, Hie Mangorō, developed the Kyōgen aspects of the theater by founding three schools that would be the principal influences on Kyōgen for hundreds of years. The Ōkura and Sagi schools flourished under the patronage of the shogunate in Edo and the Izumi school was supported by the imperial court in Kyoto.

THE MEIJI PERIOD (1868–1912) AND KYŌGEN TODAY.

The fall of the military shogunate and restoration of the emperor in 1868 brought about the end of the samurai class. At a stroke, this left both Nō and Kyōgen without patronage and without financial support.

For most Japanese arts this was a difficult period, as the country turned toward the West in search of modern ideas in politics, science, education, and culture. While the classical characteristics of Nō continued to receive respect, the comical aspects of the Kyōgen dramas were regarded with little more than embarrassment. Facing such a decline in popular support, the Sagi school closed down completely during the Taishō period (1912–26).

Despite this, Kyōgen actors continued quietly to practice and develop their art.

During the post-World War II years, there was a need to rebuild many aspects of Japanese life and one facet— the possibility of laughter—was encouraged. Kyōgen was again celebrated as the classical comic drama of Japan.

While the principal family lines of the Ōkura and Izumi schools died out during the Meiji period, the representative Yamamoto and Shigeyama family lines of actors continue the work of the Ōkura school. The Izumi school is represented by the Nomura Manzō line, and in 1963 the troupe of Nomura Manzō toured the United States and other countries to great critical acclaim.

At the start of the twenty-first century Kyōgen is experiencing something of a boom. Although still performed as interludes between Nō plays, independent Kyōgen performances have become very popular and are introducing Kyōgen to many more people. To young and appreciative audiences, actors are performing not only the classical repertoire but also new plays (even science fiction!) and adaptations of Shakespeare. Following the great commercial success of "Super Kabuki," there is now also "Super Kyōgen," based on the work of the same man, Umehara Takeshi (b. 1925), who wrote Kabuki's *Yamatotakeru. Ōsama to Kyōryū* ("The King and the Dinosaur") was also staged in Paris in 2004.

PLAYS

The classical Kyōgen repertoire consists of approximately two hundred and sixty short plays, each typically about thirty minutes in length. For convenience, the plays are classified into groups according to their subject matter. The most common groups for each school can be seen in the table below.

ŌKURA SCHOOL PLAYS	IZUMI SCHOOL PLAYS
Waki kyōgen—plays in which gods appear.	*Kami mono*—about gods.
Daimyō kyōgen—about rather gullible feudal lords.	*Kahō mono*—auspicious plays about helping people without the expectation of a reward.
Shōmyō kyōgen—about the servant called Tarōkaja.	*Hyakushō mono*—about farmers.
Muko onna kyōgen—about sons- and mothers-in-law.	*Daimyō mono*—about feudal lords.
Oni yamabushi kyōgen—about *yamabushi*, a sect of ascetic wandering Buddhist priests, and their battles with devils.	*Tarōkaja mono*—about the character Tarōkaja.
	Muko mono—about sons-in-law.
Shukke zatō kyōgen—about Buddhist priests and blind men.	*Onna mono*—about women.
	Oni mono—about devils.
Atsume kyōgen—plays about any subjects not included in the above. These may be about old people, townsmen, friends, thieves, and so forth.	*Yamabushi mono*—about *yamabushi*.
	Shukke mono—about Buddhist priests.
	Zatō mono—about blind men.
	Zatsu mono—similar to the *atsume kyōgen* of the Ōkura school.

Within any of the groups there are also subdivisions detailing the sort of stories involved. In the *oni kyōgen* category, for example, there are two subcategories, one consisting of five plays dealing specifically with stories about Enma, the king of hell, while a further four plays are about devils in general. Similarly, *zatō mono* is divided into six plays about blind men and two plays about people with other disabilities.

There are no known Kyōgen playwrights and the plays are the result of many minor amendments and alterations to the texts by successive generations of actors. Although the subject matter of the two schools is very similar, there can be considerable variation between them.

COSTUMES & MASKS

The principal difference between a Kyōgen and a Nō actor is his costume. Kyōgen costumes are much simpler than those used for Nō and are somewhat stylized versions of the actual dress worn in medieval Japan.

Masters, for example, wear the formal *kamishimo*, consisting of the shoulder-winged vest called the *kataginu* and the long trailing *nagabakama* loose trousers. Servants like Tarōkaja also wear a similar costume but rather more garish and less formal, with only the shorter *hakama* wide trousers. The *tabi* socks worn by Nō

actors are white; those worn in Kyōgen are yellow.

There are no formalized male or female role specialists, and so when Kyōgen actors play women they drape a long cloth (*binankazura*) over their heads: this hangs down past their ears to their chests, like long hair. They make no attempt to use the falsetto voice of the Kabuki *onnagata*.

In Kyōgen, actors do not normally use masks, although there are about fifty plays where masks are employed, usually for supernatural characters such as gods, devils, and for animals.

Tsurigitsune: Shigeyama Masakuni as a fox. (Ōkura School)

Susugigawa: an example of the *binankazura* head covering that represents hair. Shigeyama Shigeru as a wife. (Ōkura School)

Tarōkaja—the wily servant

The most popular of all Kyōgen characters is Tarōkaja, and, apart from the miscellaneous groups, his is the largest category of Kyōgen plays.

Tarōkaja is the wily servant to a master, and the pair—occasionally together with another servant called Jirōkaja—manage to get themselves into a variety of scrapes. In Nō and Kabuki the aristocracy are almost always portrayed either with great respect or as really evil characters.

Kyōgen takes a more personable approach to life, and so its feudal lords are subject to their equal share of the usual human failings. Many of the plays deal with the consequences of Tarōkaja failing to carry out his duties successfully and ending with the master angrily chasing after him. Although Tarōkaja sometimes succeeds in getting the better of his master, it is often debatable which of them is the more dim-witted.

Shigeyama Shime as Tarōkaja (left), Shigeyama Sengorō as Jirōkaja (center) and Shigeyama Akira as the master (right) in *Bōshibari*. (Ōkura School)

PERFORMANCE

As in Nō, the principal Kyōgen actor is called the *shite*, but the secondary actor is called the *ado* rather than *waki*. If there are more secondary characters, they are called the third or fourth *koado*.

NANORI

When the first character appears on stage it is common for him to introduce himself to the audience with a short speech, called a *nanori*. The place on the stage when he makes this introduction is called the *nanori-za*.

FACIAL EXPRESSION

Nō characters, whether wearing masks or not, deliberately keep an expressionless face. Kyōgen, on the other hand, requires exactly the opposite—exuberant and exaggerated facial expressions.

POSTURE

Although Kyōgen is in many respects a realistic drama, some of the acting techniques are rather stylized. Immediately obvious will be the *hakobi* walking styles and the stiff *kamae* posture, both techniques seen in Nō.

The *kamae* posture is the basic one in which both Nō and Kyōgen actors stand. The back is kept ramrod straight, with a slightly forward lean from the hips. The legs are planted firmly with the feet slightly apart, and the arms are held to the sides, slightly forward of the body. Female feet are placed together, and the hands hold the *binankazura* cloth that represents hair.

The *hakobi* walking method is designed to avoid up and down movements while moving along. The heels are kept in contact with the floor at all times and slide along the stage (*suriashi*). As in Nō, the male characters take longer strides than females. The female characters walk more slowly holding the *binankazura*. Strong characters tend to take longer strides than weaker ones. *Hakobi* is employed even when hurrying.

Other simple gestures such as covering ones eyes with the palm of the hand (*shiori*) are also taken from Nō, but in Kyōgen the character may also make a comical weeping sound (*ehe, ehe, ehe*) as well.

Kamae

Hakobi

Laughing

Crying

Praying

Shigeyama Shime in the *ado* role in *Tsurigitsune*.
(Ōkura School)

Sleeping

ONOMATOPOEIA

This brings us to another of Kyōgen's more comical characteristics, the use of onomatopoeia—words formed in imitation of sounds associated with a particular action.

Breaking a bowl

Pulling down a scroll picture

Eating sweets

Sawing

A mosquito

Washing clothes

Opening a heavy door

A fox

A dog barking

ENDINGS

There are numerous ways of bringing a Kyōgen play to an end, the majority of which fall into either the "resolved" or "unresolved" categories.

The most famous and most frequently seen unresolved category is the *oikomi dome*, or "chasing close." This typically occurs in Tarōkaja plays when, having done something exceptionally stupid, his master chases after him trying to catch him. The inclusion of this in the "unresolved" category is because we never get to see what happens when Tarōkaja is finally caught. Other unresolved endings are the *kusame dome*, the ending with a sneeze,

and the *shikari dome*, in which the character gets a scolding.

Examples of the "resolved" ending include the *shagiri dome*, which closes with a musical postlude featuring the flute, and the *warai dome*, or "laughing close," in which the actors face the audience and laugh heartily ("Ha, ha, ha, ha, ha!") at what they have been doing on stage.

In addition to the resolved and unresolved endings there are also the *utai dome*, which closes with a song, the *ukare dome*, which closes with a musical postlude, and the *serifu dome*, in which an actor brings things to a close with a concluding speech.

Oikomi dome

PROPS

The two most important props used in Kyōgen are the fan and the large lacquer barrel called the *kazuraoke*.

The folding fan is not only an adjunct to what the well-dressed man (or woman) is wearing, it also has a major function as a mime tool just as it does in Japanese dance. Fans (either folded or open) can represent a whole variety of everyday objects such as pens, paper, saké bottles, saké cups, or bows and arrows. It can also be waved as a gesture of beckoning, or held up like a threatening weapon.

The decorative *kazuraoke* can be used both as a rather fine stool and as the imaginary holder of different objects. It can serve as a somewhat abstract symbol of a tree, for example, and, most amusingly, its lid can be used as a huge saké cup for serious drinkers.

The *kazuraoke* used as a saké cup.

Nomura Mansaku as Suppa (left), Nomura Mansai as Chūgoku no mono (right) and Nomura Mannosuke as Mokudai (center) in *Chatsubo*. (Izumi school)

SYNOPSES

NŌ

Aoi no ue ("Lady Aoi")

Fourth category: *zatsu mono*.
Author: unknown, revised by Zeami.
Principal characters:
A Shaman (*tsure*)
Princess Rokujō (*shite*; deigan mask)
The Saint of Yokawa (*waki*)
Princess Rokujō (*nochijite*; hannya mask)

Lady Aoi no ue is the official wife of Prince Genji, the handsome and ever amorous hero of *Genji monogatari*. Often hailed as the world's first novel, this literary classic was written by Murasaki Shikibu and completed in 1004. It is the source, as here, for a great many Nō dramas and continues to be an inspiration for other theater forms to this day.

Lady Aoi's presence is indicated by a brocade robe placed at the front of the stage. She is pregnant with Genji's child, but has been stricken by some mysterious illness and now lies on her sickbed close to death. A local shaman is called in to exorcise whatever spirit is possessing her, and the shaman summons the spirit by plucking on a bow-string.

The living phantom of Princess Rokujō appears. It is she who possesses Aoi no ue because she is filled with jealousy and rage. She is one of Prince Genji's past lovers and is still deeply attached to him. Furthermore, at the recent Kamo Festival, her carriage was damaged and ruthlessly forced aside in favor of Lady Aoi's. This incident, which caused great loss of face for Rokujō, has left her much embittered.

Rokujō declares her identity and describes her past life of luxury and privilege at the imperial court. Yet now, she says, she withers like the morning glory and has come to vent her hatred. Moving toward the sickbed, she strikes at its head.

The shaman is powerless against so strong an adversary, and eventually the Buddhist mountain ascetic known as the Saint of Yokawa must be fetched. Arriving at the mansion, it is only once he has begun his prayers that Rokujō's spirit grows afraid. Hearing the sound of the scriptures, her passion is assuaged, her soul casts off its bonds, and Rokujō at last finds enlightenment and peace.

Atsumori ("Atsumori")

Second category: *shura mono*.
Author: Zeami.
Principal characters:
Renshō, a priest (*waki*)
A Young Reaper (*maejite*; without mask)
A Villager (*ai*)
The Ghost of Atsumori (*nochijite*; Atsumori or Jūroku mask)

Based on an episode in the epic *Heike monogatari*, the play is set in the late twelfth century during a time of civil war between two military clans—the Heike, now in decline, and the victorious Genji. The main characters are the refined and aristocratic youth Atsumori, a warrior of the Heike clan, and Kumagai from the eastern provinces, a general of the Genji troops. After defeating Atsumori in battle and taking his head, Kumagai felt such remorse that he became a monk to pray for his soul, taking the religious name Renshō.

Renshō appears and declares that he is setting out for the battleground at Ichinotani, where he slew Atsumori. His intention is to pray for the youth's soul on its path to enlightenment. He soon arrives, and is surprised to hear the sound of a flute. He decides to wait for the one who plays it in order to question him about the place. Out of the twilight comes a young reaper and his companions, who bemoan their lonely existence trudging repeatedly between the hill and the nearby shores of Suma Bay.

When Renshō admits surprise that one of their station should be playing the flute so beautifully, the young reaper rebukes him for despising those below him in status, arguing with unexpected sophistication that the simple woodsman's song and the reaper's flute are well known in classical poetry and bring solace to men on their journey through this world. Even common bamboo washed up by the sea can be fashioned into flutes of great renown.

Suddenly the reaper's companions disappear. He alone has remained to request prayers, saying he is one of the deceased Atsumori's family. Renshō agrees and begins to chant, upon which the young reaper is pleased and vanishes from sight.

After an interlude in which a local villager repeats the tale of the battle, the young reaper reappears in his true form as the ghost of Atsumori. Now that Renshō is praying for his soul, Atsumori agrees that, though once enemies, they are now friends on the path to Amida Buddha's paradise.

Atsumori recounts the days of the Heike clan's glory that passed as swiftly as a dream, and also recalls the hardships after their downfall. Renshō remembers the night before the battle of Ichinotani when he heard a flute being played in the enemy camp, the very instrument that Atsumori took with him into battle and which Renshō (then Kumagai) found on his person after taking his head. Briefly, Atsumori feels again the bitterness of defeat at Kumagai's hand, but the two are reconciled once more in holy prayer.

Dōjōji ("The Temple of Dōjōji)

Fourth category: *zatsu mono*.
Author: uncertain, possibly Kanze Kojirō Nobumitsu, or Kan'ami.
Principal Characters:
The Head Priest of Dōjōji (*waki*)
A Dancer (*maejite*; *shakumi* mask)

The Temple Servants (*ai*)
The Serpent Demon (*nochijite*; *hannya* mask)

The action takes place at Dōjōji, a temple situated in the hills of Kii Province (modern day Wakayama Prefecture). The head priest enters and explains that, for a very good reason that he cannot disclose, there has been no bell hanging in the belfry for many years. He has ordered a new bell, however, and on this day it is to be raised into the tower. He calls his servants and tells them to hoist the new bell at once.

The heavy bell is carried in and, after great exertion, the servants manage to accomplish their task. The head priest declares that the dedication ceremony will be held today, but he stipulates that no women are permitted to attend.

Shortly after, a woman approaches the temple. She is a dancer from a remote village and she comes hoping to improve her chances of salvation. Arriving before dusk, she requests admittance but is refused because she is a woman. She argues that she is a *shirabyōshi* dancer who has come to perform at the ceremony. One of the specialties of such *shirabyōshi* was a dance performed in male costume and the servant lets her in, supposing that she does not count as a real woman. He gives her a male courtier's cap called an *eboshi*, which she puts on before beginning.

Then follows the famous highlight of the play, the *ranbyōshi* ("mad rhythm") dance, which gradually becomes faster and more intense as it progresses. The chorus and dancer describe the origin of the temple and the spring evening when the cherry blossoms scatter and the moon sinks. At last, she approaches the bell itself and starts to strike it. As the bell falls to the ground, the dancer jumps up, seeming to disappear inside it completely.

The frightened servants report the incident to the head priest, who scolds them for allowing a woman to enter the temple grounds, and tells them why women are prohibited. Many years ago, a mountain priest made an annual pilgrimage to nearby Kumano Shrine, always putting up at the house of a local steward on his way. The steward had a young daughter and, jokingly, he told her that the priest would be her future husband. The girl believed his words and some years later she confronted the priest, demanding to know when he would make her his wife. The amazed priest turned the girl away and stealthily crept out of the house, escaping all the way to Dōjōji, where the temple priests hid him under the great bell. The girl pursued him and, upon reaching Hidaka River, her frustration and rage turned her into a great serpent that swam across. On arriving at Dōjōji, the serpent coiled itself around the bell, breathing out flames and lashing at it with its tail. The bell grew scorching hot and the priest was roasted alive.

Now all the priests pray with all their might to raise this new bell. When it lifts of its own accord, the demon serpent once again appears. As it struggles with the head priest, we hear of its attempts to rush at the bell. Eventually, its body burning in its own fire, the serpent is described leaping into Hidaka River, where it vanishes.

Eguchi ("Eguchi")

Third category: *katsura mono*.
Author: uncertain, possibly Kan'ami and Zeami.
Principal Characters:
A Priest (*waki*)
A Woman (*maejite*; *waka onna* mask)
A Villager (*ai*)
The Lady of Eguchi (*nochijite*; *waka onna* mask)
Two Women Companions (*tsure*; *ko-omote* masks)

A priest decides to make a tour of holy sites in the surrounding provinces. He departs by boat with some companions and soon reaches the riverside village of Eguchi. Disembarking, he notices a burial mound and asks a villager who is buried there. The man replies that it is the Lady of Eguchi, a prostitute who lived long ago. She was also a poetess said to be the living manifestation of the Buddhist deity Fugen. The poet priest Saigyō (1118–1190) once visited her and they exchanged poems. The villager goes off.

The priest recalls the famous verse that

Saigyō composed when the lady refused him a night's lodging at her house. In Saigyō's poem he accused her of begrudging him even "a moment's refuge," seeming to cling to it selfishly.

Mysteriously, a woman appears asking why the priest recited that poem just now. She, too, remembers the occasion but insists that the Lady of Eguchi clung to no "moment's refuge." She asks the priest to recall the lady's answering verse. In it she warned Saigyō that he should not seek lodging at the house of a prostitute, because it was improper for one who had renounced the world as a priest. He himself was wrong to seek "a moment's refuge." The lady showed religious understanding because the "moment's refuge" was also a metaphor for the human body which, even as a prostitute, she realized was merely a temporary abode.

The priest asks the identity of this woman and, just as twilight shadows begin to envelop her, she admits that she is the Lady of Eguchi's ghost and disappears.

The villager returns and relates the tale of another holy man named Shōkū (910–1007), who desired to worship the bodhisattva Fugen. He was told to go to Eguchi, where he should see the chief prostitute. He went and looked upon her and when he closed his eyes he did indeed see her transformed as Fugen. The villager again retires.

The priest begins to recite sutras when beneath the moonlight a boat suddenly appears with the lady and women singing. Their song tells of the vanity of love, which is like foam upon the water. As the cycle of birth and death continues, even those blessed with human form are immersed in sin and often lack any aspiration to enlightenment. They fail to realize that all will pass—whether it be the spring blossoms and autumn leaves, the comfort of friends, or even the intimacy of lovers. None can escape sorrow in this world for even when they do realize, human desire and the longing for love run deep. It is hard not to yearn for "a moment's refuge."

It was against this, the lady says, that she warned Saigyō. As she repeats it to the priest now, she reveals herself once more as the all-knowing bodhisattva Fugen. The chorus describes her mounted upon her pure white elephant rising into the western clouds as she fades from view.

Funa Benkei ("Benkei Aboard Ship")

Fifth category: *kiri nō.*
Author: Kanze Nobumitsu.
Principal Characters:
Benkei (*waki*)
Yoshitsune (*kokata*)
Shizuka-gozen (*maejite*; *waka onna, ko-omote,* or *fukai* mask)
A Boatman (*ai*)
The Ghost of Tomomori (*nochijite*; *mikazuki,* or *awa otoko* mask)

Set during the Heike–Genji civil wars of the late twelfth century, *Funa Benkei* is based on the fifteenth-century classic *Gikeiki* ("Chronicles of Yoshitsune"), and on the *Heike monogatari.* The play depicts an episode in the life of the brilliant young Genji commander Yoshitsune, who is now a fugitive escaping the jealous wrath of his older brother, the shogun Yoritomo.

The year is 1185. Yoshitsune and a small band of followers are fleeing the capital, pursued by his own brother's forces. His right-hand man, the warrior priest Musashibō Benkei, leads them westward and before long they arrive at the Bay of Daimotsu. They ask for lodging and for a ship from a local boatman.

Also in their group is Yoshitsune's lover, the dancer Shizuka-gozen. As the only woman among them, Benkei feels that her presence is improper and he advises that she should be sent back to the capital. Yoshitsune agrees, and Benkei goes to deliver the message. Hearing the surprising news that she must be parted from her beloved, Shizuka fears that Yoshitsune's affections have shifted, but then it occurs to her that this has been Benkei's idea all along. She insists on giving her reply directly to Yoshitsune.

Once Yoshitsune has confirmed the plan, Shizuka is ashamed to have doubted Benkei and apologizes. Though greatly saddened, she

agrees to leave, hoping that one day they will be reunited. Yoshitsune orders a cup of "chrysanthemum wine" (representing longevity) to be offered to Shizuka. She is to sing and perform a farewell dance, and they give her a dancer's cap and robe.

Echoing Yoshitsune's own situation, her song tells the tale of an ancient Chinese king, who was defeated by a rival forced into hiding in the mountains. After waiting for twenty years, the strategy of his chief advisor was finally successful and the king was reinstated. Shizuka's performance ends with a poem spoken by the Buddhist deity of mercy, Kannon, telling people simply to trust in her, for despite their hardships she will save them in the end. Shizuka departs in tears.

The boatman comes to commiserate, and to announce that their ship is ready. Much affected by the separation from his lover, Yoshitsune wishes to stay a while longer, but Benkei is impatient with such delay and urges his lord to continue at once. At last, all board the ship and they put out to sea. Though the weather starts off unusually fine, once they are some distance from land a black cloud suddenly appears. A fierce storm whips up and great waves begin to attack the ship. Fearing for their safety, Benkei tells everyone to pray hard.

Looking out, Benkei then sees the ghosts of all the drowned Heike men floating above the waves. It was at this very spot that Yoshitsune defeated the Heike in a decisive sea battle, and now the spirits of his enemy have returned to seek revenge. Their leader is the Heike general Tomomori, who declares his identity and vows to drown Yoshitsune just as he himself met his death. Tomomori repeatedly charges at the ship brandishing his halberd and spewing out poisonous fumes.

Though Yoshitsune unsheathes his sword to challenge the enemy, Benkei knows that only a spiritual force can defeat such a foe. With his prayer beads he recites the names of the five Buddhist Mantra Kings, and the evil ghost is repelled. Struggling again and again to attack the ship, Tomomori is finally drawn back by the tide and is gone.

Hagoromo ("The Feather Mantle")

Third category: *katsura mono*.
Author: unknown.
Principal Characters:
Hakuryō, a fisherman (*waki*)
An Angel (*shite*; *zō-onna* mask)

It is spring at the pine-clad Bay of Mio. A fisherman named Hakuryō appears and praises the scenery, describing the mists rising from the sea and the bright moon lingering in the sky to create a feeling of peace that lifts the heart.

As Hakuryō approaches the shore, mysteriously flowers come falling all about him and a wonderful fragrance pervades the air. He notices a beautiful feathered cloak (*hagoromo*) hanging on a pine bough and decides to take it home. Suddenly, a maiden calls out that the cloak belongs to her. Appearing before him, she says it is a celestial cloak and that he has no business taking it. She is an angel, and without the cloak she cannot fly home to Heaven. Hearing this, however, the fisherman is all the more intent on keeping his newfound treasure and hides it before turning to go.

Lost without her robe, the angel begins to suffer the signs of weakness that lead to an angel's death. She gazes up at the sky, feeling envious of the free-floating clouds, and finds that the song of the bird of heaven grows faint to her ears. Watching her, Hakuryō can bear it no longer and relents. He decides to give back the cloak on condition that she dance for him. She agrees, but must have the cloak back before she does so. Hakuryō is immediately suspicious and refuses, claiming that she will simply fly away without performing a single step, but the angel shames him by saying that such falsehood belongs to the human world and is unknown in Heaven. At last he gives her back the cloak.

Putting it on, the angel begins. We hear a description of the Moon Palace, made from an axe of jade, before which thirty angels robed in black or white dance nightly. In the moon the *katsura* tree is in full bloom, while here on earth the spring is lovely, too, with the moon gleaming above the snowy slopes of Mt. Fuji. The gods themselves gave birth to the imperial line and his majesty's realm endures for as long as the rocks that are brushed only rarely by a feathered robe.

Heavenly music filters through the clouds on which Amida Buddha descends to welcome spirits of the deceased. The angel pays tribute to the bodhisattva Seishi, whose power to lead souls to paradise is manifested by the moon. Onward the angel dances. Gradually, the feathered cloak rises into the air and floats above the pines of Mio Bay and on past the slopes of Mt. Fuji, until, mingling with the mists of heaven, the angel disappears from sight.

Izutsu ("The Well-Cradle")

Third category: *katsura mono*.
Author: Zeami.
Principal Characters:
A Priest (*waki*)
A Woman (*maejite*; *waka onna* mask)
A Villager (*ai*)
The Lady of Izutsu (*nochijite*; *waka onna* mask)

The play *Izutsu* is based on episode twenty-three of the *Ise monogatari*, a tenth-century classic said to have been written in part by the court poet and lover, Ariwara no Narihira. It is he and his fictional wife who feature in this play.

A priest traveling through the country comes upon the Ariwara Temple, the site where Narihira and his wife lived many years together. He decides to pray for the couple when a woman appears alone to place an offering at the grave mound nearby.

The priest asks if she has some connection with Narihira, at which she replies that thoughts of him still fill her heart. She begins to relate the couple's married life here. Despite their happiness, Narihira had an affair with another lady in a distant province and would divide his time between the two women. On one occasion, just after he had left his wife, she sang a song expressing anxiety for his safety along the treacherous road ahead. He heard the song and decided never again to leave.

The woman goes on to describe a boy and a girl who also lived here next door to each other. They grew up as friends and played often together, even measuring their heights on the well-cradle, the wooden frame built around the communal well. As the years passed they grew shy, but both still harbored secret thoughts of romance. Finally, the boy sent a poem to the girl indicating that, though now grown up, he still thought of her. She replied with another poem: though her long hair was now that of a mature woman, who but he should put it up for her as her husband? Soon after that the two were married.

The woman who tells all this to the priest is none other than the lady of the stories, and as soon as she discloses her identity she disappears. A villager comes by and is asked by the priest to tell the story of this place, at which he repeats the above tales. He advises the priest to chant holy sutras to comfort the deceased couple and the priest agrees to do so.

It grows late, and the priest prepares to sleep. Just then, the lady returns dressed in the outer robe and hat that once belonged to Narihira. As she dances, she laments how time has flown since the old days, and yet she still pines for her husband.

Beneath the moon she approaches the well, parts the pampas grass by its side, and glances down at the moon's reflection in the water. As she does this she recalls the poem that Narihira sent her. Though she now wishes to see his reflection in the water it is only her own, wearing his coat and hat, that appears. The temple bell signals the dawn and her form fades.

Kantan ("Kantan")

Fourth category: *zatsu mono*.
Author: uncertain, possibly Zeami or Konparu Zenchiku.
Principal Characters:
A Woman Innkeeper (*ai*)
Rosei, a young man (*shite*; Kantan otoko mask)
An Imperial Envoy (*waki*)
A Dancer (*kokata*)

A woman innkeeper in the village of Kantan in China has been given a magic pillow by a monk. Whoever sleeps on the pillow awakens to the truth after dreaming of the past and future, and she allows visitors to use it when they stay with her. One day a man named Rosei passes by and decides to put up at the woman's inn. He is on his way to find a great sage from whom he wants to learn about enlightenment. When the woman hears of this, she offers him the pillow and he lies down to sleep.

An imperial envoy arrives with the message that Rosei has been given the throne of the Kingdom of So. Despite his astonishment at this sudden news, he agrees to enter the jeweled palanquin that is provided for him, and is borne away towards his new land.

On arrival at his new palace, court officials and a dancer enter, and we hear of others pouring in, bearing priceless jewels as offerings. Rosei sees before him a magnificent vision of gleaming towers and parks with sparkling sands. To the east and the west lie mountains of pure silver or gold.

A minister then announces that Rosei has already ruled for fifty years, and offers him the elixir of youth so that he may rule for a thousand more. He is to drink it out of a precious goblet, the same as that used by the immortal sages. As he drinks, the dancer performs for him the graceful "dream dance" to lyrics that describe the land's prosperity and the precious dew that drops unendingly from the chrysanthemums.

At last, Rosei himself begins to dance and he sees another vision of passing days and nights, spring blossoms giving way to autumn leaves as the seasons turn before him. The fifty years of glory, we hear, all melt into nothingness for they all happened in a dream.

Suddenly, the innkeeper wakens Rosei. He realizes that all he witnessed took no more time to pass than it takes to cook millet. A lifetime comes and goes with all its hopes of glory and happiness, and yet it remains as insubstantial as a dream. Thanks to the Pillow of Kantan, Rosei is spiritually enlightened at last, and he decides to make his way home.

Matsukaze ("Pining Wind")

Third category: *katsura mono*.
Author: Zeami.
Principal Characters:
A Priest (*waki*)
Matsukaze (*shite*; *waka onna* mask)
Murasame (*tsure*; *ko-omote* mask)
A Villager (*ai*)

A priest is travelling to the western provinces and arrives at the Bay of Suma, famous as Prince Genji's place of exile in the classic *Genji monogatari*, which strongly influences the text of this play. On the shore the priest notices a solitary pine tree with a sign before it and a poem-slip attached to its branches. Wondering about this tree, he asks a local villager to tell its history.

The villager relates that once two sisters lived here whose occupation was to gather seawater to make salt. Their names were Matsukaze, "Pining Wind," and Murasame, "Autumn Rain." They passed away in loneliness and the villager asks the priest to pray for the repose of their souls. This he does, but upon finishing, he sees that the sun has set and that he must take shelter for the night. He decides to approach a nearby salt house.

Two women appear, one drawing a small wagon behind her and the other carrying a pail of seawater. They lament their lonely existence and the hard labor that is their daily lot. One notices her reflection in a pool, and they compare their abandoned state to a pool of seawater left stranded by the receding tide. The text goes on to describe the beauties of autumn evenings at Suma, where the distant calls of fishermen are heard, geese fly homeward across the moon, and flocks of plovers dart to and fro along the shore. Glancing down, the sisters see the moon reflected in their buckets.

They return to their salt house and come across the priest, who requests a night's lodging. Though at first they refuse him, saying that their house is unfit to receive guests, they at last relent when they find out that he is a priest. He recalls a sad poem written by the courtier Ariwara no Yukihira, who was also exiled to Suma, and again asks the sisters about the pine tree. At this, they begin to weep. Surprised that the poem should have had such an effect, the priest asks the women's identity.

The sisters reveal that they are indeed the ghosts of Matsukaze and Murasame, and that during his three years of exile here, Yukihira courted them both. Then he returned to the capital, after which they heard news of his early death. Still they long for him, and their attachment prevents them from attaining spiritual peace.

Yukihira left them his outer robe and court hat as keepsakes but, taking them up, Matsukaze complains that they only remind her of her sorrow. When she puts them on she seems to slip into madness. She claims to see Yukihira before her now and insists she is right even when Murasame tells her it is only the pine tree. But then Murasame, too, agrees that the pine stands for Yukihira himself, for the poem he gave them as he departed promised that if they pined for him, he would certainly return.

Blinded by their love for him, the sisters beg the priest to give them comfort through his prayers. At last dawn breaks, and the chorus informs us that the priest heard nothing but the autumn rain, and that nothing lingers except the sound of the wind in the pines.

Shakkyō ("The Stone Bridge")

Fifth category: *kiri nō*.
Author: unknown.
Principal Characters:
Jakushō, a priest (*waki*)
A Youth (*maejite*; *dōji* mask)
Shishi Lion (*nochijite*; *shishi gashira* mask)

The Japanese priest Jakushō, formerly known as Ōe no Sadamoto, arrives in China at the site of the holy stone bridge on Mt. Seiryō. He wishes to cross over the bridge, for on the other side lies the Paradise of the Buddhist deity Monju, the protector of wisdom. The priest waits for someone to come and tell him the bridge's history.

Suddenly a youth appears carrying firewood

on his back. As he enters, the verses tell of the flower petals that have scattered upon his wood, making it seem covered in snow. The song of the woodcutter and the flute of the herdsman can be heard, for many are the occupations of man as he makes his way through this life. Here in the mountains, the youth has spent his time among the clouds hiding his footprints, listening only to the pounding river in the valley below that drowns out the pine wind. The youth alludes to an old Chinese tale about a woodcutter who, thinking that he has spent a mere half day in the mountains, returns to his home village to discover that many generations have passed.

Coming upon the priest, the youth confirms that this is indeed the famous stone bridge, and when Jakushō expresses his desire to cross it, the youth warns him that even the most virtuous holy men have spent months in severe training before attempting such a feat. Crossing the bridge is an extremely dangerous act. Having existed since the first parting of heaven and earth, it is also called "Heaven's Floating Bridge".

The youth says that many other famous bridges exist throughout the world, all serving mankind well in saving him from drowning beneath the raging waters and allowing him to cross to safety on the other side. This bridge, however, appeared of its own accord as a miracle, hanging precariously between one jagged rock and another. Its surface is moss-covered and slippery, its breadth very narrow, and its span a distance of over thirty feet. Below the bridge is a valley so deep that its depths may reach to hell itself, and into this abyss, from out of the clouds there tumbles a threadlike cascade. Looking up at the bridge, it appears like a rainbow after a shower or a tightly drawn bow. Without special holy powers, who could ever cross to the Paradise on the other side? In that miraculous landscape, flowers come falling in the sky and the beautiful music of pipes, flutes, and other instruments are heard filtering through the evening clouds about a setting sun. The youth tells Jakushō to wait where he is for soon, before his very eyes, a heavenly apparition will appear. With this the youth disappears.

In the final brief section of the play, a *shishi* lion comes to dance before the priest and to cavort among the fragrant peony bushes nearby. (According to which version of the play is being performed, there may be one lion, a pair of lions, or even an entire group.) The *shishi* is a holy beast associated with the deity Monju, who is frequently depicted seated upon a *shishi*'s back. Here the lion dances frenziedly, displaying its majestic power as the King of Beasts, and the verses end auspiciously, saying that it will continue to dance for a thousand autumns and ten thousand years.

Sotoba Komachi ("Komachi on the Stupa")

Fourth category: *zatsu mono*.
Author: Kan'ami.
Principal Characters:
A Priest (*waki*)
Ono no Komachi (*shite*; *uba* or *rōjo* mask)

The main character in this play is the legendary courtier and poetess Ono no Komachi (fl. early ninth century). Famed for her beauty, she is said to have had many suitors, but rejected them all with cruel disdain. In this play she is portrayed abandoned and alone in extreme old age, and while she still exhibits supreme intelligence, she is also victim to bouts of madness.

A priest from Mt. Kōya enters with a companion and states that he is on the way to the capital. Since the death of the first Buddha Shakyamuni, human lives, he says, are spent in a dreamworld awaiting the coming of the future Buddha. Blessed with human form and knowledge of the Buddha's Word, he has devoted himself to the priesthood and has renounced all earthly ties. As a pilgrim, a thousand miles is nothing to him as he sleeps in open fields and rests among the hills.

Komachi appears. She bemoans her present decrepit state and recalls the past. Then, her glorious beauty was such that her long, sleek tresses resembled the sweeping branches of the weeping willow. Yet now, close to a hundred, she has been deserted by former friends and must wander about as an outcast. She is exhausted and rests upon a decaying wooden post.

Noticing her, the priest tells her to get up for the post is, in fact, a holy stupa—a symbol of the Buddha. There follows a series of questions and answers on Buddhist doctrine in which Komachi demonstrates the excellence of her knowledge. Why should she not sit on the stupa, she asks, for it is already fallen. Contrary ways may also lead to salvation for reality is void and the Buddha vowed to save all mankind, whether ignorant or wise. The priest is astounded by her erudition and pays homage.

Komachi reveals her true identity and the priest pities her sadly changed appearance. In contrast to the past, she must now subsist on meager provisions, her clothes are ragged and her straw rain coat and sedge hat are damaged. Once a famous court beauty, she is now reduced to begging for alms.

Suddenly, Komachi demands alms from the priest. She is possessed by the spirit of one of her old suitors and goes mad. The suitor was a captain named Fukakusa no Shōshō, whom Komachi cruelly obliged to travel to her house every night for one hundred consecutive nights. Obsessed by his love for her, he almost succeeded but then died on the ninety-ninth night. We hear of his trials as he trudged through the rain, wind, and snow to carve his mark each time on a wooden bench, and finally, of the bitter pain of his death. Coming to her senses once more, Komachi vows evermore to pray for salvation in the afterlife.

Takasago ("Takasago")

First category: *kami nō.*
Author: Zeami
Principal Characters:
Tomonari, a priest (*waki*)
An Old Man (*maejite*; *kōshijō* mask)
An Old Woman (*tsure*; *uba* mask)
A Villager (*ai*)
The God of Sumiyoshi (*nochijite*; *Kantan otoko* mask)

Tomonari, the chief priest of the Aso Shrine in Kyushu, makes a journey to the capital. On the way he stops at the Bay of Takasago, where an elderly couple approaches him. The old man carries a rake and the old woman, a broom, and they begin to sweep the pine needles from beneath a great pine tree.

When Tomonari asks them which is the famous Takasago pine, the old man replies that it is the very one under which they are sweeping. The pines of Takasago and Sumiyoshi are said to be paired, and it turns out that while the old woman comes from Takasago, the old man originally comes from Sumiyoshi. The woman adds that, though the pines are separated by physical distance, two hearts joined as one will always find their way to each other.

The paired pines also symbolize a blessed reign, they say, for the Takasago pine represents the ancient *Manyōshū* poetry collection, and the Sumiyoshi pine represents the *Kokinshū* collection of the present age (the early tenth century, when the play is set). The pines symbolize unending leaves of speech, which stand in constant praise of His Majesty. Here, the spring is mild and the world's oceans are calm, for all is peaceful in this land ruled by the emperor. Despite its advanced age, the Takasago pine remains evergreen and signals blessing.

At last, the two reveal themselves to be none other than the spirits of the Takasago and Sumiyoshi pines. As Tomonari watches, they board a boat and set off across the sea for Sumiyoshi.

The priest then asks a local villager to tell him the story of the Takasago pine. The villager explains that the evergreen pine needles are compared to the enduring strength of poetry in this land. The gods of Takasago and Sumiyoshi are said to be husband and wife, and when they visit each other they communicate through the sacred pines. That is why the pine trees are said to be paired, for the two gods are supposedly one in spirit. The villager is shocked to hear of the old man and woman who were just here, and advises Tomonari to travel at once to Sumiyoshi, where the gods will surely be waiting for him. He himself has a new boat and offers to take the priest there. They board and set off immediately.

Once they arrive, the god of Sumiyoshi alone comes to perform for the priest, and the lyrics refer to ancient Bugaku dances that all have auspicious themes. All are wished a thousand autumns of peace and ten thousand years of long life.

Yamanba ("The Mountain Crone")

Fifth category: *kiri nō*.
Author: Zeami.
Principal Characters:
A Dancer (*tsure*; *ko-omote* mask)
Her Attendant (*waki*)
A Woman of the Mountains (*maejite*; *fukai* mask)
A Villager (*ai*)
The Mountain Crone (*nochijite*; *Yamanba* mask)

A dancer from the capital who is famous for a particular work featuring *yamanba*, or the "mountain crone," decides to go on a pilgrimage to Zenkōji temple in the province of Shinano. Accompanied by an attendant and servants, she sets off at once. Reaching the vicinity, the group asks a local villager to be their guide, and he explains that there are three ways to reach Zenkōji. The most difficult is the path straight over the mountains, which Amida Buddha himself is said to have created. This is the path they elect to follow and the villager leads on.

The path proves to be very steep and difficult, and it begins to grow dark earlier than usual. The group is looking for somewhere to spend the night when suddenly a woman appears and offers them her humble hut. In return, she requests that the dancer perform the *Yamanba* dance.

When the attendant refuses, the woman is angered, revealing that she herself is the *yamanba* of whom the song speaks. She is resentful that a work about her has made the dancer famous and successful. If she witnesses the dance, perhaps she can escape the pain of this world and her wrongful attachment to it. The dancer is frightened to think what might happen if she continues to refuse and agrees at once. The woman tells her to wait until the

moon is high when she herself will appear in her true shape and perform together with the dancer. Suddenly, the woman disappears.

The attendant asks the villager to tell them about the *yamanba*, and he repeats three of the local legends about her identity, each one sounding more implausible than the last.

Finally, the moon rises and the crone appears with a walking staff, telling the dancer to begin. (In fact, only the crone performs.) The lyrics of the song tell of the painful wanderings of the crone as she makes her endless rounds of the mountains. They describe the magnificent scenery, the mountain peaks that soar upwards towards religious truth, and the plunging valley depths that represent the Buddha's teaching "pouring" downwards. We hear of the crone herself, an ogre without a home who dwells among the mist-shrouded hills. At times, unseen, she comes to help woodcutters carry their heavy burdens, or helps weaver girls at their looms.

At last the crone must leave to continue her rounds, which are compared to the revolving wheel of birth and death. Ever onward through the four seasons she goes, from one mountain to another until she is gradually lost from view.

Yashima

Second category: *shura mono*.
Author: Zeami.
Principal Characters:
A Priest (*waki*)
An Old Fisherman (*maejite*, *asakura-jō* mask)
A Young Fisherman (*tsure*)
A Villager (*ai*)
Yoshitsune (*nochijite*; *heida* mask)

Like *Atsumori*, this play, too, is based on an episode from the *Heike monogatari*, which chronicles a time during the late twelfth century when a civil war raged between the Heike and the Genji clans.

A priest and companions from the capital decide to visit Shikoku. On their way, they stop at the shores of Yashima and, as night is about to fall, they seek refuge at a nearby salt house.

Before long, the inhabitants of the salt house return. They are an elderly man and his younger companion, and both are fishermen. When the priest requests lodging, the old fisherman at first refuses, saying their humble abode is not good enough, but he relents when he hears that the priest is from the capital. Mention of that place seems to stir the old man strangely.

The priest has heard that a great battle was fought on this beach and asks the fishermen to tell the story. The old man begins to describe how, at the time, the Heike fleet was some way out at sea when the Genji forces rode onto the sand, led by their young general Yoshitsune. The Heike responded by putting ashore and a contest of strength ensued between the Heike commander Kagekiyo and the Genji warrior Mihonoya no Shirō. The two eventually fell to hand to hand combat. During the fight, Kagekiyo seized the neck-plate of Mihonoya's helmet and pulled backwards. The strength of both men was such that the neck-plate broke and they fell to the ground.

Soon after, Noritsune, Lord of Noto, aimed an arrow at Yoshitsune that would have struck its intended target had the loyal Genji warrior Tsuginobu not ridden his horse in front of his lord to block the arrow's path. The arrow pierced and killed Tsuginobu instead. Then Noritsune's personal page was struck down. Both sides withdrew in sadness.

The priest is taken aback by the preciseness of the fishermen's account and demands that they declare their identity. Before doing

so, however, the fishermen vanish.

Soon, a local salt maker arrives at the house and is shocked to see the priest and companions inside. The house, in fact, belongs to him. The priest asks for another account of the battle that took place here and the salt maker obliges in a manner that is far cruder than that of the old fisherman before. The salt maker realizes that it must have been the ghost of Yoshitsune himself who was here and advises the priest to remain in the house for the spirit is sure to come back.

Yoshitsune does indeed reappear, this time in full battle dress, and he explains that emotional attachment to this world has prevented him from achieving salvation. He recalls another episode from the battle when, riding into the sea, he dropped his bow into the water. Not wishing it to fall into enemy hands, he rode after it and barely managed to evade the enemy's hooks before it was retrieved. Yoshitsune was challenged by his men for so foolish an act, but he replied that he did not wish rumors of his small stature and small bow to spread among their opponents lest it tarnish his reputation as a warrior. More than his life, it is a warrior's honor that he holds most dear.

Finally, Yoshitsune recalls the sea battle at Dannoura, where he defeated the Heike army once and for all. Yet his attachment to such worldly events makes him increasingly agitated. Only with the light of coming dawn does his figure fade at last, leaving no sign except the howl of a morning gale through the pine trees.

KYŌGEN

Bōshibari ("Tied to a Pole")

Shōmyō kyōgen, tarōkaja mono.

The master's problem is that every time he makes plans to go away, his servants Tarōkaja and Jirōkaja steal his saké. This time, however, he has a plan. He recruits Tarōkaja into tying Jirōkaja's arms to the far ends of a pole placed across his shoulders. Tied up like this he can

hardly move, let alone steal anything. Then, when Tarōkaja is not looking, the master quickly ties his hands behind his back too. He leaves thinking that his saké is sure to be safe this time.

The hapless servants decide they are thirsty and manage to open up the saké cabinet. They try to use the lid of a lacquer barrel (*kazuraoke*) as a cup, but Jirōkaja cannot drink with his arms tied to the pole. He holds the lid out for Tarōkaja, who manages to drink from it. Likewise, Tarō-kaja cannot drink because his hands are tied behind his back, but he manages to hold it for Jirōkaja. They both start to get drunk and begin to sing and dance.

The master then returns. Surprised, the master angrily tries to strike them, but Jirōkaja chases the master brandishing a pole.

Busshi ("The Buddhist Sculptor")

Shukke zatō kyōgen, shukke mono.

A country bumpkin builds himself a shrine to hold a Buddhist effigy. He also needs a fine effigy to fill it, and so sets out for the city to buy one. The city, however, is so large that he cannot find a Buddhist sculptor anywhere. By chance he runs into a city slicker who, seemingly very kindly, asks him what he is looking for. The man, really a swindler who preys on innocent country types, tells him that this is his lucky day and that he is just such a sculptor. He tells the country bumpkin to come by tomorrow and pick up his new effigy.

The next day the man dutifully goes to the sculptor's house and finds a newly finished statue. (The Buddhist effigy is played by the same actor who takes the part of the swindler, wearing a mask.)

However, there is something wrong with the effigy and the country bumpkin decides that the hand positions are not as they should be. (These matters are set by centuries of Buddhist tradition and are very important.)

He decides that he must have the hand positions fixed, so he calls to the sculptor who cleverly changes from being the effigy back into the swindler by removing his mask. Alterations are made but the man still isn't satisfied. Every time he wants the hand positions changed the swindler has to put his mask back on quickly and become the effigy again. Eventually, the country bumpkin catches the cheat out.

Busu ("Sugar")

Shōmyō kyōgen, tarōkaja mono.

The master decides to go on a trip. Sugar was a rarity at this time and the master has a store of which he is very fond. He needs his servants Tarōkaja and Jirōkaja to take good care of it during his absence. However, as he is sure they will try to eat it, he tells them that the substance in the pot is actually a very strong poison. It is very dangerous and they must on no account go near it.

The master leaves, and at first Tarōkaja and Jirōkaja are very wary of this strong poison. However, they are also fascinated by it and decide to take a look. The substance appears harmless enough, so they try fanning it a little. It still looks quite safe and so the next step is to dip a finger in and try it on the tip of the tongue. They soon realize, of course, that their master has fooled them and that such sweet stuff must be sugar. They end up eating the whole lot.

While they are having fun eating all the sugar, the clumsy pair manages to tear one of their master's favorite hanging scrolls and also break a precious bowl. The master returns to find them desolate and in tears. He sees the damage and they tell him that they were attempting a bout of sumo wrestling during which they broke the objects. To atone for these misdeeds they decided to commit suicide by eating the poison. But so far nothing has happened, and they still haven't died!

Chatsubo ("The Tea Caddy")

Atsume kyōgen, zatsu mono.

A drunken man has fallen asleep by the roadside. On his back, rather like a rucksack, he is carrying a fine tea caddy. A thief comes along and spots the drunken man, thinking him an easy target. He sees the tea caddy and decides to steal it. First of all, he manages to release the right shoulder strap from the sleeping man but, however much he tries, he cannot. Then he decides to put his hand through the left shoulder strap and sleep.

Finally, the drunk wakes up and is surprised to find that he is being robbed. He accuses the thief, who in turn accuses *him* of being the robber. The only way to settle things is to ask the help of a judge. The drunk explains to the judge that he was asleep when the man tried to rob him. Hearing this, the thief tells exactly the same story.

Trying to sort out the truth, the judge asks when the tea was put in the caddy. They both give him an answer, but he comes nowhere nearer to forming a judgment. The only solution the judge can find is the old one: he decides that the tea caddy should be his. He goes off with it with the pair in hot pursuit.

Kagyū ("The Snail")

Oni yamabushi kyōgen, yamabushi mono.

The master is searching for medicine for his ailing father and tells Tarōkaja to go and look for snails, the ingredient of a cure. Tarōkaja, however, has never seen a snail and has no idea what they look like. The master explains that they live among the bamboo, have a shell on their backs and have black crowns with horns. Some can even grow as big as a man!

Tarōkaja decides to look for snails and, among the bamboo, he finds a sleeping *yamabushi*. *Yamabushi* are a sect of traveling mountain ascetics who wear distinctive costumes, including a small black hat rather like a crown.

Tarōkaja wakes up the *yamabushi* and asks him if he is a snail and to come with him. Amused by this rather dim-witted servant, the *yamabushi* tells him that he is indeed a snail but can't move for lack of songs and dances. Tarōkaja decides to sing and dance. The master observes this and objects that he is, in fact, a *yamabushi*. The *yamabushi*, however, insists that he is a snail. Finally, the *yamabushi* sings and dances for them and they are persuaded that he is, indeed, a snail. In the end, they sing and dance together and exit.

In the Izumi school, the master gets angry and Tarōkaja recovers his senses. Finally they chase after the *yamabushi*.

Shimizu ("The Spring")

Oni yamabushi kyōgen, tarōkaja mono.

There is a spring at Nonaka from which fine water may be drawn. A master would like some of this water in order to perform the tea ceremony and so he orders Tarōkaja to go there and draw some for him. Tarōkaja, however, thinks this is a very troublesome assignment and does not want to go. He leaves the mansion but goes only a short distance and then comes running home, saying that he has been threatened by a devil and could not go on.

The master believes him, but is not happy that Tarōkaja left behind the very good bucket which he had taken with him to hold the water. He tells Tarōkaja that he himself will go and get the bucket. Tarōkaja is surprised by this and, fearing that he will be found out, he runs on ahead to the spring and puts on a devil mask in order to frighten his lord. The master is indeed frightened and runs off.

However, he begins to think about this and becomes suspicious that the devil's voice was exactly like Tarōkaja's. He was also rather surprised that this "devil" asked him to provide Tarōkaja with a mosquito net for his bed and told him to give Tarōkaja lots of saké to drink. He decides to return to the spring. Tarōkaja is still there, disguised as a devil, but the master finds him out and angrily chases after him.

Suō otoshi ("Dropping the Robe")

Shōmyō kyōgen, tarōkaja mono.

The master is to go on a pilgrimage to the Great Shrine at Ise. He sends Tarōkaja to the house of the master's uncle to invite him along too. For his trouble, however, the uncle offers him saké which he drinks from the lid of a lacquered barrel.

As a parting gift he gives Tarōkaja a *suō*, a splendid robe, and he returns home. On the way, Tarōkaja, much the worse for drink, begins to think that if he appears with such a splendid present, his master will be sure to take it from him. He decides that at all costs he must hide the robe from his lord. The only thing to do is to hide it in his clothing.

The master spots Tarōkaja's drunkenness immediately. Tarōkaja offers to sing and dance for him, but lets the robe drop by mistake. The master picks up the robe and teases him. Finally, Tarōkaja gets it back and he runs away.

In Izumi school's performance the hapless Tarōkaja runs after the master as the latter makes off with the prize.

Susugigawa ("Washing in the River")

Shinsaku kyōgen.

In this household the husband is weak and continually henpecked by his wife and mother-in-law. He even has to do the family washing in the river behind the house. Today is washday and, as usual, while he is doing the washing, his wife and mother come to watch and give him a further list of things he needs to do.

This time, there are so many jobs for him that they have written him a list. Tired of all this work, he agrees to do everything on the list, as long as they promise that he need do nothing that is *not* on the list.

While he is washing a kimono sleeve he mistakenly drops it in the river. His wife tries to catch the sleeve but she too falls in the river. The mother-in-law calls for him to fish her out, but as that job was not on the list, he decides not to bother! She begs him and apologizes for being so hard on him in the past. Mollified, he fishes his wife out and she, furious, chases after him. The mother-in-law decides it is best to tear up the list of things to do.

Tōzumō / Tōjinzumō ("Chinese Sumo")

Waki kyōgen, zatsu mono.

A Japanese sumo wrestler is in China where he is employed by the emperor as one of his guards. However, he tells the emperor that he wishes to return home. The emperor agrees but says that he wishes to see him wrestle one more time before he leaves.

The sumo wrestler fights with Chinese men, but is so strong that he beats them one by one. The Chinese wrestlers do not use the "push out" and "under-arm throw" techniques of Japanese sumo, but instead are very acrobatic, and the actors do backflips and various other acrobatic tricks while playing this part.

The failure of all his guards to beat the Japanese wrestler is very vexing to the emperor, so he decides to wrestle the man himself. The emperor is likely to be defeated, but then suddenly the Chinese guards all jump on Japanese wrestler.

Tsurigitsune ("Hunting a Fox")

Atsume kyōgen, zatsu mono.

There is an old fox whose entire family has been killed by a hunter. He wants to stop the hunter from further carnage and, as Japanese foxes possess magical powers, he changes himself into the form of the hunter's uncle, a monk called Hakuzōsu.

Having transformed, the fox goes to the hunter's house to tell him a story about killing a fox, and how this will bring great misfortune on him and his household.

The hunter, hearing this story, promises the monk that he will cease hunting the fox. To prove this, he also throws away his traps. Happily, thinking he has achieved his objective, the fox–monk leaves for home. On the way, however, he finds some of the hunter's bait and, turning back into a fox, eats it.

The hunter has his doubts about this monk and, following him, finds the scraps of bait and is sure that, in fact, the monk was a fox. Determined to get his revenge, he sets another trap and lies in wait for the fox to reappear.

The fox eventually comes by again and gets caught in the trap. He fights his way out, however, and runs away.

Chapter 5

CONTEMPORARY THEATER

CONTEMPORARY THEATER
PLAYS, MUSICALS, AND BUTŌ

Tokyo is a large and dynamic center for theater comparable to New York or London. Unlike Broadway or the West End, however, Tokyo theaters are scattered around the city, with most being in Ginza, Hibiya, Shinjuku, Shibuya, and Shimokitazawa.

Although the words "Japanese theater" generally conjure up an image of Kabuki or Nō, there is also much contemporary theater on offer. Popular commercial plays and musicals attract large audiences, and there is a lively fringe theater scene. Japan also possesses a good number of cutting-edge writers, directors, and actors—in particular, Japanese directors have won critical acclaim worldwide for their unique interpretation of Shakespearean plays. In addition, theater companies from around the world regularly tour Japan.

In Europe and the United States the word "theater" basically covers all theatrical genres, and actors can play in any type of play if they have the appropriate talent and ability. In Japan, however, while Kabuki and Nō actors are free to play in contemporary theater, the severe training required for the traditional forms make it virtually unheard of for contemporary theater actors to participate in Kabuki and Nō. This makes crossover between traditional and contemporary difficult, but there is an increasing

Kamereonzu rippu ("Chameleon's Lip"), directed by Keralino Sandorovich.

number of collaborations seeking to create a new expressive style.

While much has been written about traditional Japanese theater, little has been written on contemporary theater in Japan. This section is intended to address that imbalance and provide an overview of the wide range of contemporary theater genres available. Many play titles are given with the year they were first staged, often thirty or more years ago, but all the plays mentioned here are frequently staged even today. For practical purposes, all names are given in the Japanese style, with family name first and given name second.

Okepi! ("The Orchestra Pit"), a musical written and directed by Mitani Kōki.

Pandora no kane ("Pandora's Bell," 1999)

Written by Noda Hideki. It was staged in 1999 by NODA MAP, directed and performed by Noda, and another performance the same year was directed by Ninagawa Yukio. The play is set both in prewar Nagasaki and Nagasaki of the Old Kingdom, when the queen of the Old Kingdom sacrifices herself to save the country. Noda's intention was to highlight the atrocity of the atomic bombs dropped by the U.S. as well as the Shōwa Emperor's war responsibility. Noda was awarded the government's Art Encouragement Prize and the Kinokuniya Drama Award. NODA MAP received the Yomiuri Theater Award for their production.

Doro ningyo ("The Muddy Merman," 2003)

Written and directed by Kara Jūrō, and first staged by Kara-gumi. Many of Kara's plays take themes from actual incidents. This drama is based on the Isahaya Bay reclamation project, which caused a major dispute between the government and fishing people, treated in a fantastical and emotive manner. Kara received the Yomiuri Literature Award, the Kinokuniya Drama Award, and the Tsuruya Nanboku Drama Award for this play.

Warai no daigaku
("College of Laughter," 1996)

Written by Mitani Kōki. This play is performed by just two actors, who depict a comedy writer and a censor. The play is set in the militaristic Tokyo Metropolitan Police Headquarters when Japan is about to go to war with the U.S.A. The censor at first looks down on the comedies, but gradually begins to realize how interesting comedy can be, and begins to cooperate with the writer to make the scripts even better. As here, many of Mitani's comedies have a story in which people in opposition finally reach mutual understanding and reconciliation.

Tōkyō nōto ("Tokyo Notes," 1994)

Written and directed by Hirata Oriza, and first staged by Seinendan Theater Company. The stage is the lobby of a small art museum in Tokyo, and the play is set in a near future when Europe is at war. Various men and women entering and leaving the lobby are depicted in detail. An early example of the "quiet theater" of the 1990s, in which all the characters whisper.

Mizu no tawamure
("Play of Water," 1998)

Written and directed by Iwamatsu Ryō. Haruki, a single, middle-aged tailor, is in love with the widow of his brother, who committed suicide thirteen years ago. Haruki marries her, but their marriage does not go well and, in a fit of jealousy, he kills her.

Aterui ("Aterui," 2002)

Written by Nakashima Kazuki and directed by Inoue Hidenori, first staged by Gekidan Shinkansen and produced by Shochiku. Nakashima received the Kishida Kunio Drama Award and the Asahi Performing Arts Awards' Akimoto Matsuyo Prize for this play. The play is set in the eighth and ninth centuries in the Tōhoku district of northern Japan. After bringing Tōhoku under his control, the hero Aterui is attacked by the Yamato Government, which was trying to unify the whole of Japan using guerrilla tactics. The conflict between Aterui and the Yamato general Tamuramaro is vividly depicted in this drama. Ichikawa Somegorō VII as Aterui was awarded the government's Art Encouragement Prize for New Artists.

Hebunzu sain ("Heaven's Sign," 1998)

Written and directed by Matsuo Suzuki, and first staged by Otona Keikaku. This play depicts a female college student committed to a mental hospital. Having been sexually abused by her uncle since her teens, the young woman frequently attempted suicide and also killed her neighbor's cats. This play is based on a real incident about a Japanese woman who killed herself, having previously announced on the Internet that she would do so when she turned twenty. Matsuo depicts the ailing society of Japan through aggressive laughter.

Toki no monooki ("Time's Storeroom," 1994)

Written and directed by Nagai Ai, first staged by Nitosha. A comical drama about the family of a middle school teacher who hopes to be a writer. The play is set in Tokyo in the early 1960s, a time of rapid change in Japan, when neighbors would flock to his house to watch television for the first time. It is the first play in Nagai's *Postwar Life* trilogy.

Daruma san ga koronda ("Danger! Mines!" 2004)

Written and directed by Sakate Yōji, first staged by Theatre Company RINKO-GUN. This play comprises four stories dealing with problems caused by landmines. Gangsters are ordered to acquire landmines, Japanese Self-Defense Force soldiers are sent overseas as part of an international peace-keeping force, and villagers become refugees from the damage caused by landmines. Ultimately, though, the play resembles a traditional Japanese children's game, with sometimes comical or surreal scenes.

Keshō ("Makeup," 1982)

Written by Inoue Hisashi and directed by Kimura Kōichi, first staged by Chijinkai Theatre Company. This play has been translated into several languages and has been performed by Nuria Esper of Spain, Francis de la Tour of Britain, and Kim Kumfa of Korea. The heroine of the drama, the chairwoman of a popular theater troupe, tells her story both backstage and onstage, with an unexpected ending.

TRENDS AND PERSONALITIES

SHINGEKI

Shingeki (literally, "new theater") was created in the early twentieth century, when Japan was undergoing rapid modernization based on Western models in most areas of society, from education to industry. *Shingeki* too reflected that trend, being modeled primarily on European theater. Today most *shingeki* plays are written by contemporary Japanese playwrights, although many European and American plays are staged in translation as part of the repertoire.

Many *shingeki* troupes have relatively long histories, such as Bungaku-za (est. 1937), Bunka-za (1942), Haiyū-za (1944), Mingei (1950), Seinen-za (1954), Tokyo Engeki Ensemble (1954), Theater Echo (1956), Subaru (1963), Seinen Gekijō (1966), En (1975), and Mumeijuku (1975). These are all non-profit troupes and are based in and around Tokyo. Also regarded as *shingeki* troupes are Chijinkai Theatre Company (est. 1981), led by the director Kimura Kōichi and Komatsu-za (est. 1983), associated with the playwright Inoue Hisashi.

A number of famous playwrights came from the *shingeki* tradition. Of those who emerged after World War II, the most remarkable were the well-known novelists Mishima Yukio (1925–70) and Abe Kōbō (1924–93)

who also wrote for the theater, and the leading feminist playwright Akimoto Matsuyo (1911–2001). The *shingeki* playwrights Kinoshita Junji (b. 1914), Miyamoto Ken (1926–88), Fukuda Yoshiyuki (b. 1931) and Yamazaki Masakazu (b. 1934) are particularly known for their plays addressing social issues.

Unique among the *shingeki* troupes is the Shiki Theatre Company (est. 1954), led by the director Asari Keita and featured in this chapter. Shiki specializes in musicals and has been hugely successful, enabling Shiki to open several theaters throughout Japan.

Yūrei wa koko ni iru ("The Ghost is Here"), written by Abe Kōbō.

SHŌGEKIJŌ

The *shōgekijō* (literally, "small theater") movement emerged in Tokyo in the 1960s against the backdrop of student protests. Young unknown actors and directors took to borrowing or renting cheap, small spaces and turned them into rehearsal rooms or theaters. Being free of the influence of mainstream theater groups enabled them to stage ambitious experimental plays and explore new territories. Unlike the realism-oriented *shingeki*, they chose to depict non-reality rather than reality, dreams and fantasies rather than daily life. Reflecting its somewhat political nature, this alternative theater movement was also known as *angura*, the Japanese abbreviation of "underground." Although *angura* had died out by the end of the 1970s, the experimental spirit of the movement still inspires new generations and can be seen in *shōgekijō* today.

Many of the people who started out in the *shōgekijō* movement in the 1960s are still active, and are featured in this chapter, such as the well-known directors Ninagawa Yukio, Suzuki Tadashi,

Shōjo kamen (see text) performed in a red tent.

Aohigekō no shiro ("Bluebeard's Castle"), written by Terayama Shūji, directed by Ryūzanji Show.

and Kushida Kazuyoshi, and playwrights Kara Jūrō, Betsuyaku Minoru, Shimizu Kunio, Satō Makoto (b. 1943), Ōta Shōgo, and Saitō Ren. Among those now deceased are Terayama Shūji (1935–83), part of the "eternal avant-garde," whose troupe Tenjō Sajiki staged a number of radical experimental plays including performances overseas, and whose plays are still frequently staged.

Sunafukin no tegami ("A Letter from Snufkin"), written and directed by Kōkami Shōji.

Although *shōgekijō* started out in small theaters, in the 1980s some of the troupes achieved widespread popularity, such as Noda Hideki's Yume no Yūminsha, and Daisan Butai, led by Kōkami Shōji (b. 1958), a gifted playwright-director whose works are staged today as KOKAMI@network series. With the support of commercial enterprise, they took to playing long-run performances at large theaters. In short, the "small theater" movement that had once staged mainly non-profit experimental plays began to change with the times.

The standard-bearers of the early *shōgekijō* movement were severely critical of *shingeki*, and there were strong antagonistic feelings between the two groups. Today, however, the differences between *shingeki* and *shōgekijō* are much less clearly defined, and both are now often referred to under the general term *gendaigeki*, or "contemporary drama."

WRITERS, DIRECTORS, AND ACTORS

In contemporary Japanese theater, and especially in *shōgekijō*, playwrights are also often troupe leaders, directors, and sometimes even actors in their own productions. The following are examples of such all-round talents.

KARA JŪRŌ

Kara Jūrō (b.1940) is a symbol of the *shōgekijō* movement. He started out with Jōkyō Gekijō from 1963 to 1988, and established the Kara-gumi troupe in 1988. Since 1967, he has rejected indoor theaters in favor of holding performances throughout Japan in a red tent, once even being arrested for performing in a Tokyo park without a permit.

Kara's plays are replete with fantastic and complicated storylines, sweet lyricism, popular laughter, and wild vitality. They give the audience a feeling of freedom as well as a sense of liberation. *Doro ningyo* ("The Muddy Merman," 2003) received the Yomiuri Literature Award, the Kinokuniya Drama Award, and Tsuruya Nanboku Drama Award. Kara has been a professor at Yokohama National University since 1997.

Shōjo kamen **("The Virgin's Mask," 1969)**
A drama set in a cafe run by a woman who is a self-styled Takarazuka star, analyzing the relationship between body and action. This play was awarded the prestigious Kishida Kunio Drama Award in 1970, just when Kara was establishing himself as a first-class playwright.

Kyūketsu ki **("The Vampire Princess," 1971)**
The unconventional career of a nurse, adapted from the popular love story *Aizen Katsura* that was made into a film in 1938.

Shōjo toshi kara no yobigoe
("A Cry from the City of Virgins," 1985)
A fantasy depicting the incestuous love of a young man for his sister.

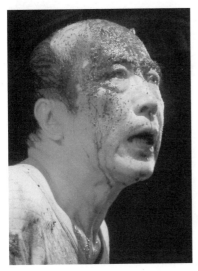

Doro ningyo (see text)

NODA HIDEKI

Noda Hideki (b. 1955) is known for eccentric and creative large-scale dramas. Noda established his Yume no Yūminsha troupe while at Tokyo University. The eccentric ideas, bohemian playfulness and light lyricism in his plays made him very popular with young people and he became the representative Japanese playwright of the 1980s. *Nokemono kitarite* ("Here Comes a Wild Beast," 1984) was performed at the Edinburgh Festival in 1987 and he returned the following year with *Hanshin* ("The Demi-God"). In 1988 he also performed *Suisei no shisha* ("Comet Messenger Siegfried") in New York. At the peak of his popularity in 1992, Noda disbanded Yume no Yūminsha and went to England for a year, after which he established his current company, NODA MAP. He is still so popular that his performances are usually sold out in advance.

Since the 1990s, Noda's plays have begun to criticize both the Japanese nation and society. *Pandora no kane* ("Pandora's Bell," 1999), dealing with the U.S. dropping of the A-bombs and the Emperor's war responsibility, was awarded the Yomiuri Drama Award. In 2003 he directed and staged an English-language version of his *Akaoni* ("The Red Demon Akaoni") in London using a British cast.

Hanshin (see text), by Noda Hideki (center).

Akaoni (see text)

Noda's experimental plays are far from realistic and invite the audience to a mysterious labyrinthine world. Often impressive climaxes solve all the puzzles presented during the play. His dramas are not always easy to understand, but they attract large audiences because of their magnificent storylines, fast stage development, and charming mysteries.

Nokemono kitarite ("Here Comes a Wild Beast," 1984)

A boxer who made his debut on the day the Apollo mission landed on the moon meets the two Heian-period authors Murasaki Shikibu and Sei Shōnagon. Two totally different dimensions are united in this typical Noda drama.

Hanshin ("The Demi-God," 1986)

This play is about an operation to separate Siamese twin sisters with quite different characters and mental capacities. It is based on a short comic story by Hagio Moto, and won the Kinokuniya Drama Award.

Akaoni ("The Red Demon Akaoni," 1996)

An allegorical drama set in an island country where different cultures are received or rejected, depicting the conflict between villagers who hope to drive aliens away and women who hope to welcome them.

Nokemono kitarete (see text)

MATSUO SUZUKI

Matsuo Suzuki (b. 1962) established his troupe Otona Keikaku in 1988. Like Noda, Matsuo has distinguished himself through a storm of controversy. He ranks as one of the most aggressive playwrights of the 1990s.

Matsuo depicts what he calls "reality worse than a nightmare" in a wild style that highlights the weaknesses of his characters. His stories are similar to manga-type caricatures, but often turn into serious tragedies. Influenced by the works of Kurt Vonnegut, Matsuo's plays pivot around absurdist, horrifying dramas filled with black humor.

In *Fankī—uchū wa mieru tokoro made shika nai* ("Funky—Space Is Just As Far As You Can See," 1996), for example, Matsuo dealt with the incestuous relationship between a paralyzed girl and her father. Handicapped people rarely appear in Japanese theater, movies, or TV dramas, but if they do they are generally depicted as being "noble." Here, however, Matsuo's self-proclaimed intention was to "make handicapped people the true target of laughter."

Other well-known works by Matsuo include *Hebunzu sain* ("Heaven's Sign," 1998), *Haha o nigasu* ("Let Mother Loose," 1999), and *Erosu no hate* ("Future of Eros," 2001). *Ningen gowasan* ("People Starting Afresh," 2003) is about a character who wants to become a great playwright and wishes classic authors Nanboku and Mokuami could take him on as their student, and stars the Kabuki actor Nakamura Kankurō V.

Eros no hate ("Future of Eros," 2001)
Set in 2019, the year the protagonist Saigo—who was born in a whorehouse and abandoned by his mother—turns twenty, when Eros has lost all eroticism. The play poses the question "What is the ultimate eroticism?"

Ningen gowasan (see text), by Matsuo Suzuki (left)

COMEDY WRITERS

Comedy is very popular in contemporary Japanese theater, especially with young audiences. Until the 1950s and 1960s, when *shingeki* entered the mainstream of the theatrical world, audiences preferred realistic social dramas. Some *shingeki* playwrights wrote comedies, such as Iizawa Tadasu (1909–94) who specialized in high satire, and it was seen as a branch of *shingeki*. This began to change in the 1970s, and Inoue Hisashi and Tsuka Kōhei, in particular, found a greater role for the genre.

INOUE HISASHI

Born in Tōhoku in northern Japan, Inoue Hisashi (b. 1934) first won popularity as a TV and radio drama writer. Soon after, his comedy *Nihonjin no heso* ("The Navel of the Japanese," 1969) created a sensation, in the wake of which he published such master-pieces as *Yabuhara kengyō* ("Yabuhara, the Blind Master Minstrel," 1973) and *Ame* ("Rain," 1976). Inoue is also popular as an author of humorous novels. Most of his dramas are comedies rich in surprising ideas and entertaining elements, as well as sharply pointed social criticism. Inoue's attitude has been likened to that of Molière, who

Yabuhara kengyō (see text)

said, "The duty of comedy lies in correcting people while pleasing them." Inoue himself says he has been influenced by Brecht. He also writes musical comedies strongly criticizing society.

Many of Inoue's plays are written in the form of biographies depicting the life of the literati. Representative works in this genre include *Īhatobo no geki-ressha* ("Drama Train from Īhatobo," 1980), about Miyazawa Kenji, a well-known fairy tale writer and poet; *Zutsū katakori Higuchi Ichiyō* ("Headache, Stiff Shoulders—Higuchi Ichiyō," 1984), about Higuchi Ichiyō, a Meiji period female author; and *Ningen gōkaku* ("Worthy to be Human," 1989), which comically depicts the life of Dazai Osamu, an author notorious for his bohemian lifestyle and suicide. Another excellent play is *Keshō* ("Makeup," 1982), performed by a single actress depicting the female leader of a popular troupe.

In 1984, Inoue founded the Komatsu-za troupe in Tokyo in order to stage his own plays. His plays are also staged by the Chijinkai Theatre Company led by the director Kimura Kōichi, as well as at the New National Theatre. Inoue was the first president of Nihon Gekisakka Kyōkai ("Japan Playwrights Association") from 1993–1998.

Yabuhara kengyō ("Yabuhara, The Blind Master Minstrel," 1973)
Set in the Edo period, this is the story of a poor blind boy from North Japan who rises in the world, accumulating various evils as he does so.

TSUKA KŌHEI

A second generation Korean living in Japan, Tsuka Kōhei (b. 1948) started his theatrical activities at Keio University in Tokyo, and was an overnight sensation in *Atami satsujin jiken* ("The Atami Murder Case," 1973). He established the Tsuka Kōhei Jimusho troupe in 1974.

Teaming up with other actors of his generation, he directed many of his own works, including *Yūbinya-san chotto* ("Hey, Mailman"), *Shokyū kakumei kōza—hiryū den* ("Revolution for Beginners: Legend of the Flying Dragon"), and *Sensō de shinenakatta otōsan no tame ni* ("For Father, Who Couldn't Die in the War"). He became very popular with the younger generation. After publishing *Kamata kōshinkyoku* ("The Kamata March," 1980), which was made into a film, Tsuka stopped working in theater for five years and concentrated on writing novels. In 1987 he returned to the theater, but the plays dating from that time are mostly revisions of his past works, and are less effective.

The Tsuka boom in the 1970s was largely due to the ironical, warped nature of his comedies that appeared to reflect the sense of emptiness felt by many young people after the failure of the student protest movement. Tsuka's plays strip Japanese people of their superficial modesty and depict them as they really are. The principles of postwar democracy and left-wing ideology are likewise mercilessly unmasked and made the target of laughter. His objective, critical eyes are always conscious of himself as a Korean living in Japanese society. Tsuka's comedies had a strong influence on the playwrights of the younger generation.

Atami satsujin jiken
("The Atami Murder Case," 1973)
Three detectives investigate a suspect with unusual and dramatic methods.

Kamata kōshinkyoku
("The Kamata March," 1980)
This play depicts the unusual relationship between an arrogant star actor, an actress (his lover), and a bit-part actor.

Atami satsujin jiken (see text)

NAGAI AI

Nagai Ai (b. 1951) began as an actress but turned to writing and directing. She founded the Nitosha group in 1981 with Ōishi Shizuka, also a former actress. She is well known as a writer of comedies dealing with social problems from a feminist point of view.

Her works have been constantly in print since the 1990s, and she became the president of the Japan Playwrights Association in 2002. Recently Nagai has written many new plays for various troupes and theaters other than her own Nitosha company.

Nagai depicts the changing society of Japan from the viewpoint of ordinary people rather than the machinations of the elite. Typical is her trilogy, *Sengo seikatsu shigeki* ("Postwar Life"), set in postwar Tokyo, comprising *Toki no mono oki* ("Time's Storeroom," 1994); *Papa no demokurashī* ("Daddy's Democracy," 1995), a comedy of civilian life in Tokyo in the aftermath of World War II; and *Boku no Tōkyō nikki* ("My Tokyo Diary," 1996), depicting the life of students, actresses, and others in an apartment house in Tokyo in the midst of the radical political movements of the early 1970s.

Women are always at the center of Nagai's plays as in *Miyo hikōki no takaku toberu o* ("Behold How High the Plane Is Flying," 1997), which

Hagike no san shimai (see text)

sympathetically depicts a group of girl students who start a strike against the management of a women's teaching college in the Meiji Period, 'Ra' nuki no satsui ("Murderous Impulse without 'Ra'," 1997), a comedy attacking the structure of the contemporary Japanese language and its frequent use of masculine expressions, and Hagi-ke no san shimai ("The Three Sisters of the Hagi Family," 2000), a study of contemporary women's lives, shifting the setting of Chekhov's "Three Sisters" to contemporary Japan.

MITANI KŌKI

Mitani Kōki (b. 1961) is one of Japan's most popular comedy writers for both stage and TV. He established a troupe called Tokyo Sunshine Boys in 1983

and has been working as a freelance writer since 1994. Mitani has been influenced greatly by popular American culture such as the films of Billy Wilder and the plays of Neal Simon. Although he started out in shōgekijō, Mitani has no interest in avant-garde plays. His works depict real life, are very easy to understand, and are filled with warm laughter. Unlike Inoue Hisashi and Nagai Ai, who write comedies dealing with social problems, Mitani pursues the fun of comedy as pure entertainment. Since the 1990s, his works have been staged mostly at the Parco Theater in Tokyo.

The content of Mitani's quick-witted comedies varies greatly. Shō masuto gō on ("The Show Must Go On," 1991), Radio no jikan ("Radio Time," 1993), and Yū ā za toppu— Koyoi no kimi ("You Are the Top—

Matoryōshika (see text)

You, Tonight," 2002), depict the entertainment world of theatrical troupes and radio stations, while *Hikoma ga yuku* ("Hikoma, the Hero," 1990) and *Ryoma no tsuma to sono otto to aijin* ("Ryoma's Wife, and Her Husband and Lover," 2000) are both period dramas. *Matoryōshika* ("The Russian Doll," 1999) is full of intrigue, while *12-nin no yasashii Nihonjin* ("Twelve Gentle Japanese"), a Japanese version of Reginald Rose's play *Twelve Angry Men*, comically depicts the characteristics of Japanese people who are not good at thinking logically and tend to sheepishly follow each other. Matani's masterpiece is *Warai no daigaku* ("College of Laughter," 1996), performed by just two actors.

Matoryōshika ("The Russian Doll," 1999)
An audition held by a veteran actor to find his successor on the stage gives an unexpected result. This play full of suspense was first staged by Theatre IX, a company created by the Kabuki actor Matsumoto Kōshirō IX to produce top modern Japanese theater.

"WELL-MADE" PLAYS

During the 1990s, playful and skillful playwrights such as Mitani Kōki emerged with so-called *ueru meido purei*—literally, "well-made plays"—that are easy-to-understand, popular entertainment. Sometimes criticized as superficial or commercial, these plays simply aim to entertain, in contrast to the dramas dealing with serious issues that make up the mainstay of contemporary Japanese theater.

MAKINO NOZOMI

Makino Nozomi (b. 1959) heads a troupe called MOP in Kyoto, but he lives in Tokyo and allows his plays to be performed by other troupes too. Makino's best-known works include *Tōkyō genshikaku kurabu* ("Tokyo Atomic Club," 1997); *Mazā—Kimi shini tamau koto nakare* ("Mother—Please Don't Die," 1994), a humorous portrayal of Meiji-period literati such as the poet Yosano Akiko; *Fuyuhiko* ("Fuyuhiko," 1997), a comedy about the essayist and physiscist Terada Torahiko and his family. *Akashatsu* ("Red Shirt," 2001) is an eccentric comedy based on Natsume Sōseki's famous novel *Botchan* (1907), but whereas the novel is written from the perspective of Botchan, a young teacher with a strong sense of justice, the play is written from the viewpoint of a villain. Another excellent drama is *Takaki kanomono* ("That Thing on High," 2000), about a mentally retarded teenage student trying for college.

Tōkyō genshikaku kurabu
("Tokyo Atomic Club," 1997)

This play is modeled on Tomonaga Shinichirō, Japan's Nobel Prize-winning atomic physicist. Although Japan is the only country to have suffered the disaster of two atomic bombs, this play reveals the fact that Japan too had a project to develop A-bombs during World War II. Complex feelings are unleashed when the physicist protagonist states that he would not hesitate to develop an atomic bomb for the purpose of "research into the laws of nature." Although the play has a serious theme, it unfolds in a humorous way, a characteristic of this new generation of playwrights.

Tōkyō genshikaku kurabu (see text)

Hōōchō no hinin hō ("Rhythm Method," 1994)

Hōōchō no hinin hō ("Rhythm Method") is a comedy cowritten by Iijima Sanae and Suzuki Yumi, and first staged by the all-female troupe Jitensha Kinqureat's Company in 1994. It is about Ogino Kyūsaku, a Japanese obstetrician and gynecologist, who, before World War II, invented the "Ogino-style Contraceptive Method."

Hōōchō no hinin hō

Ginga senritsu (see text)

CARAMELBOX

Another playwright popular with younger theater audiences is Narui Yutaka (b. 1961), leader of the troupe Caramelbox established in 1985. Caramelbox began as *shōgekijō*, but they are so popular that they have been giving long-run performances at large theaters since the 1990s. Narui's best works include *Fushigina kurisumasu no tsukurikata* ("Recipe for a Strange Christmas," 1988), *Ginga senritsu* ("Stardust Melody," 1989), and *Hakkuruberī ni sayonara o* ("Farewell My Huckleberry," 1991).

GEKIDAN SHINKANSEN

Gekidan Shinkansen was founded by the students of Osaka University of Arts in 1980 under the director Inoue Hidenori (b. 1960), with plays written by Nakashima Kazuki. It rapidly gained in popularity, and now also performs in Tokyo, with shows featuring heavy metal rock music and such charismatic

actors as Furuta Arata. Some plays set in Japan's legendary past directed by Inoue are called "Inoue Kabuki" because of their strong appeal and highly entertaining elements. These include *Dokuro-jō no shichinin* ("Seven Souls in Skull Castle,"1990), *Yajūrō kenzan* ("Beast is Red," 1996) and *Rosuto sebun* ("Lost Seven," 1999). In collaboration with Shochiku, Gekidan Shinkansen staged *Ashura-jō no hitomi* ("Blood Gets in Your Eyes," 1987) in 2000 and 2003, and also *Aterui* ("Aterui," 2002), both starring the young Kabuki actor Ichikawa Somegorō VII, to great acclaim.

Dokuro-jō no shichinin (see text)

THEATER OF THE ABSURD

The Japanese translation of Samuel Beckett's *Waiting for Godot* (1953), one of the best-known plays of the theater of the absurd, was published in 1956, and the Bungaku-za first staged it in 1960. Its influence on Japanese playwrights and directors has been far-reaching.

BETSUYAKU MINORU

Strongly influenced by *Godot* during his college days, Betsuyaku Minoru (b. 1937) is the playwright who established the theater of the absurd, or *fujōrigeki*, in Japan. Betsuyaku's plays always feature well-spoken male and female petit bourgeois characters, and take place on a simple stage, almost devoid of sets or props.

Betsuyaku first shocked his audiences with *Zō* ("The Elephant," 1962), which, with surprising style and sensi-

Macchi uri no shōjo (see text)

tivity, depicts people suffering from the aftermath of the atomic bomb against the background of a hospital in Hiroshima. Another early work, *Macchi uri no shōjo* ("The Little Match Girl," 1966), critically depicts Japan's postwar social systems, employing the motif of Andersen's fairy tale. Betsuyaku is a prolific writer and has already published more than a hundred dramas, including *Nishi muku samurai* ("The Samurai Facing West," 1977), *Mazā, mazā, mazā* ("Mother, Mother, Mother," 1979), *Byōki* ("Sickness," 1981) and *Giobanni no chichi e no tabi* ("A Journey toward Giovanni's Father," 1987). He was the president of the Japan Playwrights Association from 1998 to 2002.

Macchi uri no shōjo
("The Little Match Girl," 1966)
A young woman visits the home of a middle-aged couple claiming she is their daughter who died in an accident when she was a little girl.

Nishi muku samurai
("The Samurai Facing West," 1977)
A drama about two couples who are forced to lead a homeless life, and a beggar who becomes their victim.

Furōzun bīchi
(see text)

KERALINO SANDOROVICH (KERA)

Keralino Sandorovich (b. 1963) is Japanese, but uses a European pen name. He started out as a rock musician, but in the 1980s began to write plays, and established his troupe Nylon 100°C in 1993. He is highly acclaimed as a writer of absurdist comedies with black humor. The multitalented KERA has written plays in various styles. *Uchi wa sobaya ja nai* ("We Aren't a Noodle Shop," 1992) is a farce, while *Karafuru merii de ohayo* ("Good Morning with Colorful Merry," 1988) is written in the "I-novel" confessional style, and is based on his father's death. Other well-known plays are *Kafukazu dikku* ("Kafka's Dick," 2001), a unique, critical biography of Kafka portrayed from the viewpoint of the women around him; and *Subete no inu wa tengoku e iku* ("Every Dog Goes to Heaven," 2001), an absurdist-style Western for an all-female cast.

Furōzun bīchi ("Frozen Beach," 1998)
First staged by Nylon 100°C, and awarded the Kishida Kunio Drama Award. This suspenseful comedy is played out by four women living in a villa on an island.

MIYAZAWA AKIO

Another playwright influenced by Beckett is Miyazawa Akio (b. 1956), who established the theater group U-enchi Saisei Jigyōdan. His main works include *Hinemi* ("Hinemi," 1992), *Suna no kuni no tōi koe* ("A Distance Voice from the Country of Sand," 1994), and *Suna ni shizumu tsuki* ("The Moon Sinking into the Sand," 1999).

Hinemi ("Hinemi," 1992)
A man born in a town called Hinemi, which is now lost, tries to draw a map of that town. It was awarded the Kishida Kunio Drama Award.

Hinemi (see text)

"QUIET" THEATER

Many new theaters opened in Tokyo and Osaka during the bubble economy of the 1980s, and entrepreneurs began inviting Broadway shows to perform in Japan. In the 1990's, however, the bubble burst, plunging the country into a prolonged recession. This mood of the time was reflected in a more subdued style of acting depicting quiet moments in daily life, in contrast to the large scale and fast action of plays by, for example, Noda Hideki or Kōkami Shōji. This movement came to be known as *shizuka na engeki*, or "quiet" theater.

HIRATA ORIZA

Hirata Oriza (b.1962) established the Seinendan Theater Company in 1983. At first influenced by Noda Hideki, Hirata changed his style toward the end of the 1980s, and began to write what he calls "contemporary colloquial theater," portraying ordinary life directly on the stage with dialogues that dispassionately unfold as tender miniatures. Hirata's best-known works include *Sōru shimin* ("Citizens of Seoul," 1989), *Minami e* ("To the South," 1990), *Hokugen no saru* ("Northernmost Monkeys," 1992) *Kataku ka shura ka* ("Burning House, or a Shambles?" 1995), and *Barukan dōbutsuen* ("The Balkan Zoo," 1997).

In Hirata's plays actors speak almost in a whisper, and sometimes multiple conversations are held simultaneously. Stage sets are unchanging and there is no music. Hirata has said he aims to avoid producing plays that assert any doctrine, striving instead to create dramas that directly portray the world. This is clearly seen in *Tōkyō nōto* ("Tokyo Notes," 1994), which has also been staged in Europe, the United States, and Australia. This play was inspired by *Tōkyō monogatari* ("Tokyo Story"), the 1953 classic movie directed by Ozu Yasujirō (1903–63).

HASEGAWA KŌJI

Hasegawa Kōji's (b. 1956) Hirosaki Gekijō theater company is based in Aomori Prefecture, and also performs at theaters throughout Japan and abroad. Originally influenced by Kara

Ie ni wa takai ki ga atta (see text)

Jūrō, Hasegawa changed his style in the late 1980s and took to writing plays about people living in provincial cities. Like Hirata, Hasegawa avoids making any assertions in his dramas but instead depicts ordinary men and women in realistic speech, often with local dialect. His representative works include *Ie ni wa takai ki ga atta* ("A House with a Big Tree," 1994). Himself a high school teacher, Hasegawa has written plays in a school setting, such as *Shokuin shitsu no gogo* ("Afternoon in the Staff Room," 1995) and *Kyūkei shitsu* ("The Rest Room," 1997).

IWAMATSU RYŌ

Iwamatsu Ryō (b. 1952) caught the attention of the public as a house writer for Gekidan Tokyo Kandenchi ("Tokyo Dry Cell Theater Group"), led by Emoto Akira in the 1980s. His *Chōnai-geki* ("My Town") trilogy comically depicts the town's residents, in *Ocha to sekkyō* ("Tea and Remonstrance," 1986), *Daidokoro no tomoshibi* ("The Kitchen Lamp," 1987), and *Ren'ai gohatto* ("Love is Forbidden," 1987)

in which Iwamatsu reportedly tried to maintain a lazy lack of tension, intentionally avoiding dramatic climaxes. His *Futon to daruma* ("Bedding and a *Daruma* Doll," 1988) was awarded the Kishida Kunio Drama Award.

Iwamatsu left Gekidan Tokyo Kandenchi in 1992 and began to write plays about rather more mysterious and deeper human relationships. He wrote and directed plays to high acclaim for the popular actors' project Takenaka Naoto no Kai, including *Gekkō no tsu-tsushimi* ("The Moonlight," 1994) and *Terebi deizu* ("TV Days," 1996). *Mizu no tawamure* ("Play of Water," 1998) seems to hint at Chekhov's *Uncle Vanya*. Iwamatsu likes to depict the inner chaos of the human situation, and he leaves much of the drama to the imagination of the audience. *Natsu hoteru* ("Hotel Summer," 2001) by Theatre IX, the story of a magician and his troupe's members set in the hotel where Chekhov died; *Wani o sude de tsuka-maeru hōhō* ("To Catch an Alligator with Bare Hands," 2004); and *Shibuya kara tōku hanarete* ("Far Away from Shibuya," 2004) were well received.

Natsu hoteru
(see text)

PLAYWRIGHTS WITH A SOCIAL CONSCIENCE

Some playwrights, like Inoue Hisashi, who was referred to in the Comedy section, depict the reality of life in Japan in a critical light. Strongly influenced by Bertolt Brecht, Inoue vividly depicts social themes in a casual, humorous way, while others take a more serious approach.

SAITŌ REN

Saitō Ren (b.1940) is an independent writer whose works range from period plays and biographical dramas to musicals. His best known works are *Shanhai bansu kingu* ("Shanghai Vance King," 1979); *Kusuko* ("Kusuko," 1982), based on the Kusuko Incident of 810; *Gurei Kurisumasu* ("Gray Christmas," 1983); and *Burehito Opera* ("Brecht Opera," 1999).

SAKATE YŌJI

Sakate Yōji (b. 1962) established his Theatre Company RINKO-GUN in 1983, and it is known for its radical anti-authority and critical stance. Many of Sakate's plays deal with social

Tennō to seppun ("The Emperor and the Kiss")

issues: *Kamuauto* ("Come Out," 1989) depicts lesbians in Japan; *Buresuresu* ("Breathless," 1990) deals with the garbage problems facing Tokyo; and *Kujira no bohyō* ("Epitaph of the Whales," 1993), is about the whaling fishermen forced to give up their work. Other remarkable plays are *Kamigami no kuni no shuto* ("The Capital of the Country of Gods," 1993), a biographical drama about the author Lafcadio Hearn; and *Daruma san ga koronda* ("Danger! Mines!" 2004).

KANESHITA TATSUO

Kaneshita Tatsuo (b. 1964) established THE GAZIRA Theater Company in 1987. Most of his plays depict people in extreme situations such as crime and war. His major works include *Tatsuya* ("Tatsuya," 1991), about a serial killer; *Kanka* ("Ice Blossoms," 1997), about the Korean independence activist who assassinated the Japanese politician Ito Hirobumi; and *Musabori to ikari to orokasa to* ("Greed, Anger, and Foolishness," 1998), which depicts a family falling apart as the bubble economy collapses.

Musabori to ikari to orokasa to (see text)

DIRECTORS

Since the 1960s, theater in Europe and the United States has centered around directors, with such big names as Peter Brook, Giorgio Strehler, Jurij Ljubimov, Jerzy Grotowski, and Robert Wilson. In Japan it is less common to specialize in a particular aspect of a play's production, and there are fewer specialist directors in the all-powerful Western sense. Kara Jūrō, Tsuka Kōhei, Noda Hideki, Nagai Ai, Mitani Kōki, Hirata Oriza, Matsuo Suzuki and Sakate Yōji, for example, are all playwrights who also direct their own works. There are, however, a few individuals who have proved themselves gifted and creative directors in their own right.

NINAGAWA YUKIO

Ninagawa Yukio (b. 1935) is the artistic director of the Theatre Cocoon in Tokyo, and is the best-known Japanese director internationally. He became a professor at Toho Gakuen College of Drama and Music in 1993 and its president in 2003. Having started out as a *shingeki* actor, Ninagawa formed a *shōgekijō* troupe called Gendaijin Gekijō in 1968. The next year he directed *Shinjō afururu keihakusa* ("Such a Serious Frivolity") written by Shimizu Kunio (b. 1936), which depicted a quarrel between people waiting in a line and a young couple. His style of directing, with stunning

Shinjō afururu keihakusa (see text)

visual effects and vitality, was an overnight sensation. Ninagawa has since directed a number of plays by Shimizu. He is adept at handling large-scale productions, while his background in *shōgekijō* has given him in an interest in the experimental.

Since 1974, Ninagawa has directed highly popular Shakespearean and Greek tragedies for Toho, one of Japan's major entertainment companies. He always respects the text of the play: even when directing a classical play, he rarely omits any lines or adapts it in any way. He does, however, frequently place it in a Japanese or Asian setting, to rich visual effect. His first Asia-oriented Greek tragedy was *Medea* by Euripides, first staged in 1978, and with the male actor Hira Mikijirō in the role of Medea, reminiscent of the *onnagata* of Kabuki. The sixteen members of the Chorus were all men, too, and played the *tsugaru jamisen*, a traditional Japanese musical instrument. From 1983 *Medea* was staged in Rome, Athens, London, and New York, to critical acclaim. Ninagawa's production of *Macbeth*, first staged in 1980, was also a big hit. Ninagawa's Shakespeare plays are dealt with in more detail on page 251.

SUZUKI TADASHI

Suzuki Tadashi (b. 1939) is a director in total contrast to Ninagawa. Both directors have adapted Greek tragedies and Shakespeare, but whereas Ninagawa creates spectacular, large-scale productions, Suzuki removes all unnecessary decoration to create sparse, concentrated theater. Ninagawa could be likened to the flamboyant Kabuki, while Suzuki's work is more akin to the refined Nō.

Suzuki started directing at Waseda University in Tokyo. In 1966 he founded a troupe called Waseda Shōgekijō with the playwright Betsuyaku Minoru, and their first production was Betsuyaku's *Macchi uri no shōjo*. However, Betsuyaku resigned from the troupe in 1968. Teaming up with the actress Shiraishi Kayoko, Suzuki then successfully directed *Gekiteki naru mono o megutte II* ("On the Dramatic Passions Part II," 1970). The play depicts an insane woman (excellently played by Shiraishi) confined in a room, reenacting fragments of famous dramas. Suzuki's direction and Shiraishi's shocking performance won great praise. Since 1972 this play has been repeatedly staged in both Europe and the United States.

Suzuki has also successfully directed classical dramas such as his epoch-making version of Euripides's *The Trojan Women* in 1974. The original play is about the passions of Trojan women after their defeat in the Trojan War. Suzuki treated the drama as a "Trojan fantasy" of an old Japanese man living in the ruins of a fire after World War II. Employing traditional Japanese clothes, customs, and manners, a play was created that was both Greek tragedy and Japanese drama. *The Bacchae* (1978), *King Lear* (1984), and *Dionysos* (1990), all of which also toured Europe and the United States, are further examples of such reconstructions. Suzuki rarely stages dramas as they are written and often interprets them in his own way or combines them with other works. Unlike Ninagawa, Suzuki is the type of director who makes up his own plays, rather than devote himself to a slavish interpretation of the writer's text.

He is also known internationally for his "Suzuki Method" of training actors (not to be confused with the music education method of the same name), which is inspired by the acting techniques of traditional Japanese theater and is effective for dramas requiring a more stylized mode of acting.

Dionysos (see text)

KUSHIDA KAZUYOSHI

Kushida Kazuyoshi (b. 1942) started out in the 1960s in *shōgekijō*, and is well-known for his unique style of directing. He is also an actor, and frequently appears in his own productions. Having dropped out of the Nihon University College of Art in Tokyo, he studied at the Haiyū-za Theatre Company actors' studio and went on to act in the *shōgekijō* troupe Gekidan Jiyū Gekijō formed by graduates of the Haiyū-za in 1966. In 1976, Kushida formed the On Theatre Jiyū Gekijō troupe.

Kushida is a "hands on" director, and his productions use a great deal of music, often requiring the actors to play the instruments themselves, such as *Shanhai bansu kingu* (written by Saitō Ren, with music by Koshibe Nobuyoshi) in which the actors must play the prewar jazz for themselves. This play became a great hit, and has also been made into a film. Other plays directed by Kushida include *Motto naiteyo furappā* ("Cry More, Flapper," 1977), a musical about gangs, show girls, and newsrooms in Chicago in the 1920s; *Kusuko* ("Kusuko," 1982); *Sukapan* ("Scapin," 1994); and *A Midsummer Night's Dream*, 1994.

Partly helped by the great popularity of *Shanhai bansu kingu*, On Theatre Jiyū Gekijō went under contract to Theatre Cocoon in Tokyo, and Kushida became the theater's art director. Since 1994 Kushida has been working with the Kabuki actor Nakamura Kankurō V to produce the "Cocoon Kabuki" series, a stimulating blend of traditional and contemporary theater (see page 241). On Theatre Jiyū Gekijō disbanded in 1996 and Kushida became a freelance director. He is now a professor in the Nihon University College of Art, and in 2003 he became artistic director at Matsumoto Performing Arts Centre in Nagano Prefecture.

Good Woman of Setsuan, written by Brecht, directed by Kushida Kazuyoshi.

Shanhai bansu kingu (see text)

MATSUMOTO YŪKICHI

Having started out in *shōgekijō*, Matsu-moto Yūkichi (b.1946) has created a unique dramatic world with his troupe Ishinha. After majoring in fine arts at Osaka University, he founded Nihon Ishinha in Osaka in 1970, and has been writing and directing all of the troupe's plays since 1974. Ishinha, as they have been known since 1987, are noted for their large-scale outdoor performances. The troupe members themselves build the temporary out-door theater with huge stage sets that contribute to the visual impact of their plays. Their productions take the form of unique musicals called "Jan-Jan Opera" in which the actors do not sing, but rather speak rhythmically and chant the lines in an Osaka accent. Set to the dynamic music of Uchihashi Kazuhisa, the effect is rather like rap.

Matsumoto's plays center around boys and girls rather than adults. Chil-dren are often depicted as orphans in a large city, as strong beings able to live on their own, apart from the power and systems of the grownups. In *Aozora* ("Blue Sky," 1994) war orphans band together and manage to survive in a ruined city in the aftermath of World War II, while *Mizumachi* ("Water City," 1999) deals with boys and girls in a slum in an industrial area of Osaka in the early twentieth century. In 2000, Ishinha created a sensation with their performance of *Mizumachi* at the Adelaide Festival in Australia.

Nokutān ("Nocturne"), directed by Matsumoto Yūkichi.

KIMURA KŌICHI

The *shingeki* director Kimura Kōichi (b. 1931) has been with the Chijinkai Theatre Company since 1981. A Tokyo University graduate, Kimura first joined Bungaku-za, one of Japan's major *shingeki* troupes. He made his debut as a director for Arnold Wesker's *Kitchen* in 1963, and went on to direct many plays, including Tennessee Williams' *A Streetcar Named Desire* and Miyamoto Ken's *Utsukushiki mono no densetsu* ("Legend of the Beautiful"), a play about men and women in the theater and socialist movements in Tokyo in the 1910s and 1920s that was first staged by Bungaku-za in 1968. He has also directed Inoue Hisashi's *Yabuhara kengyō*, *Ame*, and *Kobayashi Issa* ("Kobayashi Issa, Haiku Poet," 1979), for which he was highly praised.

Kimura left Bungaku-za in 1980 and established Chijinkai Theatre Company the following year, since when he has directed five or more plays every year, including many by Inoue. He is enthusiastic about performing overseas, and Inoue's one-woman

Utsukushiki mono no densetsu (see text)

play *Keshō*, and *Yabuhara kengyō* were enthusiastically received in both Europe and the United States. Kimura's directing is well-balanced, making a play's theme clear, while creating elaborate visual effects. He often translates European and American dramas into Japanese.

KURIYAMA TAMIYA

After graduating from Waseda University, Kuriyama Tamiya (b. 1953) first worked as an assistant to Kimura Kōichi. He made his debut as a director of Beckett's *Waiting for Godot* in 1983, and was sent to England by Japan's Agency for Cultural Affairs in 1988 to study for a year. As a freelance director, he has worked on a variety of plays ranging from *shōgekijō* to *shingeki* and commercial theater. He has directed many of Inoue Hisashi's plays, such as *Nihonjin no heso*, *Kokugo gannen*, *Mokuami Opera* ("Mokuami Opera"), and *Yume no sakeme* ("A Rift in the Dream"). Kuriyama has also directed a number of translated plays such as *Ghetto* by Joshua Sobol, *Kinder Transport* by Dianne Samuels, and *Long Day's Journey Into Night* by Eugene O'Neill. Kuriyama also directed *Okuni* ("Dancer Okuni") written by Suzuki Satoshi, a musical drama about the female dancer said to be the founder of Kabuki. Since 2000, he has been the art director of the theatrical department of the New National Theatre in Tokyo.

TRADITIONAL MEETS CONTEMPORARY

Being modeled on European theater, *shingeki* has taken a very different direction from the traditional Nō, Kyōgen, Bunraku, and Kabuki theaters. However, some connection between them has been attempted. Mishima Yukio, for example, wrote a number of new Kabuki plays, and also wrote eight excellent one-act plays called *Kindai nōgakushū* ("Collection of Modern Nō Plays") in the 1950s. These stories from Nō plays adapted to a contemporary setting have been translated into several languages, and are frequently staged aboard. While Mishima's Nō plays were written to be performed realistically with no attempt to blend traditional and contemporary theater acting techniques, others have looked for ways to fuse the two theaters.

NOMURA MANSAI

The Kyōgen player Nomura Mansai (b. 1966) is also a popular movie actor, and is the artistic director of the Setagaya Public Theatre in Tokyo. In 1991, Mansai's father, Nomura Mansaku, directed and starred in *Hora zamurai* ("The Braggart Samurai") by Takahashi Yasunari, a Kyōgen-style adaptation of Shakespeare's *The Merry Wives of Windsor*, staged in both Japan and England. In 1994 Mansai went to England for a year on the artist overseas training system promoted by the Agency for Cultural Affairs in order to observe English theater, and in particular new ways of directing the classics. This experience helped him to formulate a Kyōgen-style adaptation of Shakespeare's *The Comedy of Errors*, entitled *Machigai no kyōgen* ("The Kyōgen of Errors," 2001), with a cast of male Kyōgen actors. It was first staged in Tokyo by Mansaku no Kai, with Mansai as director and in the role of

Hora zamurai (see text)

Hamlet, directed by Jonathan Kent.

one of the twin servants, and was staged in July of the same year at Shakespeare's Globe Theatre in London to critical acclaim. Mansai also starred in *Hamlet,* directed by the British director Jonathan Kent at the Setagaya Public Theater in 2003, and in London later the same year. The cast consisted of male actors only, with Ophelia played by the Kabuki actor Nakamura Shinobu I.

SHIGOSEN NO MATSURI ("REQUIEM ON THE GREAT MERIDIAN," 1979)

Shigosen no matsuri is a voluminous work by Kinoshita Junji that attempts to fuse *shingeki* and traditional theater.

Shigosen no matsuri (see text)

Kinoshita is a well-known *shingeki* playwright. His masterpiece *Yūzuru* ("The Twilight Crane," 1949), based on a traditional Japanese folk tale, has been adapted to opera. *Shigosen no matsuri* is based on an episode of the classic *Heike monogatari*, written in dramatic verse. It was new staged by the New National Theatre in 1999 with a cast of young actors, including Nomura Mansai and the Kabuki actor Ichikawa Ukon I.

SUPER KABUKI

Super Kabuki was first produced by the Shochiku company in 1986, starring Ichikawa Ennosuke III (b. 1939). Super Kabuki is an attempt to create a spectacular and popular entertainment with a contemporary pace and new stage facilities, sets, lighting, and sound technology. All the scripts are new, and Ennosuke directs and stars in all of them. The first production was *Yamatotakeru* ("Prince Yamatotakeru," 1986), based on a Japanese myth and written by Umehara Takeshi, a philosopher with a deep knowledge of Japan's history and culture. *Yamatotakeru* was followed by such plays as *Oguri* ("Oguri Hangan," 1991), *Hakkenden* ("The Legend of Eight Warriors," 1993), *Kaguya* ("Kaguya," 1996), and *Shin sangokushi* ("A New History of Three Countries," 1999). These are all spectacular shows drawing on techniques and stage tricks (*keren*) of traditional Kabuki, such as *chūnori* (flying), *hayagawari* (quick onstage costume changes), and *tachi-mawari* (stylized fight scenes).

COCOON KABUKI

Cocoon Kabuki began in 1994 at the Theater Cocoon in Tokyo with a collaboration between artistic director Kushida Kazuyoshi and the popular Kabuki actors Nakamura Kankurō V and Nakamura Hashinosuke III. Their productions are all from the traditional Kabuki repertoire, starting with *Tōkaidō Yotsuya kaidan* in 1994, followed by *Natsumatsuri Naniwa kagami* in 1996, *Kamikakete sango taisetsu* in 1998, *Sannin Kichisa* in 2001 and *Natsumatsuri Naniwa kagami* again in 2003.

Since 1996 Kushida has been in charge of the stage and art direction, which depart significantly from traditional Kabuki. To start with, he removed the seats at the front of the auditorium to make the stage and the seating area the same size. He opened the doors of the backstage loading area so that the street behind is in full view of the audience, and a police patrol car appeared onstage in *Natsumatsuri Naniwa kagami*. Kushida has said that the aim of Cocoon Kabuki is "not to preserve Kabuki as a classic, but to produce a living Kabuki for the present day." Cocoon Kabuki has become very popular and is frequently sold out.

According to Nakamura Kankurō's book *Kabukitta* (1999), the idea of Cocoon Kabuki was sparked by a wildly energetic performance of *Hebihimesama* ("The Snake Princess: Nadja in My Heart") written and directed by Kara Jūrō in 1977. It occurred to Kankurō that such vitality must have been a feature of Kabuki in its early days. Finding classical Kabuki to be somewhat staid, he wished to reintroduce this energy into new-style Kabuki performances.

KANKURŌ AND NODA'S KABUKI

Kankurō has also collaborated with Noda Hideki, starting with Noda's version of *Togitatsu no utare* ("Revenge on Togitatsu"), a *shin kabuki* play first staged in 1925 about two samurai brothers who pursue a former merchant turned samurai. *Noda-ban Togitatsu no utare* was rewritten and directed by Noda and starred Kankurō. Noda used sets, lighting, and costumes designed by people with no experience in Kabuki. He injected a witty playfulness together with new visual effects in order to surprise the audience and make them laugh, and Kankurō's comic acting contributed to the success of the show. Also highlighting social issues, the performance became so controversial that the Kabuki-za, where the play was staged, was sold out every day. The show was awarded the Grand Prix of the Asahi Performing Arts Awards, while Kankurō received an Asahi Performing Arts Award for his performance. In 2003, Noda staged *Noda-ban Nezumi Kozō* ("Noda's Rat Bandit Kozō").

Ōta Shōgo (b. 1939), a playwright and director of the same generation as Suzuki Tadashi (see page 234), creates original "quiet theater" dramas in modern Nō. Music and even speech is rare in his plays, and the actors move extremely slowly. In *Komachi fūden* ("The Legend of Komachi," 1977) they take five minutes just to walk two meters. *Komachi fūden* is based on *Sotoba Komachi* ("Komachi on the Stupa"), a Nō play, and was first staged at a Nō theater in Tokyo. *Mizu no eki* ("Water Station," 1981) is a silent drama in which water runs continuously from a roadside tap as travelers come and go. In the 1980s it was staged in twenty-four countries throughout Europe, the United States, Australia, and Asia. In *Chi no eki* ("Earth Station," 1985), another silent drama by his troupe Tenkei Gekijō, the stage set is made up of accumulated industrial waste such as TV sets, washing

Mizu no eki (see text)

machines, and cars, amidst which men and women come and go without a word. In *Suna no eki* ("Sand Station"), solitary travelers come and go on a stage covered in sand. This drama was first staged in Berlin in 1991, and a revised edition was staged in Fujisawa City in 1993. After Tenkei Gekijō disbanded, Ōta became the artistic director of the Fujisawa Public Theater, on the outskirts of Tokyo, from 1990 to 2000. He continues to direct plays while teaching at Kyoto University of Art and Design.

Komachi fūden (see text)

HANAGUMI SHIBAI

Actor and director Kanō Yukikazu (b. 1960) founded the troupe Hanagumi Shibai in 1987 in order to produce so-called "Neo-Kabuki" dramas. As in Kabuki, Hanagumi Shibai uses male actors for the female roles, but they generally parody classical plays set to traditional Japanese, European classical, and rock music. The troupe's first performance was *Za Sumidagawa* ("The Sumida River," 1987), and it has since staged various plays including *Iroha Yotsuya kaidan* ("Iroha Yotsuya Ghost Story," 1987), *Kabuki-za no kaijin* ("The Phantom of the Kabuki-za," 1989), *Okujochūtachi* ("The Ladies-in-Waiting," 1992), and *Izumi Kyōka no tenshu monogatari* ("Izumi Kyōka's Donjon Story," 1997). Hanagumi Shibai's repertoire also includes *Tenpesuto arashi nochi hare* ("The Tempest —Clear Sky after the Storm," 1994), an adaptation of Shakespeare's *The Tempest*. Recently, Kanō has also directed commercial plays.

Kabuki-za no kaijin (see text)

Okujochūtachi (see text)

MUSICALS IN JAPAN

TAKARAZUKA

Takarazuka Kagekidan ("Takarazuka Revue") occupies a unique position in Japan's entertainment world. Founded in 1913 with its headquarters in Takarazuka City in Hyōgo Prefecture, the company stages colorful musicals and revues performed exclusively by unmarried women. Their performances can be viewed throughout the year at the Takarazuka Grand Theater in Takarazuka City as well as at the Tokyo Takarazuka Theater. Many of the stars go on to careers in theater, TV, and movies after leaving the troupe.

ORGANIZATION

The Takarazuka company comprises approximately four hundred actresses divided into five troupes: *hana gumi* ("Flower Troupe"), *tsuki gumi* ("Moon Troupe"), *yuki gumi* ("Snow Troupe"), *hoshi gumi* ("Star Troupe") and *sora gumi* ("Cosmos Troupe"), the newest of which is the Cosmos Troupe founded in 1998. Each troupe operates separately, although sometimes two or more teams give joint performances.

Altogether, almost one thousand people are employed by the company, including actresses, trainees, and staff members. The company owns the Takarazuka Grand Theater (capacity 2,527), the Takarazuka Bow Hall (capacity 500), and the Tokyo Takarazuka Theater (capacity 2,500). It also runs the Takarazuka Music School to train young actresses, and has its own inhouse orchestra, production crews, directors-playwrights, choreographers, and stage artists.

To become a Takarazuka member, girls must first graduate from the Takarazuka Music School. For that reason all the Takarazuka members are called "students" even if they are stars, and all the production crew, including directors, are called "teachers." With the motto of "Purely, Correctly, and Beautifully," the large company is highly disciplined. The rule that actresses may stay with the troupe only as long as they are unmarried may seem anachronistic today, but Takarazuka remains true to the rules set down by its founder Kobayashi Ichizō (1873–1957).

MALE AND FEMALE ROLE PLAYERS

The charm of the traditional Japanese theatrical tradition of men playing female roles is reversed in Takarazuka. New members are allotted either male or female role parts according to their height, body shape, and vocal range. Most of the Takarazuka fans range from teenagers to middle-aged or older

Berusaiyu no bara (see text)

women, and the overwhelmingly popular stars are those who take the male roles. The central character of a play is always the male role, and it is these actresses who usually continue their acting careers after leaving Takarazuka. The male role actresses Ōtori Ran, Asami Rei, Daichi Mao, Anju Mira, Suzukaze Mayo, Ichiro Maki, and Amami Yūki, for example, all went on to successful acting careers after retiring from Takarazuka.

Although the conventions are not as strict as in Nō or Kabuki, the male-role players do have distinctive techniques for elocution, makeup, hairstyles, and movements that characterize their performance. Just why the predominantly female audience is so fanatical about the male-role actresses has often been questioned. The consensus appears to be that

Takarazuka's male-role players represent a stylized, idealistic, and romanticized image of women's vision of the ideal man. Though lacking in reality, that image expresses a longed-for male charm and sex appeal. That image is perhaps "safer" for women precisely because it is devoid of realism.

REPERTOIRE

Takarazuka's repertoire consists mostly of popular musicals and revues. Takarazuka Kagekidan means literally "Takarazuka Opera," but the company does not stage classical European operas. A program usually comprises two parts: the first is a musical play with a storyline, and the second is a revue. Many of the plays are original, written by the company's own directors. Sometimes novels and dramas are adapted for their shows, including many translated works such as *War and Peace* (1988) and *The Great Gatsby* (1991), as well as classical Japanese literature set to traditional Japanese music and dance, such as *Shin Genji monogatari* ("The New Tale of Genji," 1981) and *Chūshingura* ("The Faithful Forty-Seven," 1991). A European-style orchestra is, however, used to accompany the Japanese plays, too.

Other famous productions include *Berusaiyu no bara* ("La Rose de Versailles," 1974), based on the popular comics for girls by Ikeda Riyoko (adapted by Ueda Shinji and directed by Hasegawa Kazuo). It was an instant hit and led to a "Beru-bara" boom. The tempestuous storyline is set against the background of the eighteenth-century French court, where the commander of the royal guard is a girl disguised as a man, who later participates in the Revolution. From 1974 to 1976, all four Takarazuka troupes staged *Berusaiyu no bara*, drawing a total audience of 1.6 million. *Berusaiyu no bara* was restaged between 1989 and 1991, and again drew an audience of 2.9 million, sparking a second "Beru-bara" boom.

From the 1980s, the Western musicals *Guys and Dolls* (1984), *Me and My Girl* (1987), *Kiss Me Kate* (1988 and 2002), and *Grand Hotel* (1993) were also performed. The central characters of all of these translated musicals are men, following the Takarazuka rule for the star of the show to be a male role. An interesting example was the Snow Troupe's staging of the Viennese musical *Elizabeth*, adapted and directed by Koike Shūichirō in 1996. The heroine is a beautiful Austrian empress called Elizabeth. However, the Takarazuka deliberately shifted the central role from Elizabeth to a character called Tod (meaning "death" in German), performed by a male-role actress. *Elizabeth* proved to be a great hit, and was performed in turn by the Star Troupe in 1997, the Cosmos Troupe in 1999 and by the Flower Troupe in 2002. In 2000, 2001, and 2004, the commercial production company Toho retranslated *Elizabeth* and staged it with a cast of male and female actors, again with Koike as director.

THE HISTORY OF TAKARAZUKA

Takarazuka was created by Kobayashi Ichizō, the founder of the electric railroad Hankyu Corporation and the film and theater production company Toho, who was well-known for his original management concepts. Wishing to attract passengers to Hankyu's Takarazuka Line, a private railroad in the Kansai area, Kobayashi built a hot spring resort in Takarazuka City. As entertainment for the hot spring visitors, in 1913 he founded the Takarazuka Shōkatai ("Takarazuka Singing Troupe") composed entirely of teenage girls. Takarazuka Shōkatai began staging musical plays in 1914, and became more and more successful, eventually opening the Takarazuka Grand Theater in 1924 and Tokyo Takarazuka Theater in 1934 with a capacity of four thousand.

During the 1920s the Takarazuka production crew visited Europe and the United States on the look-out for new ideas. *Mon pari* ("My Paris," 1927), directed by Kishida Tatsuya, was the first revue to be produced in Japan. Another Takarazuka director, Shirai Tetsuzo, was influenced by the *Ziegfeld Follies* he had seen in New York, and staged a successful revue called *Parisette* in 1930. Takarazuka toured Europe for the first time in 1938, and the United States in 1939.

With the outbreak of World War II, Takarazuka found itself caught up in Japan's militarism, and was mobilized to Manchuria to entertain the troops. After the war, Takarazuka was revived, and performances resumed at the Takarazuka Grand Theater in 1946. Its first tour of the United States was in 1959, since when it has toured many countries throughout the world. 1993 saw the reconstruction of the Takarazuka Grand Theater, and the Tokyo Takarazuka Theater was remodeled in 2001. In 2002 Takarazuka gave a total of 920 performances, attracting approximately two million people, despite the national recession in which many other troupes were suffering a decline in audience figures.

TOHO MUSICALS

Toho is one of Tokyo's major theater and film production companies and, like Takarazuka, belongs to the electric railroad Hankyu Company. Toho today produces both plays and musicals.

Soon after the end of the war, a theater producer and president of the Imperial Theatre, Hata Toyo-kichi, began staging small-scale musicals starring the former Takarazuka star Koshiji Fubuki (1924–80). This initiative was inspired by Kikuta Kazuo (1908–73), a playwright-director and executive of the Toho company, who initiated the "Toho Musicals" in 1955. A Japanese-language version of *My Fair Lady* was also staged at the Tokyo Takarazuka Theater in 1963. This was the first full-scale performance of a Broadway musical in Japan, and was a big hit with the audience.

Since then many famous Broadway musicals have been translated and staged at the theaters under the Toho banner. Toho today produces and stages both musicals and plays. Musicals are generally staged at their large theaters, such as the Imperial Theatre (capacity 1,917), and their repertoire consists mostly of translated European or American musicals. Popular stars form the core of their casts, and runs are usually limited to one or two months. If a musical becomes a hit, Toho restages it every few years. *Man of La Mancha*, for example, has been staged repeatedly since 1969 and marked its 1000th performance in 2002. The star is the Kabuki actor Matsumoto Kōshirō IX (formerly called Ichikawa Somegorō), who has played the central character for thirty-three years. In 1970

Man of La Mancha, in which Kōshirō IX played on Broadway.

Kōshirō was invited to New York to play the central character in English for ten weeks.

GEKIDAN SHIKI AND ASARI KEITA

Gekidan Shiki, or "Shiki Theatre Company," founded in 1953 under the direction of Asari Keita (b. 1933), comprises about eight hundred actors, actresses, technicians, and management staff. Shiki has its headquarters in Yokohama, and owns five theaters in Tokyo, with others in Nayoga, Osaka, Kyoto, and Fukuoka. Although Shiki stages plays, its main repertoire is musicals. In 2003, they produced 2,660 performances, mobilizing an audience of 2.55 million, with box office sales grossing 20.9 billion yen.

Shiki was founded as a *shingeki* troupe to stage plays by the French dramatists Jean Giraudoux and Jean Anouilh, but from 1969 they focussed more on musicals drawing on Asari's experience as a producer at Shiki's Nissay Theatre. He had been closely involved with musical there, and had invited *West Side Story* from Broadway in 1964, and also produced and directed a large number of original musicals for the "Musicals for Children" series staged by Shiki every year at the Nissay Theatre. In 1973, he directed a Japanese version of the enormously popular *Jesus Christ Superstar* using Kabuki-style makeup.

Shiki staged *Cats* for the first time in Japan in 1983, building a temporary theater in the Shinjuku area of Tokyo, where they could attempt an unlimited run. *Cats* ran for an entire year, and went on to runs of a year and a month in Osaka, a year in Nagoya, seven months in Fukuoka and eleven months in Sapporo. Such long runs were unheard of in Japan at that time. Other Shiki hits include *The Phantom*

Ri Kōran (see text)

Yuta to fushigi na nakama tachi (see text)

of the Opera (1988), *The Beauty and the Beast* (1995), *The Lion King* (1998), and *Mamma Mia!* (2002).

Shiki also stages original musicals such as *Ri Kōran* ("Ri Kōran," 1991), composed by Miki Takashi and directed by Asari, about the life of Yamaguchi Yoshiko, a singer and actress during the Japan-China war. Other popular examples include *Yume kara sameta yume* ("A Dream Within a Dream," 1987), based on a novel of the same title by the popular author Akagawa Jirō (1987); *Yuta to fushigi na nakama tachi* ("Yuta and Enchanting Friends," 1989), based on the novel of the same title by Miura Tetsuo; and *Ikoku no oka* ("An Exotic Hill," 2001).

ONGAKU-ZA

Ongaku-za was founded in 1977 by Yokoyama Yoshikazu, Ueda Seiko, and others, to stage Japanese musicals, but disbanded in 1987. New Ongaku-za was started in 1988 and has created such musicals as *Madomoazeru Mōtsuaruto* ("Mademoiselle Mozart," 1991), *Hoshi no ōjisama* ("The Little Prince," 1993) based on Antoine de Saint-Exupery's book; and *Ai rabu Botchan* ("I Love Botchan," 1993), based on Natsume Sōseki's novel.

Ai rabu Botchan (see text)

FURUSATO CARAVAN

The group Furusato Caravan was founded in 1983 in Tokyo and stages musicals about Japanese life. Their playwright and director is Ishizuka

Labor of Love (see text)

the troupe has made musicals about white-collar city workers and factory workers, such as *Yū ā mai sanshain* ("You Are My Sunshine," 1990) and *Sararīman no kin medaru* ("Gold Medal for a White-Collar Worker," 1992).

MIYAMOTO AMON

The former dancer Miyamoto Amon (b. 1958) studied in London and New York, and attracted attention as a director with the success of *Ai gatto māman* ("I Got Merman"), which he wrote, directed, and choreographed. He directed and choreographed Stephen Sondheim's *Pacific Overture* (first staged on Broadway in 1976, and in Japan in 2000), portraying late nineteenth-century Japan. Sondheim himself praised Miyamoto's version, which was also staged with an all-American cast in New York in 2004.

Katsuhiko (b.1937), and their composer is Teramoto Tateo. They began by making musicals about life in farming villages in contemporary Japan, such as *Oyaji to yomesan* ("Dad and his Wife," 1983), *Anchan* ("Brother," 1985), and *Za kekkon* ("The Marriage," 1986). In 1991 Furusato Caravan staged a Japan-U.S. coproduction called *Labor of Love*, depicting exchanges between Japanese and U.S. rice farmers. It was performed in both Japan and the United States with a cast of Japanese and American actors. Since the 1990s

Pacific Overture (see text)

SHAKESPEAREAN DRAMA IN JAPAN

Shakespearean plays are enormously popular in Japan. During 2003 in the Tokyo metropolitan area alone, as many as forty-seven Shakespearean dramas, some rewritten or adapted, were staged by both Japanese casts and visiting British, Russian, and Korean troupes.

The first Shakespeare play staged in Japan was a Kabuki-style version of *The Merchant of Venice* in Osaka in 1885. The play was set in Japan, turned into one act, and performed by Kabuki actors. In 1901, the Geki-dan Shinpa ("New School Troupe")—created in the Meiji era to rival the "old school" Kabuki—staged a translation by Tsubouchi Shōyō of *Julius Caesar*. This too was an adaptation consisting mainly of its assassination scene, with the setting once again in Japan. In addition the female roles were mainly played by Kabuki *onnagata*. However, most troupes later started interpreting Shakespearean dramas in the traditional

The Comedy of Errors by Shakespeare Theatre.

European style. When the Royal Shakespeare Company (R.S.C.) toured Japan in 1970 with Trevor Nunn's *The Winter's Tale*, followed by Peter Brook's *A Midsummer Night's Dream* in 1973, Japanese audiences saw yet another new approach to Shakespeare.

In the six years from 1975 through 1981, a troupe of young actors led by the director Deguchi Norio and calling themselves Shakespeare Theatre staged all thirty-seven of Shakespeare's plays in a small theater in Shibuya, Tokyo. The actors wore casual modern dress, with simple sets, accompanied by rock music. This group was the first to introduce such plays as *Henry VI*. Since then, Japanese directors have done much to popularize innovative approaches to classic drama worldwide.

NINAGAWA'S SHAKESPEARE

Ninagawa Yukio is perhaps best-known in the West for his Shakespeare productions. His first was a Toho production of *Romeo and Juliet* that he directed at the Nissay Theatre in 1974. Matsumoto Kōshirō IX (then called Ichikawa Somegorō) played Romeo in a production in which Ninagawa's infusion of the youth and wild energy of *shōgekijō* somewhat shocked the conservative commercial theater.

In 1980 Ninagawa directed *Ninagawa Macbeth* at Toho, putting his own name in the title to emphasize his interpretation of one of Shakespeare's best-known plays. This *Macbeth* was played as a drama within a drama, on a stage set as a huge Japanese Buddhist altar dedicated to the deceased. The play was set in sixteenth-century Japan, and while the characters retained their

Pericles (see text)

original names, all the characters, including Macbeth, appeared in kimono. The three witches were played in an *onnagata* style. The production was inspired by Kurosawa Akira's film *Kumonosujō* ("The Throne of Blood," 1957), a version of *Macbeth* set during Japan's pre-Edo period civil wars, and Ninagawa's intention was to draw the drama closer to the history of the Japanese people in order to make the play easier for them to understand. *Ninagawa Macbeth* was also a hit at the 1985 Edinburgh Festival, and was staged in London in 1987, and New York in 1990 and 2002.

In 1997 Ninagawa directed *The Tempest* with the subtitle "A rehearsal at the Nō stage on Sado." Sado Island in the Japan Sea is where Zeami (1363–1443), the founder of Nō, was exiled and Ninagawa drew on the similarities between the situations of Zeami and

Macbeth, directed by Ninagawa. (see text)

Prospero. This version of *The Tempest* was also staged at the National Theatre in London in 1992. Ninagawa has also staged his own productions of *A Midnight's Summer Dream* (1994) and *Pericles* (2003) in both Japan and London.

Since 1998, Ninagawa has been working on the *Sai no kuni* Shakespeare series, a thirteen-year project to stage all of Shakespeare's plays at the Saitama Arts Theater just north of Tokyo. The project included a coproduction of *King Lear* with the R.S.C. in 1999. Twenty-four British actors and actresses, headed by Nigel Hawthorne, appeared in this drama, and Sanada Hiroyuki took the role of the fool.

King Lear, directed by Suzuki. (see text)

King Lear directed by Ninagawa with the R.S.C. (see text)

SUZUKI TADASHI'S CRITICAL SHAKESPEAREAN DRAMAS

Suzuki Tadashi is also well-known for his Japanese-style Shakespeare. Suzuki emphasizes a strict, severe order with highly stylized acting, more in the manner of Nō, in contrast to Ninagawa's more flamboyant Kabukiesque style. While Ninagawa faithfully follows the original text, Suzuki plays free with it, omitting parts, adding his own, and transforming the characters at will. In *Atorie No. 3—Yoru to tokei* ("Atelier No. 3—Night and Clock," 1975), for example, he transposes Macbeth into the dramatic realm of Maxim Gorky's *The Lower Depths* and Beckett's *Waiting for Godot*. In 1988, Suzuki directed *King Lear* as a coproduction with four American regional theaters, including the Arena Stage and the Milwaukee Repertoire Theater. This version displayed *King Lear* as the illusions of a solitary old man in a contemporary hospital, with a cast of twelve American actors all wearing Japanese-style costumes and staged in both Japan and the United States.

OTHER SHAKESPEARE PERFORMANCES

BROKEN HAMLET (1990)

From the 1980s there were many *shingeki* and *shōgekijō* productions of Shakespeare, often adapted to Japanese cultural themes. One such example was *Broken Hamlet*, written and directed by Uesugi Shōzō, and with him in the starring role. The play caricatured Hamlet as a powerless youngster.

Broken Hamlet

RYŪZANJI MACBETH (1988)

Adapted and directed by Ryūzanji Show, this version set *Macbeth* in a wartime jungle in Southeast Asia, reminiscent of Vietnam. The three witches were homeless women who frequented the battlefield.

Ryūzanji Macbeth

NODA HIDEKI'S SHAKESPEARE

Noda Hideki also daringly transformed Shakespeare with his original ideas. *Noda Hideki no kara sawagi* ("Noda Hideki's Much Ado About Nothing," 1990) was set in the world of Sumo. *Noda Hideki no manatsu no yo no yume* ("Noda Hideki's A Midsummer Night's Dream," 1992) turned the forest in Athens into an amusement park at the foot of Mt. Fuji, against a setting of Japanese food and chefs. *Sandaime Richādo* ("Richard III," 1990) was set in the world of traditional flower arrangement, and took the form of an eccentric court drama with Shakespeare himself appearing as a public prosecutor.

Sandaime Richādo

HIMAWARI ("SUNFLOWER," 1988)

Written and directed by Takeuchi Jūichirō (b. 1947), this is a humorous drama of three sisters and their father, skillfully linking Shakespeare's *King Lear* with a family in contemporary Japan. The father abandons his role as a father and is now called "Mom," while hiring someone to play the role of the father. Takeuchi creates a dra-

Himawari

matic world about a family falling apart, with references to *King Lear* and Chekhov's *The Three Sisters*.

KANADEHON HAMLET (1992)

Unique among this series of Japanese Shakespeare is *Kanadehon Hamlet* by Tsutsumi Harue (b. 1950), a playwright living in the United States. The drama unfolds against the background of the Morita-za Kabuki theater in Tokyo in 1897, which decides to stage *Hamlet* for the first time in Japan in the translation by Tsubouchi Shōyō. The Kabuki actors, however, are unacquainted with European drama, and try to play it using the acting methods of the famous Kabuki play *Kanadehon chūshingura*. As the drama unfolds, it becomes clear that these two popular dramas, representing the West and Japan respectively, share many similarities. Both stories deal with the theme of revenge, and the central characters both undertake a "performance" to deceive their enemies. *Kanadehon Hamlet* was staged in New York in 1997, London in 2001, and Moscow in 2004.

Kanadehon Hamlet

BUTŌ

Butō is a genre of avant-garde dance started by Hijikata Tatsumi and Ōno Kazuo during the late 1950s and early 1960s. Just as the *shōgekijō* movement of the 1960s revolutionized the world of drama, so Butō shook up the world of modern dance to produce a genre that is uniquely Japanese. Since the 1970s, Butō has gained international acclaim for its extraordinary physical expression. Butō dancers are characterized by heavy white makeup covering their face and body, and many of the male dancers shave their heads. This white makeup represents their transformation to something strange and grotesque, something that takes us beyond the confines of our daily lives.

HIJIKATA TATSUMI

Hijikata Tatsumi (1928–86) learned modern dance in his hometown in Akita Prefecture, before moving to Tokyo in 1949. In 1959, he made his shocking debut with *Kinjiki* ("Forbidden Colors"), based on homosexuality. The modern dance mainstream disapproved of this radical theme, which was widely perceived as perverted. However, Hijikata also received powerful support, notably from the novelist Mishima Yukio, and from 1961 named his dance style *Ankoku butōha* ("Dance of Utter Darkness School"). *Anma* ("Masseur: A story That Supports Passion," 1963) and *Barairo dansu* ("Rose-Colored Dance: To Mr. Shibusawa's House," 1965) shocked audiences with Hijikata's charisma and outstanding technique, as well as his violent physical expression and extreme eroticism.

With *Nikutai no hanran—Hijikata Tatsumi to nihonjin* ("The Rebellion of the Body—Tatsumi Hijikata and the Japanese," 1968), Hijikata began to leave his Western realm and return to Japanese themes. *Shiki no tame no nijūnana ban* ("Twenty-Seven Nights for Four Seasons," 1972), staged for four consecutive weeks, evoked memories of his native Tōhoku, including the sound of the freezing wind, the footsteps of speeding horses, *tsugaru jongara* folk music, the chorus of cicadas, and the whistle of a train. Hijikata fasted before this performance so that he could dance like a weak beggar or emaciated Buddhist ascetic. After this he choreographed a series of dances under the title of *Tōhoku kabuki keikaku* ("Tohoku Kabuki Project").

ŌNO KAZUO

Ōno Kazuo (b. 1906), twenty-two years older than Hijikata, created a totally different type of Butō—a brilliant and pure universe in contrast to Hijikata's grotesque, dark world. Ōno was born in Hakodate, Hokkaido, and became interested in modern dance while teaching gymnastics at school. He was drafted during World War II, and returned to dance in 1949. In collaboration with Hijikata, he danced in *Anma* and *Barairo dansu*. After a

La Argentina Shō (see text)

long period away from the stage, Ōno returned at the age of seventy-one to perform *La Argentina Shō* ("Admiring La Argentina," 1977), a tribute to the Spanish dancer La Argentina, whose performance he recalled seeing in Tokyo in 1929. In 1980, Ōno toured Europe, also participating in the Nancy Festival. He danced in New York in 1981, at the Munich Festival in 1982, and at Avignon Festival in 1983. In contrast to Hijikata, who stopped performing at the age of forty-five, Ōno—over ninety at the time of writing—is still active.

Kaiin no uma (see text)

Juku, Bishop Yamada's Hoppō Butōha, Murobuse Kou's Sebi, Osuga Isamu's Byakkosha, and Tamura Tetsurō's Dance Love Machine, which all retain some element of spectacle inherited from Dairakudan.

DAIRAKUDAKAN

Maro Akaji (b. 1943), a former student of Hijikata and a once popular actor with the Jōkyō Gekijō troupe, established the Butō dance group Dairakudakan in 1972. As the director and choreographer of Dairakudakan, Maro staged such works as *Yōbutsu shin tan* ("The Story of Male-Sex Deity," 1972), *Arashi* ("The Storm," 1976), and *Binbō na hitobito* ("People in Poverty," 1979). He also took *Kaiin no uma* ("The Sea Dappled Horse," 1982) to the American Dance Festival in North Carolina in 1982 and 2001, and to the Avignon Festival. Dairakudakan's performances are characterized by highly visual and dramatic spectacle, replete with absurdity and abundant follies. A variety of groups have been formed by former Dairakudakan dancers, including such groups as Amagatsu Ushio's Sankai

SANKAI JUKU

Sankai Juku was formed in 1975 as an all-male dance troupe led by Amagatsu Ushio (b. 1949), and frequently tours abroad to considerable acclaim. Sankai Juku has refined Butō both visually and in terms of physical expression. Although the troupe maintains the white makeup and the spectacular performances that characterize Butō, it has carefully eliminated grotesque strangeness and over-emotional physical expressions, instead placing bodies like symbols in strictly pictorial compositions. This refined aesthetic sense has made Sankai Juku a globally popular dance troupe. Sankai Juku's best known works include *Kinkan shōnen* ("The Kumquat Seed," 1978),

Hibiki (see text)

Jōmon shō ("Homage to Prehistory," 1982), *Unetsu* ("The Egg Stands out of Curiosity," 1986), *Shijima* ("The Darkness Calms Down in Space," 1988), *Omote* ("The Grazed Surface," 1991) and *Hibiki* ("Resonance from Far Away," 1998). Since 1982, Sankai Juku's new work has been premiered at Théâtre de la Ville in Paris. In 2001, it staged six dances, including its latest *Kagemi* ("Beyond the Metaphors of Mirrors," 2000), at the Setagaya Public Theater in Tokyo to commemorate the troupe's twenty-fifth anniversary.

TANAKA MIN

Tanaki Min (b. 1945) started out in modern dance. He established Shintai Kishō Kenkyūjo ("Body Meteorology Laboratory") in 1978, and performed his *Hyper Dance Projection 1824 Hours*, in which he danced naked (something he does often) for 76 days at 180 locations throughout Japan. Tanaka then met Hijikata and became a Butō dancer, and in 1981 formed the troupe Maijuku, which disbanded in 1997. In 1985, Tanaka established the Shintai Kishō Nōjō ("Body Weather Farm") at Hakushū-chō in Yamanashi Prefecture, where members of his troupe study dance daily while also working on the farm growing crops and tending poultry. In 1995 Tanaka established the Buyō Shigen Kenkyūjo ("Institute of Dance Resources") at Hakushū-chō in order to research ethnic dances in Japan and around the world. In 2000, he formed Tōkason buyōdan ("Peach-blossom Village Dance Troupe"), a group of mainly young dancers that performs throughout Japan, the United States, and Europe.

THEATER LISTINGS GUIDE

A number of English-Language newspapers, magazines, and free entertainment guides give details of performances. None of the ticket agencies have websites in English, although they may be able to provide information in English on the telephone. Some, but not all, of the theaters have websites in English. Tourist Information offices and hotels often provide information on current performances and, in some cases, can assist with purchasing tickets. Tickets may be purchased through ticket agencies and the theater box offices. If you purchase tickets by telephone, you will need to give an address in Japan to which the tickets will be mailed. All prices are given as a general guide only and are subject to change.

TICKET AGENCIES

Ticket Pia (10:00–18:00)
TEL: 0570–029999, 0570–029988

Lawson Ticket (10:00–20:00)
TEL: 0570–000403

e+ (10:00–18:00)
TEL: 03–5749–9911

CN Play Guide (10:00–22:00)
TEL: 03–5802–9999 (Kantō and Tōhoku area)
  06–6776–1199 (Kansai area)
  052–968–0099 (Tōkai and Hokuriku area)

* * *

For Kabuki or Bunraku, it is best to purchase tickets direct from the theater box office as you can choose seats.

Ticket-phone Shochiku
(Kabuki—Kabuki-za, Shinbashi Enbujō)
TEL: 03–5565–6000 (10:00 to 18:00)

Ticket-phone Shochiku, Osaka
(Kabuki—Minami-za, Osaka Shochiku-za)
TEL: 0570–000–489
  06–6214–2200 (10:00 to 18:00)

Tokyo National Theatre Ticket Center
(Kabuki/Bunraku—Tokyo National Theatre,
Nō/ Kyōgen—National Noh Theatre)
TEL: 03–3230–3000 (10:00 to 17:00)

Tele-seat Misono (Kabuki—Misono-za)
TEL: 052–222–1481 (10:00 to 17:00)

Hakata-za Telephone Center
(Kabuki—Hakata-za)
TEL: 092–263–5555 (10:00 to 18:00)

National Bunraku Theatre
(Bunraku—National Bunraku Theatre)
TEL: 06–6212–1122/1081 (10:30 to 16:00)

GENERAL INFORMATION

Dentō Kabuki Hozon-kai
TEL: 03–5212–1243
E-MAIL: info@kabuki.or.jp
This organization is helpful in giving information on Kabuki performances.

Nōgaku Association
TEL: 03–5925–3871
WEBSITE: www.nohgaku.or.jp
E-MAIL: office@nohgaku.or.jp

Japan Playwrights Association
TEL: 03–5738–3150
E-MAIL: office@jpwa.jp

The Japan Foundation
TEL: 03–5562–3530
WEBSITE: www.jpf.go.jp/e/index.html
The English website provides information about contemporary theater, with over 100 synopses.

KABUKI

Kabuki is usually shown in month-long runs starting on the 1st or 2nd day of the month and ending on the 24th or 26th. The Kabuki-za in Tokyo is the only theater with a full year-round program of Kabuki. Other Tokyo theaters presenting Kabuki on a regular basis include the Tokyo National Theatre, Shinbashi Enbujō, Asakusa Kōkaidō, and Theatre Cocoon (Bunkamura). Outside Tokyo, Kabuki can be seen at the Minami-za in Kyoto, Osaka Shochiku-za in Osaka, Misono-za in Nagoya, Hakata-za in Fukuoka (Kyūshū), and the Kanamaru-za in Kotohirachō (Shikoku). Prices range from ¥500 for watching a single act to ¥20,000 for the whole performance in the best seats.

English earphone guides providing a running commentary on the performance are available at the Kabuki-za and the Tokyo National Theatre. For more information on earphone guides see the website:
www.asahikaisetsu.co.jp/kb_dic/bun_ eep.htm.

CALENDAR

January	*Hatsuharu (Shinshun) Ōkabuki* (New Year Special): Kabuki-za, Tokyo National Theatre, Asakusa Kōkaidō, Osaka Shochiku-za.
February	Kabuki-za, Hakata-za.
March	Kabuki-za, Tokyo National Theatre.
April	Kabuki-za, Misono-za. *Kompira Kabuki-Ōshibai* ("Kompira Grand Kabuki"): Kanamaru-za. Kabuki introductory course: Minami-za.
May	Kabuki-za.
June	Kabuki-za, Hakata-za. Kabuki introductory course: Tokyo National Theatre.
July	Kabuki-za, Osaka Shochiku-za. Kabuki introductory course: Tokyo National Theatre.
August	Kabuki-za (3 shows daily).
September	Kabuki-za.
October	Kabuki-za, Tokyo National Theatre. *Kichirei Kaomise Kōgyō:* Misono-za.
November	*Kichirei Kaomise Kōgyō:* Kabuki-za, Tokyo National Theatre.
December	*Kichirei Kaomise Kōgyō:* Minami-za, Kabuki-za, Tokyo National Theatre.

THEATER TIMES

Kabuki-za	*MATINEE:* 11:00 *EVENING:* 16:30	Matinee and evening sessions present different programs, each lasting approximately 4 to 4 ½ hours with three intervals. • Three different performances are held daily at the Kabuki-za in August
Shinbashi Enbujō Misono-za Minami-za Osaka Shochiku-za Hakata-za	*MATINEE:* 11:00 *EVENING:* 16:30 or 16:15	
Tokyo National Theatre	*MATINEE:* 11:30 or 12:00 *EVENING:* 16:30	Matinee and evening sessions present the same program lasting 3 ½ to 4 hours with three intervals.

THEATERS

Kabuki-za

ADDRESS: 4–12–5 Ginza, Chūō-ku, Tokyo 104–0061
TEL: 03–3541–3131
WEBSITE: www.shochiku.co.jp/play/kabukiza/theater
/index.html
NEAREST STATION: Higashi-Ginza (Hibiya line, Toei
Asakusa line); Shimbashi (JR Yamanote line)

a) *Sajiki*, first floor (¥16,800), second floor Nos. 1 to 8 (¥14,700) and Nos. 9 to 11 (¥10,500)

The first and second floor side balconies have comfortable seats with foot warmers (shoes must be removed). Lunch and cakes are served.

b) First Class (¥14,700)

First floor front (*kaburitsuki*) to row 15 and rows 1 to 7 on the second floor. The best seats are rows 7 to 9 in the center on the first floor. Nos. 36–39 on the first floor are on the left of the *hanamichi*. Tickets are more expensive for January and *shūmei* performances.

c) Second Class (¥10,500)

Rear seats on the first and second floors. Nos. 37 to 40 on the first floor are on the left of the *hanamichi*.

d) Third Class, A (¥4200) and B (¥2,520)

Third floor seats. "A" seats are rows 1 to 9, and "B" seats are at the back. Seats on the right have a better view of the *hanamichi*.

e) *Makumi-seki* (Single act or play seats, ¥500 to ¥1,200)

Fourth floor seats, no reservations, available for one or more acts, or entire programs, either matinee or evening. Two rows of ninety seats, and space for sixty standing. Can only be bought on the day of performance at the *makumi-seki* entrance, thirty minutes before the curtain is raised. This is a popular option for first-timers.

Tokyo National Theatre

ADDRESS: 4–1 Hayabusachō, Chiyoda-ku, Tokyo 102–8656
TEL: 03–3230–3000 (10:00–17:00)
WEBSITE: www.ntj.jac.go.jp/english/index.html
NEAREST STATION: Hanzōmon (Hanzōmon line); Nagatachō (Hanzōmon line, Yūrakuchō line)
OTHER SERVICES: A library on the third floor of the main office building, with an audio-visual room in which you can watch Kabuki and Bunraku videos (¥100 for one hour). Weekdays 10:00–12:00 and 13:00–17:00. Please call 03–3265–6479 beforehand.

The Traditional Performing Arts Information Center next door is a must for visitors interested in the traditional performing arts. There are museum pieces on the first floor, and video with on-screen narration. In the library on the second floor you can read books on the performing arts, and also reference photos and pictures on the Internet. 10:00–18:00. Please call beforehand. (*TEL*: 03–3265–7411)

a) Special Class (¥12,000, ¥8,400 for students)

First floor, rows 1 to 13, center (seats 23–36), and center ten seats of first row on the second floor.

b) First Class A (¥9,200, ¥6,400 for students)

First floor seats other than Special Class and Second Class seats, and front five rows of the second floor other than Special Class seats.

c) First Class B (¥6,100, ¥4,300 for students)

Rows 6 and 7 of the second floor.

d) Second Class (¥2,500, ¥1,800 for students)

Rows 2 to 8, left (seats 1–12) and right (seats 49–59) on the first floor; front two rows (8 and 9) on the third floor.

e) Third Class (¥1,500, ¥1,100 for students)

Rear three rows of the third floor.

Kabuki-za

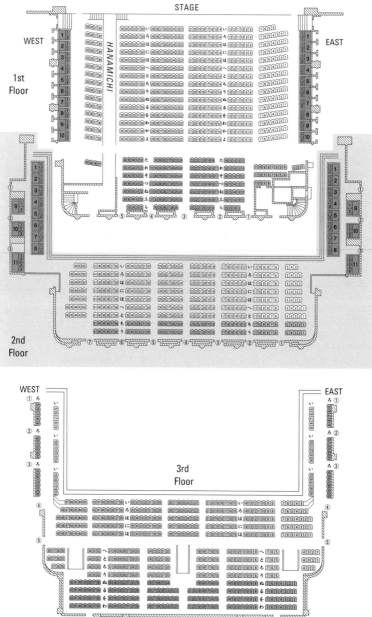

▪Tokyo National Theatre

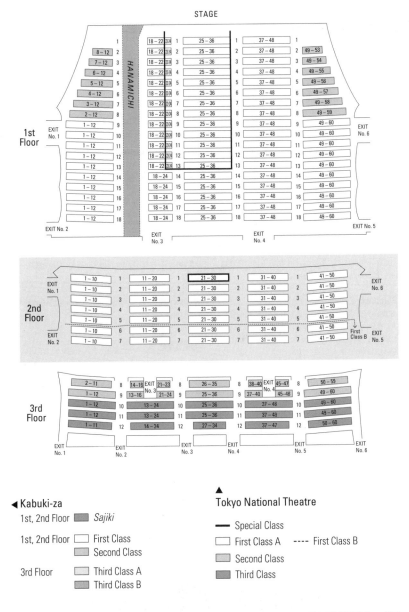

STAGE

1st Floor

2nd Floor

3rd Floor

HANAMICHI

EXIT No. 1
EXIT No. 2
EXIT No. 3
EXIT No. 4
EXIT No. 5
EXIT No. 6

◀ Kabuki-za

1st, 2nd Floor	Sajiki
1st, 2nd Floor	First Class
	Second Class
3rd Floor	Third Class A
	Third Class B

▲
Tokyo National Theatre

— Special Class
☐ First Class A   ---- First Class B
☐ Second Class
☐ Third Class

Asakusa Kōkaidō

ADDRESS: 1–38–6 Asakusa, Taitō-ku, Tokyo 111–0032

TEL: 03–3844–7491

NEAREST STATION: Asakusa (Ginza line, Tōbu Isesaki line, Toei Asakusa line)

Mitsukoshi Theater

ADDRESS: Nihombashi Mitsukoshi Department Store, 6F, 1–4–1 Nihombashi-Muromachi, Chūo-ku, Tokyo 103–8001

TEL: 03–3274–8675

E-MAIL: info@mitsukoshi.co.jp

NEAREST STATION: Mitsukoshimae (Hanzōmon line)

Nissay Theatre

ADDRESS: 1–1–1 Yūrakuchō, Chiyoda-ku, Tokyo 100–0006

TEL: 03–3503–3111

WEBSITE: www.nissaytheatre.or.jp/e/index.html

NEAREST STATIONS: Hibiya (Hibiya line, Chiyoda line, Toei Mita line); Yūrakuchō (JR Yamanote line, JR Keihin Tōhoku line, Yūrakuchō line); Ginza (Ginza line, Marunouchi line, Hibiya line)

Shinbashi Enbujō

ADDRESS: 6–18–2 Ginza, Chūo-ku, Tokyo 104–0061

TEL: 03–3541–2600

NEAREST STATION: Higashi-Ginza (Hibiya line, Toei Asakusa line)

Edo Tokyo Museum Hall

ADDRESS: 1–4–1 Yokozuna, Sumida-ku, Tokyo 130–0015

TEL: 03–3626–9974

WEBSITE: www.edo-tokyo-museum.or.jp/english/index.html

NEAREST STATIONS: Ryōgoku (JR Sōbu line, Toei Ō-edo line)

Meiji-za

ADDRESS: 2–31–1 Nihombashi-Hamachō, Chūo-ku, Tokyo 103–0007

TEL: 03–3660–3939

WEBSITE: www.meijiza.co.jp/eng/index.html

E-MAIL: meijiza@meijiza.co.jp

NEAREST STATION: Hamachō (Toei Shinjuku line)

Theatre Cocoon (Bunkamura)

ADDRESS: Bunkamura 2–24–1 Dōgenzaka, Shibuya-ku, Tokyo 150–8507

TEL: 03–3477–3244

WEBSITE: www.bunkamura.co.jp/english/cocoon/index.html

NEAREST STATION: Shibuya (JR Yamanote line, Ginza line, Hanzōmon line, Den'en Toshi line, Inokashira line, Tōyoko line)

KYOTO

Minami-za

ADDRESS: Shijō Ōhashi Higashizume Nakanomachi, Higashiyama-ku, Kyoto 605–0075

TEL: 075–561–1155

NEAREST STATIONS: Kawaramachi (Hankyū Kyoto line); Shijō (Keihan line)

OSAKA

Osaka Shochiku-za

ADDRESS: 1–9–19 Dōtonbori, Chūo-ku, Osaka 542–0071

TEL: 06–6214–2211

NEAREST STATION: Nanba (Midōsuji line, Sennichi-mae line)

NAGOYA

Misono-za

ADDRESS: 1–6–14 Sakae, Naka-ku, Nagoya 460–8403

TEL: 052–222–1481

NEAREST STATION: Fushimi (Higashiyama line, Tsuru-mai line)

Chūnichi Theatre

ADDRESS: 4–1–1 Sakae, Naka-ku, Nagoya 460–0008

TEL: 052–263–7171

NEAREST STATION: Sakae (Meijō line, Higashiyama line)

OTHER REGIONAL THEATERS

KOSAKA, AKITA

Kōrakukan
ADDRESS: 2 Aza Matsunoshita, Aza Kosaka Kōzan, Kosakamachi, Kazuno-gun, Akita 017–0202
TEL: 0186–29–3732
NEAREST STATION: Ōdate (JR Ōu line)

KOTOHIRA, SHIKOKU

Kanamaru-za
ADDRESS: 1241 Kawanishi, Kotohirachō, Nakatado-gun, Kagawa 766–0001
TEL: 0877–75–6714
WEBSITE: www.town.kotohira.kagawa.jp/english/index.html
E-MAIL: kabuki@town.kotohira.kagawa.jp
NEAREST STATION: Kotohira (JR Seto Ōhashi line)

UCHIKO, SHIKOKU

Uchiko-za
ADDRESS: 2102 Uchiko, Uchikochō, Kita-gun, Ehime 791–3301
TEL: 0893–44–2840
E-MAIL: syoukou@town.uchiko.ehime.jp
NEAREST STATION: Uchiko (JR Yosan line)

HIROSHIMA

Itsukushima Shrine Nō Stage
ADDRESS: 1–1 Miyajimachō, Saeki-gun, Hiroshima 739–0500
TEL: 0829–44–2020
NEAREST STATION: Miyajimaguchi (JR Sanyō line, Hiroshima Electric Railway) → Ferry

NAGATO, YAMAGUCHI

Renassa Nagato
ADDRESS: 818–1 Senzaki, Nagato-shi, Yamaguchi 759–4106
TEL: 0837–26–6001
E-MAIL: renassa@ymg.urban.ne.jp
NEAREST STATION: Nagato-shi (JR Mine line)

FUKUOKA, KYŪSHŪ

Hakata-za
ADDRESS: 2–1 Kawabatachō, Hakata-ku, Fukuoka 542–0071
TEL: 092–263–5555
NEAREST STATION: Nakasu-Kawabata (Hakosaki line, Kūkō line)

KUMAMOTO, KYŪSHŪ

Yachiyo-za
ADDRESS: 1499 Yamaga, Yamaga-shi, Kumamoto 861–0501
TEL: 0968–44–4004
E-MAIL: inquiry@yachiyoza.com
NEAREST STATION: Kumamoto (JR Kagoshima line) → bus or taxi

BUNRAKU

Bunraku is presented regularly at the National Bunraku Theatre in Osaka and the Tokyo National Theatre, and occasionally in other cities (usually in March and October). Programs are generally shown for one month.

BUNRAKU CALENDAR

National Bunraku Theatre	January, April, June (Bunraku introductory course), late July to early August, November.
Tokyo National Theatre	February, May, September, December. Matinee and evening shows on Sundays in December (Bunraku introductory course).

THEATER TIMES

Matinees are usually at 11:00 and evening shows at 16:30, with performances lasting 4 hours. When three performances are given in a day, each lasts 2 to 3 hours.

THEATERS

National Bunraku Theatre

ADDRESS: 1–12–10 Nipponbashi, Chūō-ku, Osaka 542–0073
TEL: 06–6212–1122 (10:30–16:00)
WEBSITE: www.ntj.jac.go.jp/english/index.html
NEAREST STATION: Nipponbashi (Sennichimae line, Sakaisuji line, Kintetsu line)

a) First Class (¥5,800, students ¥4,100)

b) Second Class (¥2,300)
Rear two rows.

c) Day ticket discount.

d) *Makumi-seki* (Single act seats, ¥500 to ¥2,000)

Tokyo National Theatre

ADDRESS: 4–1 Hayabusachō, Chiyoda-ku, Tokyo 102–8656
TEL: 03–3230–3000 (10:00–17:00)
WEBSITE: www.ntj.jac.go.jp/english/index.html
NEAREST STATIONS: Hanzōmon (Hanzōmon line); Nagatachō (Hanzōmon line, Yūrakuchō line)

a) First Class (¥6,000, students ¥4,200)

b) Second Class (¥5,000, students ¥2,500)
Rear two rows.

c) Third Class (¥1,500, students ¥1,100)
Only 7 seats nearest to the *gidayū*.

d) Day ticket discount.

▪ National Bunraku Theatre

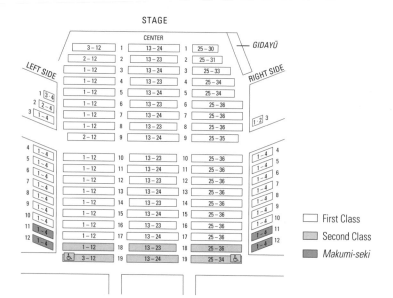

266

▪Tokyo National Theatre

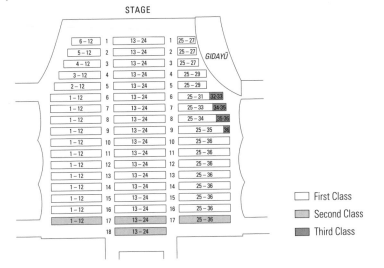

STAGE

First Class
Second Class
Third Class

NŌ

The National Noh Theatre in Tokyo is the only theater offering a regular program. Performances can also be seen in other theaters, public halls, Buddhist temples, and Shinto shrines with outdoor Nō stages (*takigi Nō*). These performances are on an irregular basis, and are advertised locally. For a helpful website providing details of forthcoming Nō performances, see www.theatrenohgaku.org/calendar/index.html.

The best seats are those in front of the stage (*shōmen*), although those in the center front of the stage (*naka shōmen*) can have the view of the stage partially obscured by a pillar and are best avoided. Seats on the left side of the stage (*waki shōmen*) near the *hashigakari* are also popular.

NATIONAL NOH THEATRE CALENDAR

Regular Programs "*Teirei-kōen*" performances	Two days every month, usually one matinee and one evening.
"*Fukyū-kōen*" performances	Once a month , usually the second Saturday.
Introduction to Nō and Kyōgen	June
Special Performances	Irregularly.

NATIONAL NOH THEATRE TIMES

Teirei- kōen	MATINEE: 13:00	2.5 hours
	EVENING: 18:30	2.5 hours
Fukyū-kōen	MATINEE: 13:00	2.5–3 hours

THEATERS

National Noh Theatre

ADDRESS: 4–18–1 Sendagaya, Shibuya-ku, Tokyo 151–0051

TEL: 03–3423–1331

03–3230–3000 (10:00–17:00, for tickets)

WEBSITE: www.ntj.jac.go.jp/english/index.html

NEAREST STATIONS: Sendagaya (JR Sōbu line); Kokuritsu-Kyōgijō (Toei Ōedo line)

OTHER SERVICES: There is a library on level B1 with an audio-visual room in which you can watch videos of the Nō stage (¥50 for 30 minutes). Weekdays 10:00–12:00 and 13:00–17:00. Saturdays, 10:00– 13:00. Please call beforehand.

Teirei-kōen and *Fukyū-kōen* performances
Shōmen: ¥4,300
Waki shōmen: ¥2,800, students ¥2,000
Naka shōmen: ¥2,300, students ¥1,600

Introduction to Nō and Kyōgen
Shōmen: ¥3,000
Waki shōmen: ¥2,500
Naka shōmen: ¥2,000
Students (all seats): ¥1,300

Cerulean Tower Noh Theater

ADDRESS: 26–1 Sakuragaokachō, Shibuya-ku, Tokyo 150–8512

TEL: 03–3477–6412

WEBSITE: www.ceruleantower-hotel.com/en/noutheater/

NEAREST STATION: Shibuya (JR Yamanote line, Ginza line, Hanzōmon line, Den'en Toshi line, Inokashira line, Tōyoko line)

Ginza Noh Theater

ADDRESS: 6–5–15 Ginza, Chūō-ku, Tokyo 104–0061

TEL: 03–3571–0197

NEAREST STATION: Ginza (Ginza line, Marunouchi line, Hibiya line)

▪ National Noh Theatre

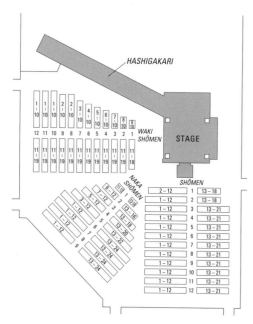

Hōshō Noh Theatre

ADDRESS: 1–5–9 Hongō, Bunkyō-ku, Tokyo 113–0033
TEL: 03–3811–4843
E-MAIL: info@hosho.or.jp
NEAREST STATION: Suidōbashi (JR Sōbu line, Toei Mita line)

Kanze Noh Theatre

ADDRESS: 1–16–4 Shōtō, Shibuya-ku, Tokyo 150–0046
TEL: 03–3469–5241
NEAREST STATIONS: Shibuya (JR Yamanote line, Ginza line, Hanzōmon line, Den'en Toshi line, Inokashira line, Tōyoko line); Shinsen (Inokashira line)

14th Kita Roppeita Memorial Noh Theatre

ADDRESS: 4–6–9 Kami Ōsaki, Shinagawa-ku, Tokyo 141–0021
TEL: 03–3491–8813
E-MAIL: info@kita-noh.com
NEAREST STATION: Meguro (JR Yamanote line, Meguro line, Toei Mita line, Namboku line)

Suginami Nō Theater

ADDRESS: 1–55–9 Wada, Suginami-ku, Tokyo 166–0012
TEL: 03–3381–2208
NEAREST STATION: Nakano-Fujimichō (Marunouchi line)

Tessen-kai Nohgaku Training Institute

ADDRESS: 4–21–29 Minami Aoyama, Minato-ku, Tokyo 107–0062
TEL: 03–3401–2285
FAX: 03–3401–2313
E-MAIL: tessen@jade.dti.ne.jp
NEAREST STATION: Omotesandō (Ginza line, Chiyoda line, Hanzōmon line)

Umewaka Nohgaku Gakuin Hall

ADDRESS: 2–6–14 Higashi Nakano, Nakano-ku, Tokyo 164–0003
TEL: 03–3363–7748
E-MAIL: office@noh-umewaka.com
NEAREST STATIONS: Higashi-Nakano (JR Sōbu line, Toei Ōedo line); Nakano-Sakaue (Marunouchi line, Toei Ōedo line)

Yarai Noh Theatre

ADDRESS: 60 Yaraichō, Shinjuku-ku, Tokyo 162–0805
TEL: 03–3268–7311
E-MAIL: kyukohkai@kanze.com
NEAREST STATIONS: Kagurazaka (Tōzai line); Ushigome-Kagurazaka (Toei Ōedo line)

Yasukuni Shrine Noh Theater

ADDRESS: 3–1–1 Kudan Kita, Chiyoda-ku, Tokyo 102–8246
TEL: 03–3261–8326
WEBSITE: www.yasukuni.or.jp/english/index.html
NEAREST STATION: Kudanshita (Tōzai line, Hanzōmon line, Toei Shinjuku line)

Fuchū-no-Mori Theater

ADDRESS: 1–2 Sengenchō, Fuchū-shi, Tokyo 183–0001
TEL: 042–335–6211
NEAREST STATION: Higashi-Fuchū (Keiō line)

Suntory Hall

ADDRESS: 1–13–1 Akasaka, Minato-ku, Tokyo 107–8403
TEL: 03–3505–1001
WEBSITE: www.suntory.co.jp/suntoryhall/english/index.html
NEAREST STATION: Roppongi-Itchōme (Namboku line)

YOKOHAMA

Yokohama Noh Theatre

ADDRESS: 27–2 Momijigaoka, Nishi-ku, Yokohama-shi, Kanagawa 220–0044
TEL: 045–263–3055
E-MAIL: nohgaku@city.yokohama.jp
NEAREST STATION: Sakuragichō (JR Keihin Tōhoku line, JR Negishi line, Yokohama City Subway)

KAMAKURA

Kamakura Nō Stage

ADDRESS: 3–5–13 Hase, Kamakura-shi, Kanagawa 248–0016
TEL: 0467–22–5557
E-MAIL: webmaster@nohbutai.com
NEAREST STATION: Hase (Enoshima Electric Railway)

Kamakura Performing Arts Center

ADDRESS: 6–1–2 Ōfuna, Kamakura-shi, Kanagawa
247–0056
TEL: 0467–48–4500
WEBSITE: www.city.kamakura.kanagawa.jp/english/
lives/map/index.htm
NEAREST STATION: Ōfuna (JR Tōkaidō line, JR Keihin Tōhoku line, Shōnan Monorail)

NAGOYA

Nagoya Nō Theater

ADDRESS: 1–1–1 Sannomaru, Naka-ku, Nagoya
460–0001
TEL: 052–231–0088
NEAREST STATION: Shiyakusho (Meijō line)

KYOTO

Kongō Nō Theater

ADDRESS: Ichijō-kudaru, Karasuma-dōri, Kamikyō-ku, Kyoto 602–0912
TEL: 075–441–7222
NEAREST STATION: Imadegawa (Karasuma line)

Kyoto Kanze Hall

ADDRESS: 44 Enshōjichō, Okazaki, Sakyō-ku, Kyoto
606–8344
TEL: 075–771–6114
NEAREST STATION: Higashiyama (Tōzai line)

OSAKA

Osaka Nōgaku Kaikan

ADDRESS: 2–3–17 Nakazaki Nishi, Kita-ku, Osaka
530–0015
TEL: 06–6373–1726
E-MAIL: nohgaku@bp.iij4u.or.jp
NEAREST STATIONS: Osaka (JR Osaka Loop line);
Umeda (Midōsuji line, Hankyū line, Hanshin line)

Ōtsuki Seiinkai Noh Theater

ADDRESS: A-7 Uemachi, Chūō-ku, Osaka
540–0005
TEL: 06–6761–8055
WEBSITE: www.noh-kyogen.com/english.htm
NEAREST STATION: Tanimachi-Yonchōme (Tanimachi
line, Chūō line)

Theater Drama City

ADDRESS: 19–1 Chayamachi, Kita-ku, Osaka
530–0013
TEL: 06–6377–3888
NEAREST STATIONS: Osaka (JR Osaka Loop line);
Umeda (Midōsuji line, Hankyū line, Hanshin line)

NARA

Nara Komparu Nō Theater

ADDRESS: Nara National Park 101 Kasuganochō,
Nara 630–8212
TEL: 0742–22–7929
WEBSITE: www.shinkokaido.jp
NEAREST STATION: Nara (JR Kansai line, Kintetsu line)

OKAYAMA

Okayama Kōrakuen Nō Theater

ADDRESS: 1–5 Kōrakuen, Okayama 703–8257
TEL: 086–272–1148
NEAREST STATION: Okayama (JR Shinkansen, JR
San'yō Main line)

HIROSHIMA

Aster Plaza Nō Theater

ADDRESS: 4–17 Kakomachi, Naka-ku, Hiroshima
730–0812
TEL: 082–244–8000
E-MAIL: naka-cs@cf.city.hiroshima.jp
NEAREST STATION: Hiroshima (JR Shinkansen, JR
San'yō Main line)

Itsukushima Shrine Nō Stage

ADDRESS: 1–1 Miyajimachō, Saeki-gun, Hiroshima
739–0500
TEL: 0829–44–2020
NEAREST STATION: Miyajimaguchi (JR Sanyō Main
line, Hiroshima Electric Railway) → Ferry

FUKUOKA

Ōhori Park Nō Theater

ADDRESS: Ōhori Park 1–2 Ōhorikōen, Chūō-ku,
Fukuoka 810–0051
TEL: 092–715–2155
NEAREST STATIONS: Ōhori-Kōenmae, Tōjinmachi
(Fukuoka City Subway)

TAKIGI NŌ

Outdoor Nō is presented on an occasional basis at the following venues. For details please check locally.

TOKYO

Hibiya City (October)
ADDRESS: 2–3–3 Uchisaiwaichō, Chiyoda-ku Tokyo 100–0011
TEL: 03–3595–0295
 03–3275–8904 (Sankei Shimbun)
E-MAIL: info@hibiyacity.com
NEAREST STATIONS: Uchisaiwaichō (Toei Mita line); Kasumigaseki (Marunouchi line, Chiyoda line, Hibiya line)

Shinjuku Gyoen (October)
ADDRESS: 11 Naitōchō, Shinjuku-ku, Tokyo, Japan 160–0014
TEL: 03–3344–3160
 (Shinjuku City Tourism Association)
WEBSITE: www.shinjukugyoen.go.jp/english/english-index.html
NEAREST STATION: Shinjuku (JR Yamanote line, JR Chūō line, JR Sōbu line, JR Saikyō line, Odakyū line, Keiō line, Marunouchi line, Toei Shinjuku line); Shinjuku-Gyoenmae (Marunouchi line); Shinjuku-Sanchōme (Toei Shinjuku line)

Zōjōji Temple (May)
ADDRESS: 4–7–35 Shiba-Kōen, Minato-ku, Tokyo 105–0011
TEL: 03–3432–1431
NEAREST STATIONS: Onarimon (Toei Mita line); Daimon (Toei Asakusa line, Toei Ōedo line)

CHIBA

Naritasan Shinshōji Temple (May)
ADDRESS: in front of the Kōmyōdō, 1 Narita, Narita-shi, Chiba 286–0023
TEL: 0476–22–2111
WEBSITE: www.naritasan.or.jp/english/index.html
NEAREST STATION: Narita (JR Sōbu line, Keisei Electric Railway)

KANAGAWA

Odawara Castle (September or October)
ADDRESS: Odawara Castle Park 6–1 Jōnai, Odawara-shi, Kanagawa 250–0014
TEL: 0465–22–5002
WEBSITE: www.city.odawara.kanagawa.jp/kanko/kanko_4/e_index.html
NEAREST STATION: Odawara (JR Shinkansen, Tōkaidō line)

NAGOYA

Atsuta Jingū Shrine (August)
ADDRESS: 1–1–1 Jingū, Atsuta-ku, Nagoya 456–0058
TEL: 052–241–3146 (Nōgaku Association)
WEBSITE: www.atsutajingu.or.jp/eng/index.htm
E-MAIL: nagoya@nohgaku.or.jp
NEAREST STATIONS: Jingūmae (Meitetsu line); Atsuta (JR Tōkaidō line)

KYOTO

Heian Jingū Shrine (June)
ADDRESS: Nishi Tennōchō, Okazaki, Sakyō-ku, Kyoto 606–8341
TEL: 075–771–6114 (Kanze Kaikan)
WEBSITE: www.heianjingu.or.jp/index_e.html
www.city.kyoto.jp/koho/index_e.html
NEAREST STATION: Higashiyama (Tōzai line),

Kyoto Station Building (August)
ADDRESS: c/o Kyoto Station Building, Shiokoji-sagaru, Karasuma-dōri, Shimogyō-ku, Kyoto 600–8216
TEL: 075–361–4401
NEAREST STATION: Kyoto (JR Shinkansen, JR Tōkaidō line, Kintetsu line, Karasuma line)

ISE, MIE

Ise Jingū Shrine (September)
ADDRESS: Gekū, 279 Toyokawachō, Ise-shi, Mie 516–0042
TEL: 0596–28–3705 (Ise Sightseeing Information)
WEBSITE: www.ise-kanko.jp/e-ok/index.html
www.isejingu.or.jp/english/index.htm
NEAREST STATION: Ise-shi (JR Sangū line, Kintetsu line)

OSAKA

Ikutama Shrine (August)
ADDRESS: 13–9 Ikutamachō, Tennōji-ku Osaka
543–0071
TEL: 06–6771–0002
NEAREST STATION: Tanimachi-Kyūchōme (Tanimachi line, Sennichimae line)

Osaka Castle (July)
ADDRESS: Nishinomaru Garden, Osaka Castle 2
Osaka-jō Chūō-ku, Osaka 540–0002
TEL: 06–6366–1848 (Yomiuri Shimbun)
NEAREST STATION: Morinomiya (JR Osaka Loop line)

Sumiyoshi Shrine (August—the oldest Nō stage in Japan)
ADDRESS: 2 Hattori Minamimachi, Toyonaka-shi
Osaka 561–0853
TEL: 06–6864–0761
NEAREST STATION: Hattori (Hankyū Takarazuka line)

HIMEJI, HYŌGO

Himeji Castle (in August)
ADDRESS: Sannomaru Plaza, Himeji Castle 68
Honmachi, Himeji-shi, Hyōgo 670–0012
TEL: 0792–81–6800
NEAREST STATION: Himeji (JR Shinkansen, JR San'yō Main line)

HIROSHIMA

Hiroshima Gokoku Shrine (May)
ADDRESS: 21–2 Motomachi, Naka-ku, Hiroshima
730–0011
TEL: 082–221–5590
NEAREST STATION: Hiroshima (Hiroshima Electric Railways) → bus or taxi

MATSUYAMA, SHIKOKU

Matsuyama Castle (October)
ADDRESS: 3–2–46 Ōkaidō, Matsuyama-shi, Ehime
790–0004
TEL: 089–927–7128 (Nankai Broadcasting Co.)
WEBSITE: www.city.matsuyama.ehime.jp/eng/index.html
NEAREST STATION: Ōkaidō (Street Car)

SHIMABARA, KYŪSHŪ

Shimabara Castle (October)
ADDRESS: 1–1183–1 Jōnai, Shimabara-shi,
Nagasaki 855–0036
TEL: 0957–62–4753
0957–63–1111
NEAREST STATION: Shimabara (Shimabara Railway)

NOBEOKA, KYŪSHŪ

Nobeoka Castle (October)
ADDRESS: Ninomaru Square, 178 Higashi Honkōji,
Nobeoka-shi Miyazaki 882–0813
TEL: 0982–33–0248
E-MAIL: nobeoka@takigihoh.com
NEAREST STATION: Nobeoka (Nippō line)

KYŌGEN

Regular performances can be seen at the National Noh Theatre. Programs usually consist of three plays each lasting 20–60 minutes, with ticket prices ranging from ¥2,000 to ¥4,000. To see Kyōgen performed with Nō, please see the listings of Nō theaters.

The offices of the main Kyōgen schools are generally very helpful with information on their school's performances.

MAIN KYŌGEN SCHOOLS

TOKYO

Izumiryū Sōke Kōen-kai
TEL: 03–3974–0506

Mansaku no Kai (Nomura Mansaku-ke, Nomura Mansai-ke, Izumi school)
TEL: 03–3997–5899
WEBSITE: www.mansaku.co.jp/english/index2.html

Ōkura-kai (Ōkuraryū Sōke)
TEL: 03–3920–6717

Yorozu Kyōgen Office (about Izumi school's Yorozu Kyōgen, and Nomura Mannojō no Gakugeki Sakuhin only)
TEL: 03–5363–1305

KYOTO

Shigeyama Kyōgen-kai (Ōkura school)
TEL: 075–221–8371

CONTEMPORARY THEATER

THEATERS

TOKYO

Shibuya / Omotesandō ───────────

Aoyama Theatre / Aoyama Round Theatre
ADDRESS: 5–53–1 Jingūmae, Shibuya-ku, Tokyo 150–0001
TEL: 03–3797–5678
WEBSITE: www.aoyama.org/english/index.html
NEAREST STATION: Omotesandō (Ginza line, Chiyoda line, Hanzōmon line)

Orchard Hall (Bunkamura) / Theatre Cocoon (Bunkamura)
ADDRESS: Bunkamura 2–24–1 Dōgenzaka, Shibuya-ku, Tokyo 150–8507
TEL: 03–3477–3244
    03–3477–9999 (Box Office)
WEBSITE: www.bunkamura.co.jp/english/orchard/institute/index.html
www.bunkamura.co.jp/english/index.html
NEAREST STATION: Shibuya (JR Yamanote line, Ginza line, Hanzōmon line, Den'en Toshi line, Inokashira line, Tōyoko line)

Parco Theater
ADDRESS: Shibuya Parco Part 1, 9F, 15–1 Udagawa-chō, Shibuya-ku Tokyo 150–8377
TEL: 03–3477–5858
NEAREST STATION: Shibuya (JR Yamanote line, Ginza line, Hanzōmon line, Den'en Toshi line, Inokashira line, Tōyoko line)

Roppongi ─────────────────

Haiyū-za Theatre
ADDRESS: 4–9–2 Roppongi, Minato-ku, Tokyo 106–0032
TEL: 03–3470–2880
WEBSITE: www.haiyuzagekijou.co.jp/ehaiyuza/etoppage.html
E-MAIL: info@haiyuzagekijou.co.jp
NEAREST STATION: Roppongi (Hibiya line, Toei Ōedo line)

Setagaya ─────────────────

Setagaya Public Theatre / Theatre Tram
ADDRESS: 4–1–1 Taishidō, Setagaya-ku, Tokyo 154–0004
TEL: 03–5432–1526
    03–5432–1515 (Box Office)
WEBSITE: www.setagaya-ac.or.jp/sept/frame-e.html
NEAREST STATION: Sangenjaya (Den'en Toshi line, Setagaya line)

Shinjuku / Shin Ōkubo / Hatsudai ──────

Kinokuniya Hall
ADDRESS: Kinokuniya book store, 4F, 3–17–7 Shinjuku, Shinjuku-ku, Tokyo 163–8636
TEL: 03–3354–0141
WEBSITE: www.kinokuniya.co.jp/english/index.html
E-MAIL: info@kinokuniya.co.jp
NEAREST STATION: Shinjuku (JR Yamanote line, JR Chūō line, JR Sōbu line, JR Saikyō line, Odakyū line, Keiō line, Marunouchi line, Toei Shinjuku line)

Kinokuniya Southern Theater
ADDRESS: Kinokuniya book store, 7F, in Takashimaya Times Square
TEL: 03–5361–3321
WEBSITE: www.kinokuniya.co.jp/english/index.html
E-MAIL: info@kinokuniya.co.jp
NEAREST STATION: Shinjuku (JR Yamanote line, JR Chūō line, JR Sōbu line, JR Saikyō line, Odakyū line, Keiō line, Marunouchi line, Toei Shinjuku line)

New National Theatre
ADDRESS: 1–1–1 Honmachi, Shibuya-ku, Tokyo 151–0071
TEL: 03–5351–3011
    03–5352–9999 (Box Office)

NEAREST STATION: Hatsudai (Keiō line)

Space Zero

ADDRESS: Zenrōsai Building 2–12–10 Yoyogi,
Shibuya-ku Tokyo 151–0053
TEL: 03–3375–8741
        03–3375–8869 (Box Office)
E-MAIL: info@spacezero.co.jp
NEAREST STATION: Shinjuku (JR Yamanote line, JR
Chūō line, JR Sōbu line, JR Saikyō line, Odakyū line,
Keiō line, Marunouchi line, Toei Shinjuku line)

Theatre Apple

ADDRESS: 1–19–1 Kabukichō, Shinjuku-ku, Tokyo
160–0021
TEL: 03–3209–0222
E-MAIL: info@theatre-apple.co.jp
NEAREST STATIONS: Seibu-Shinjuku (Seibu Shinjuku
line), Shinjuku (JR Yamanote line, JR Chūō line, JR
Sōbu line, JR Saikyō line, Odakyū line, Keiō line,
Marunouchi line, Toei Shinjuku line)

Theater Moliere

ADDRESS: 3–33–10 Shinjuku, Shinjuku-ku, Tokyo
160–0002
TEL: 03–3354–6568
NEAREST STATION: Shinjuku-Sanchōme (Marunouchi line, Toei Shinjuku line)

Theater / Tops

ADDRESS: TOPS HOUSE, 4F, 3–20–8 Shinjuku, Tokyo
160–0022
TEL: 03–3350–9696
NEAREST STATION: Shinjuku (JR Yamanote line, JR
Chūō line, JR Sōbu line, JR Saikyō line, Odakyū
line, Keiō line, Marunouchi line, Toei Shinjuku line)

The Tokyo Globe

ADDRESS: 3–1–2 Hyakuninchō, Shinjuku-ku, Tokyo
169–0073
TEL: 03–3366–4020
NEAREST STATION: Shin-Ōkubo (JR Yamanote line)

The Tokyo Globe, designed by leading architect
Isozaki Arata, opened in 1988 with a capacity of
700, dedicated primarily to performances of Shakespeare. The Globe frequently invites troupes from
around the world.

Shimokitazawa

Ekimae Theater

ADDRESS: 2–11–8 Kitazawa, Setagaya-ku, Tokyo
155–0031
TEL: 03–3414–0019
E-MAIL: office@honda-geki.com
NEAREST STATION: Shimokitazawa (Odakyū line,
Inokashira line)

"Geki" Shōgekijō

ADDRESS: 2–6–6 Kitazawa, Setagaya-ku, Tokyo
155–0031
TEL: 03–3466–0020
E-MAIL: office@honda-geki.com
NEAREST STATION: Shimokitazawa (Odakyū line,
Inokashira line)

Honda Theater

ADDRESS: 2–10–15 Kitazawa, Setagaya-ku, Tokyo
155–0031
TEL: 03–3468–0030
E-MAIL: office@honda-geki.com
NEAREST STATION: Shimokitazawa (Odakyū line,
Inokashira line)

OFF OFF Theater

ADDRESS: 2–11–8 Kitazawa, Setagaya-ku, Tokyo
155–0031
TEL: 03–3424–3755
E-MAIL: office@honda-geki.com
NEAREST STATION: Shimokitazawa (Odakyū line,
Inokashira line)

The Suzunari

ADDRESS: 1–45–15 Kitazawa, Setagaya-ku, Tokyo
155–0031
TEL: 03–3469–0511
E-MAIL: office@honda-geki.com
NEAREST STATION: Shimokitazawa (Odakyū line,
Inokashira line)

Ikebukuro / Sengoku

Sanbyakunin Theater

ADDRESS: 2–29–15 Honkomagome, Bunkyō-ku,
Tokyo 113–0021
TEL: 03–3944–5451
WEBSITE: www.bekkoame.ne.jp/~darts

E-MAIL: darts@bekkoame.ne.jp
NEAREST STATION: Sengoku (Toei Mita line)

Sunshine Theater

ADDRESS: Bunka Kaikan, 4F, in Sunshine City, 3–1–4 Higashi Ikebukuro, Toshima-ku, Tokyo 170–0013
TEL: 03–3987–5281
NEAREST STATION: Ikebukuro (JR Yamanote line, JR Saikyō line, Tōbu Tōjō line, Seibu Ikebukuro line, Yūrakuchō line, Marunouchi line)

Tokyo Metropolitan Art Space

ADDRESS: 1–8–1 Nishi Ikebukuro, Toshima-ku, Tokyo 171–0021
TEL: 03–5391–9111
03–5985–1707 (Box Office)
WEBSITE: www.geigeki.jp/english/index.html
NEAREST STATION: Ikebukuro (JR Yamanote line, JR Saikyō line, Tōbu Tōjō line, Seibu Ikebukuro line, Yūrakuchō line, Marunouchi line)

Ginza / Hibiya / Shimbashi / Yūrakuchō ——————

The Dentsu Shiki Theatre SEA

ADDRESS: 1–8–2 Higashi Shimbashi, Minato-ku, Tokyo 105–0021
TEL: 03–5776–6730
045–903–1141 (Shiki headquarters)
WEBSITE: www.shiki.gr.jp/siteinfo/english/index.html
E-MAIL: e-support@shiki.gr.jp
NEAREST STATION: Shimbashi (JR Yamanote line, Ginza line, Toei Asakusa line)

Hakuhinkan Theater

ADDRESS: 8–8–11 Ginza, Chūō-ku, Tokyo 104–8132
TEL: 03–3571–1003
WEBSITE: www.hakuhinkan.co.jp/eng/body.htm
NEAREST STATION: Shimbashi (JR Yamanote line, Ginza line, Toei Asakusa line)

Imperial Theatre (Teikoku Gekijō)

ADDRESS: 3–1–1 Marunouchi, Chiyoda-ku, Tokyo 100–0005
TEL: 03–3213–7221
NEAREST STATION: Hibiya (Hibiya line, Chiyoda line, Toei Mita line)

Le Theatre Ginza

ADDRESS: 3rd floor, Ginza Theatre building 1–11–2 Ginza, Chūō-ku Tokyo 104–0061
TEL: 03–3535–5151
NEAREST STATIONS: Kyōbashi (Ginza line); Ginza-Itchōme (Yūrakuchō line)

Nissay Theatre (see 264 page)

Shinbashi Enbujō (see 264 page)

Tokyo International Forum

ADDRESS: 5–1 Marunouchi 3-chōme, Chiyoda-ku, Tokyo 100–0005
TEL: 03–5221–9000
WEBSITE: www.t-i-forum.co.jp/english/index.html
NEAREST STATION: Yūrakuchō (JR Yamanote line, JR Keihin Tōhoku line, Yūrakuchō line)

Tokyo Takarazuka Theater

ADDRESS: 1–1–3 Yūrakuchō, Chiyoda-ku, Tokyo 100–0006
TEL: 03–5251–2001
kageki.hankyu.co.jp/english/index.html
NEAREST STATION: Hibiya (Hibiya line, Chiyoda line, Toei Mita line)

Other ——————————————————

Art Sphere

ADDRESS: 2–3–16 Higashi Shinagawa, Shinagawa-ku, Tokyo 140–0002
TEL: 03–5460–9999
E-MAIL: webmaster@sphere.tennoz.co.jp
NEAREST STATION: Tennōzu Isle (Tokyo Monorail, Rinkai line)

The Shiki Theatres, HARU, AKI, and JIYŪ

ADDRESS: 1–10–48 Kaigan, Minato-ku, Tokyo 105–0022
TEL: 03–5776–6730
045–903–1141 (Shiki headquarters)
WEBSITE: www.shiki.gr.jp/siteinfo/english/index.html
E-MAIL: e-support@shiki.gr.jp
NEAREST STATION: Hamamatsuchō (JR Yamanote line, JR Keihin Tōhoku line, Tokyo Monorail)

Theater X (pronounced "*Kai*")
ADDRESS: 2–10–14 Ryōgoku, Sumida-ku, Tokyo
130–0026
TEL: 03–5624–1181
E-MAIL: info@theaterx.jp
NEAREST STATION: Ryōgoku (JR Sōbu line, Toei Ōedo
line)

Theatre 1010 (pronounced "*Senju*")
ADDRESS: Senju Mildix, 10F, 3–92 Senju, Adachi-ku,
Tokyo 120–0034
TEL: 03–5244–1010
E-MAIL: info@t1010.jp
NEAREST STATION: Kita-Senju (JR Tōbu Isesaki line,
Chiyoda line, Hanzōmon line, Hibiya line)

SAITAMA

Saitama Arts Theater
ADDRESS: 3–15–1 Uemine, Chūō-ku, Saitama
338–8506
TEL: 048–858–5500
E-MAIL: mail@saf.or.jp
NEAREST STATION: Yono-Honmachi (JR Saikyō line)

NIIGATA

Ryūtopia (Niigata City Performing Arts Center)
ADDRESS: 2 Ichibanbori-dōri , Niigata-shi 951–8132
TEL: 025–224–7000
E-MAIL: jigyou@ryutopia.or.jp
NEAREST STATION: Niigata (JR Shinkansen, JR Shin-
etsu line)

MATSUMOTO, NAGANO

Matsumoto Performing Arts Centre
ADDRESS: 3–10–1 Fukashi, Matsumoto-shi, Nagano
390–0815
TEL: 0263–33–3800
E-MAIL: mpac@city.matsumoto.nagano.jp
NEAREST STATION: Matsumoto (JR Chūō line)

SHIZUOKA

The Shizuoka Arts Theatre
ADDRESS: The Shizuoka Performing Arts Center
(SPAC) 79–4 Ikeda, Shizuoka City, Shizuoka
422–8005
TEL: 054–203–5730

WEBSITE: www.spac.or.jp/01news01-f.html
NEAREST STATION: Higashi-Shizuoka (JR Tōkaidō line)

NAGOYA

Aichi Prefectural Art Theater
ADDRESS: Aichi Arts Center, Art Plaza 1–13–2
Higashisakura, Higashi-ku, Nagoya 461–8525
TEL: 052–971–5511
WEBSITE: www.aac.pref.aichi.jp/english/gekijyo/
index.html
E-MAIL: aaf01@aac.pref.aichi.jp
NEAREST STATIONS: Sakae (Higashiyama line,
Meijō line); Sakaemachi (Meitetsu Seto line)

Chūnichi Theatre (see 264 page)

The Shin Nagoya Musical Theatre
ADDRESS: 1–2–24 Sakae, Naka-ku, Nagoya
460–0008
TEL: 052–220–7111 (theatre)
      052–290–0800 (office)
WEBSITE: www.shiki.gr.jp/siteinfo/english/index.
html
E-MAIL: e-support@shiki.gr.jp
NEAREST STATIONS: Fushimi (Higashiyama line,
Maizuru line); Nagoya (JR Shinkansen, JR Tōkaidō
line, JR Chūō line, JR Kansai line, Meitetsu line,
Kintetsu line, Higashiyama line)

KYOTO

Kyoto Prefectural Center for Arts and Culture
ADDRESS: Hirokōji kudaru, Kawaramachidōri,
Kamikyō-ku, Kyoto 602–0858
TEL: 075–222–1046
NEAREST STATION: Furitsu Idai Byōin mae (bus or
taxi from Kyoto station)

The Kyoto Theater
ADDRESS: c/o Kyoto Station Building, Shiokoji-
sagaru, Karasuma-dōri, Shimogyō-ku, Kyoto
600–8216
TEL: 075–353–3551
WEBSITE: www.shiki.gr.jp/siteinfo/english/index.
html
E-MAIL: e-support@shiki.gr.jp
NEAREST STATION: Kyoto (JR Shinkansen, JR
Tōkaidō line, Kintetsu line, Karasuma line)

OSAKA

Festival Hall
ADDRESS: 2–3–18 Nakanoshima, Kita-ku, Osaka 530–0005
TEL: 06–6231–2221
NEAREST STATIONS: Higobashi (Yotsubashi line); Yodoyabashi (Midōsuji line, JR Osaka Loop line)

The Osaka MBS Theatre
ADDRESS: 1–3–2 Shiromi, Chūō-ku, Osaka 540–0001
TEL: 06–6966–5126 (theater)
    06–6966–5117 (office)
WEBSITE: www.shiki.gr.jp/siteinfo/english/index.html
E-MAIL: e-support@shiki.gr.jp
NEAREST STATIONS: Osakajō-Kōen (JR Osaka Loop line); Kyōbashi (JR Osaka Loop line, Tōzai line, Keihan line); Osaka Business Park (Nagahori Tsurumi-Ryokuchi line)

Umeda Koma Theater/ Theater Drama City
ADDRESS: 19–1 Chayamachi, Kita-ku Osaka 530–0013
TEL: 06–6377–7777 (Umeda Koma)
    06–6377–3888 (Theater Drama City)
NEAREST STATIONS: Umeda (Midōsuji line, Hankyū line, Hanshin line); Osaka (JR Osaka Loop line)

HYŌGO

Shinkobe Oriental Theater
ADDRESS: 1–3 Kitanochō, Chūō-ku, Kōbe 650–0002
TEL: 078–291–1100
NEAREST STATIONS: Shin-Kōbe (JR Shinkansen); Kobe (Kobe City Subway)

Takarazuka Grand Theater
ADDRESS: 1–1–57 Sakaemachi, Takarazuka City, Hyōgo 665–8558
TEL: 0570–00–5100
WEBSITE: kageki.hankyu.co.jp/english/index.html
NEAREST STATION: Takarazuka (Hankyū Takarazuka line, JR Fukuchiyama line)

FUKUOKA

Kitakyūshū Performing Arts Center
ADDRESS: 1–1–1–11 Muromachi, Kokurakutaku, Kitakyūshū-shi, Fukuoka 803–0812

TEL: 093–562–2655
NEAREST STATIONS: Kokura (JR Shinkansen, JR Nippō line, JR Kagoshima line); Nishikokura (JR Nippō line, JR Kagoshima line)

Mielparque Fukuoka
ADDRESS: 4–14–52 Yakuin, Chūō-ku, Fukuoka 810–8541
TEL: 092–525–0771
E-MAIL: miel-fukuoka@msd.biglobe.ne.jp
NEAREST STATIONS: Hakata (JR Shinkansen, JR Kagoshima line, Fukuoka City Subway); Tenjin (Fukuoka City Subway)

Nishitetsu Hall
ADDRESS: Solaria Stage Building, 6F, 2–11–3 Tenjin, Chūō-ku, Fukuoka
TEL: 092–734–1362
E-MAIL: hall@nnr.co.jp
NEAREST STATION: Tenjin (Fukuoka City Subway)

The Fukuoka City Theater
ADDRESS: Canal City Hakata, 4F, 1–2–1 Sumiyoshi, Hakata-ku, Fukuoka 812–0018
TEL: 092–271–1199 (office)
WEBSITE: www.shiki.gr.jp/siteinfo/english/index.html
E-MAIL: e-support@shiki.gr.jp
NEAREST STATION: Nakasu-Kawabata (Fukuoka City Subway)

THEATER TROUPES

These are helpful with information about their performances.

Bungaku-za
TEL: 03–3351–7265
E-MAIL: info@bungakuza.com

Bunka-za
TEL: 03–3828–2216
E-MAIL: info@bunkaza.com

Caramelbox (Narui Yutaka)
TEL: 03–5342–0220

Chijinkai Theatre Company
TEL: 03–3354–8361
    03–3354–1279 (for tickets)
E-MAIL: chijinkai@mub.biglobe.ne.jp

Furusato Caravan
TEL: 042–381–6721

Gekidan Shinkansen
(Nakashima Kazuki, Inoue Hidenori)
TEL: 03-5348-2870 (Village)

Haiyū-za Theatre Company
TEL: 03–3470–2888

Hanagumi Shibai (Kanō Yukikazu)
TEL: 03–3709–9430
WEBSITE: www.hanagumi.ne.jp
E-MAIL: office@hanagumi.ne.jp

Kiyama Jimusho
TEL: 03–5958–0855

Mumeijuku
TEL: 03–3709–7802

Ongaku-za Musical / R Company
TEL: 03–3222–1178

Seinen Gekijō
TEL: 03–3352–6922
E-MAIL: info@seinengekijo.co.jp

Seinan-za
TEL: 03–5478–8571
E-MAIL: info@seinenza.com

Shakespeare Theatre
TEL: 03–5348–6993
E-MAIL: atelier@shkspr-thr.co.jp

Shiki Theatre Company
TEL: 03–5776–6730
    045–903–1141 (Shiki headquarters)
WEBSITE: www.shiki.gr.jp/siteinfo/english/index.
html
E-MAIL: e-support@shiki.gr.jp

Subaru (The Institute of Dramatic Arts: DARTS)
TEL: 03–3944–5451
E-MAIL: darts@bekkoame.ne.jp

Takarazuka Revue
TEL: 0570–00–5100
WEBSITE: www.kageki.hankyu.co.jp/english/index.
html

Theatre Echo
TEL: 03–5466–3311
E-MAIL: info@t-echo.co.jp

The Mingei Theatre Company
TEL: 044–987–7711
E-MAIL: seisaku@gekidanmingei.co.jp

Toho
TEL: 03-3201-2400
E-MAIL: customer@toho.co.jp

Tokyo Engeki Ensemble
TEL: 03–3920–5232
E-MAIL: tee@tee.co.jp

BUTŌ TROUPES

Dairakudakan (Maro Akaji)
TEL: 0422–21–4982
WEBSITE: www.dairakudakan.com/rakudakan/e_
top.html
E-MAIL: temputenshiki@dairakudakan.com

Sankai Juku
TEL: 03-3498-9619
    01 43 07 46 30 (Paris)
WEBSITE: www.sankaijuku.com
E-MAIL: sankaioffice@yahoo.co.jp
info@sankaijuku.com

Tenshikan
TEL: 042–301–2510
E-MAIL: tenshikan-kasai@jcom.home.ne.jp

PLAYWRIGHTS, DIRECTORS, AND ACTORS

Betsuyaku Minoru
(Piccolo Theater Company, Hyōgo)
TEL: 06–6426–1940
E-MAIL: p-gyohmu@hyogo-arts.or.jp

Hasegawa Kōji (Hirosaki Gekijō)
TEL: 0172–62–0717
WEBSITE: www.hirogeki.co.jp/en/index.html
E-MAIL: office@hirogeki.co.jp

Hirata Oriza (Seinendan)
TEL: 03–3467–2743
WEBSITE: www.seinendan.org/eng/info/index.html

Iijima Sanae / Suzuki Yumi (Jitensha Kinqureat)
TEL: 03–5489–4434
E-MAIL: mail@jitekin.com

Inoue Hisashi (Komatsu-za)
TEL: 03–3862–5941

Iwamatsu Ryō
TEL: 03–3470–8581 (KOMS SIFT)

Kaneshita Tatsuo (THE GAZIRA)
TEL: 03–3411–4081 (office cottone)
E-MAIL: cottone@msh.biglobe.ne.jp

Kara Jūrō (Kara-gumi)
TEL: 03–3330–8118

Keralino Sandorovich (Nylon100°C)
TEL: 03–5458–9261
E-MAIL: sillywalk@sillywalk.com

Kimura Kōichi (see Chijinkai Theatre Company)

Kōkami Shōji (Third Stage)
TEL: 03–5772–7474

Kuriyama Tamiya (see New National Theatre)
TEL: 03–5351–3011
WEBSITE: www.nntt.jac.go.jp/english/index.html

Kushida Kazuyoshi (see Matsumoto Performing Arts Centre)

Makino Nozomi
TEL: 03–5766–5899
03–3380–3140 (MOP)
E-MAIL: staff@g-mop.com

Matsumoto Kōshirō/ Ichikawa Somegorō
TEL: 03–3455–7188/7288

Matsumoto Yūkichi (Ishinha)
TEL: 06–6763–2634
E-MAIL: info@ishinha.com

Matsuo Suzuki
(Otona Keikaku)
TEL: 03–3327–4312
E-MAIL: otona@big.or.jp

Mitani Kōki
TEL: 03–3477–5858 (plays produced by Parco only)

Miyamoto Amon
TEL: 03–5722–3831
WEBSITE: www.puerta-ds.com
E-MAIL: info@puerta-ds.com

Miyazawa Akio (U-enchi Saisei Jigyōdan)
TEL: 03–5454–0545
E-MAIL: u-ench@inter7.jp

Nagai Ai (Nitosha)
TEL: 03–5638–4587
E-MAIL: info@nitosha.net

Nakamura Kankurō
TEL: 03–5565–0003

Ninagawa Yukio
E-MAIL: ninagawa@my-pro.co.jp

Noda Hideki (NODA MAP)
TEL: 03–5423–5901

Nomura Mansai (Mansaku no Kai)
TEL: 03–3997–8778 (11:00–17:00)
WEBSITE: www.mansaku.co.jp/english/index2.html

Ōta Shōgo
TEL: 03–3399–2637
   075–791–9122 (Kyoto University of Art and
   Design)

Ryūzanji Show (Ryūzanji Company)
TEL: 03–5272–1785
WEBSITE: www.ryuzanji.com/e-index.html
E-MAIL: ok21-kk@mk1.macnet.or.jp

Satō Makoto (The Black Tent Theater)
TEL: 03–3926–4021
WEBSITE: www.ne.jp/asahi/kurotent/tokyo/english
/e_btt.html
E-MAIL: btt@tokyo.email.ne.jp

Sakate Yōji (RINKO-GUN)
TEL: 03–3426–6294
E-MAIL: rinkogun@alles.or.jp

Suzuki Tadashi
(Shizuoka Performing Arts Center)
TEL: 054–203–5730
WEBSITE: www.spac.or.jp

Tsuka Kōhei (Kita-ku Tsuka Kōhei Gekidan)
E-MAIL: mail@tsuka.co.jp

Uesugi Shōzō (UN et NEUF)
TEL: 03–3470–4905
E-MAIL: fan-mail@un-neuf.co.jp

BUTŌ

Hijikata Tatsumi
TEL: 03–3424–3062 (The Asbestos Studio Sup-
porters' Committee)
WEBSITE: www.hijikata-tatsumi.com/index-e.html
E-MAIL: asbestos@hijikata-tatsumi.com

Ōno Kazuo
TEL: 045–381–2333
WEBSITE: www.asahi-net.or.jp/~ab4t-mzht/
E-MAIL: ab4t-mzht@asahi-net.or.jp

Tanaka Min
TEL: 03–5340–3860
E-MAIL: artcamp@sf7.so-net.ne.jp

Kaiin no uma ("The Sea Dappled Horse")

KABUKI

FAMOUS PERFORMANCES ON DVD

- *Dattan/Ninin wankyū*
- *Fūingiri* from *Koi bikyaku yamato ōrai*
- *Fuji musume/Yasuna/Sagi musume*
- *Ippongatana dohyōiri*
- *Ise ondo koi no netaba*
- *Jusshukō* from *Honchō nijūshikō/Heike monogatari: Kenrei monin*
- *Kanjinchō*
- *Kōchiyama* from *Kumoni magō Ueno no hatsuhana*
- *Kumagai jinya* from *Ichinotani futaba gunki*
- *Shi-no-kiri* from *Yoshitsune senbon zakura*
- *Shiranami gonin otoko*
- *Sumidagawa/Hanabusa shūjaku jishi*
- *Terakoya* from *Sugawara denju tenarai kagami*
- *Togitatsu no utare* directed by Noda Hideki
- *Yamatotakeru* (Super Kabuki)

(English audio translations and commentaries included/All Regions)
TEL: 0120–135–335 (Shochiku)
    03–5478–0780 (NHK Software)

BANDŌ TAMASABURŌ DVDS

- *Kyōganoko musume Dōjōji*
- *Sagi musume* and others
- *Yōkihi* and others
- *Kagami jishi* and others
- *Onatsu kyōran* and others
- *Fuji musume* and others

(English audio translations and commentaries included/All Regions)
TEL: 0120–135–335 (Shochiku)

NŌ

Noh Dōjōji (English commentaries/All Regions)
TEL: 03–3363–7718 (Umewaka Rokurō Jimusho)
E-MAIL: office@noh-umewaka.com

Nohgakushi (English subtitles/All Regions)
TEL: 03–3291–2488 (Hinoki Book Store)
E-MAIL: office@hinoki-shoten.co.jp

KYŌGEN

Machigai no Kyōgen (English subtitles/Region 2)
TEL: 03–5432–1526 (Setagaya Public Theatre)
    03–3997–5899 (Mansaku no Kai)
E-MAIL: shop@so-net.ne.jp

The Nōgaku Association is helpful with information on DVDs of Nō and Kyōgen.
TEL: 03–5925–3871
E-MAIL: office@nohgaku.or.jp

CONTEMPORARY THEATER

PLAY

Gekidan Shinkansen:
- *Ashura-jō no hitomi* (2003)
- *Aterui*
(English subtitles/All Regions)

Musical:
- *Tenshi wa hitomi wo tojite* (Kōkami Shōji)
(English subtitles/All Regions)
TEL: 03–5361–3512
E-MAIL: cs@e-oshibai.net

BUTŌ

Ōno Kazuo:
- *Beauty and Strength* (English subtitles/Region 2)
- *O, Kind God!* (English and Italian subtitles/All Regions)
TEL: 045–381–2333
E-MAIL: ab4t-mzht@asahi-net.or.jp

Companies, directors, and playwrights are helpful in giving information on their own productions available on DVD, and should be contacted individually. Parco Theater DVD Shop also sells various Contemporary Theater DVDs (*TEL*: 03–5361–3853).

PHOTOGRAPHS

The following photos are reproduced with permission from each photographer, actor, theater, and company.

Jacket (front) *Kyōganoko musume Dōjōji* (2003). Kabuki-za. Hanako: Bandō Tamasaburō V. Photo by Fukuda Naotake. / *Tōmei ningen no yuge* (2004). Actors: Abe Sadao (left), Miyazawa Rie. Photo by Yakō Masahiko. (New National Theatre)

Jacket (back) *Utsubozaru* (2003). National Noh Theatre. *Saruhiki*: Nomura Mansai; *Kozaru*: Nomura Yūki. Photo by Masakawa Shinji. (Mansaku no Kai)/ *Kanadehon chūshingura* (2000). Konami: Kiritake Icchō. (Tokyo National Theatre)

P. 1 *Dōjōji* (*Tokubetsu kōen*, December 26, 1998). *Nochijite*: Umewaka Rokurō; *Waki*: Hōshō Kan; *Wakitsure*: Hōshō Kinya, Tonoda Kenkichi. Kanze school. (National Noh Theare)

PP. 2–3 *Yoshitsune senbon zakura* (2002). Heisei Nakamura-za. Taira no Tomomori no rei: Nakamura Kankurō V. Photo by Fukuda Naotake.

P. 4 *Hagoromo* (*Teirei kōen*, June 17, 1988). *Shite*: Kanze Hideo. Kanze school. (National Noh Theare)/ *Yume kara sameta yume* (2000). Photo by Yamanoue Masanobu. (Gekidan Shiki)/ *Ichinotani futaba gunki* (1990). Kumagai Naozane: Nakamura Kichiemon II. (Tokyo National Theatre)

P. 5 *Sugawara denju tenarai kagami* (2003). Kan Shōjō: Yoshida Tamao. (Tokyo National Theatre)/ *Oidipusuō* (2004). Creon: Yoshida Kōtarō. Photo by Yakō Masahiko. (Bunkamura)/ *Aoi no ue* (Introduction to Nō and Kyōgen, June 26, 1984). *Shite*: Asami Masakuni. Kanze school. (National Noh Theatre)

P. 6 *Yamatotakeru* (1986). Shinbashi Enbujō. Yamatotakeru: Ichikawa Ennosuke III. (Shochiku Co., Ltd.)

P. 7 *Dannoura kabutogunki* (1997). Akoya: Bandō Tamasaburō V; Shigetada: Nakamura Baigyoku IV; Iwanaga: Kataoka Gatō V. / *Yanone* (1990). Soga no Gorō: Onoe Shōroku IV. (both Tokyo National Theatre)

PP. 8–9 *Kanjinchō* (1998). Benkei: Matsumoto Kōshirō IX; Togashi: Nakamura Baigyoku IV; Kamei Rokurō: Ōtani Tomoemon VIII; Kataoka Hachirō:

Ichikawa Komazō XI; Suruga Jirō: Nakamura Tamatarō IV. (Tokyo National Theatre)

P. 10 *Meido no hikyaku* (2002). Chūbei: Yoshida Tamao; Umegawa: Yoshida Bungo. / *Yoshitsune senbon zakura* (2003). Tadanobu, in reality Genkurō kitsune: Yoshida Bungo; Shizuka: Kiritake Monju; Yoshitsune: Yoshida Kazuo. (both Tokyo National Theatre)

P. 11 *Shakkyō* (*Teirei kōen*, September 18, 1998). *Nochijite* (white lion): Konparu Yasuaki; *Tsure*: Tsujii Hachirō, Yamai Tunao, Inoue Yoshiaki. Konparu School./ *Tsuchigumo* (*Fukyū kōen*, August 11, 2001) *Nochijite*: Ōtsuki Bunzō; *Waki*: Hōshō Kan; *Wakitsure*: Noguchi Yasuhiro, Norihisa Hideshi, Obinata Hiroshi. Kanze School. (both National Noh Theatre)

P. 12 *Atsumori* (*Kikaku kōen*, April 27, 1995). *Nochijite*: Honda Mitsuhiro. Konparu School/ *Momijigari* (*Teirei kōen*, October 7, 1987) *Maejite*: Umewaka Yasuyuki; *Tsure*: Umewaka Shinya, Umewaka Yasunori, Yamazaki Masamichi. Kanze School. (both National Noh Theatre)

P. 13 *Susugigawa* (2001). National Noh Theatre. *Onna*: Shigeyama Shigeru; *Shūtome*: Shigeyama Senzaburō; *Otoko*: Shigeyama Shime. Photo by Iwata Akira. / *Tōzumō* (2002). Kyoto Kanze Hall. *Tōjin*: Shigeyama Shigeru, *Nihon-jin*: Shigeyama Shime. Photo by Kawanishi Yoshiki. (both Shigeyama Kyogen-kai)

P. 14 *Aoi no ue* (2002). Actors: Miwa Akihiro (left), Takuma Shin. Photo by Midō Yoshinori. (Parco)/ *Aohigekō no shiro* (2003). Actors: from left, Sasai Eisuke, Ikeda Yukiko, Hiraguri Atsumi. Photo by Miyauchi Katsu. (Ryūzanji Jimusho)

P. 15 *Gansaku sakura no mori no mankai no shita* (2002). Fukatsu Eri (back) Tsutsumi Shinichi. Photo by Yakō Masahiko. (New National Theatre)

P. 16 *Hamlet* (1998). Hamlet: Sanada Hiroyuki; Horatio: Matsushige Yutaka; Laertes: Yokota Eiji; Fortinbras: Miyawaki Takuya; Gertrude: Kaga Mariko; Claudius: Sagawa Tetsurō. Photo by Fukunaga Kōji. (Kansai Telecasting Corporation)/ *Kawa no hotori* (2002). Photo by Yamazaki Hiroto. (Dairakudakan)

P. 17 *Suō otoshi* (2003). National Noh Theatre. Tarōkaja: Nomura Mansai. Photo by Masakawa Shinji. (Mansaku no Kai)

P. 18 *Machigai no kyōgen* (2001). Globe

Theatre in London. From left, Kinjirō: Tsukizaki Haruo; Kurokusa no Tarōkaja: Nomura Mansai; Kurokusa no Ishino-suke: Ishida Yukio. (Mansaku no Kai)

P. 19 *Oidipusuō* (credit p. 5). Oedipus Rex: Nomura Mansai; Jocasta: Asami Rei.

P. 70 *Meiboku sendai hagi* (1998). Masaoka: Nakamura Ganjirō III; Sakae Gozen: Sawamura Tanosuke VI. (Tokyo National Theatre)

P. 74 *Oshiguma* of Onoe Shōroku II as Kagekiyo in *Nanatsumen* (January, 1983). Tokyo National Theatre./ *Oshiguma* of Nakamura Utaemon VI as the lion spirit in *Kagami jishi* (December, 1951). Minami-za./Double *Oshiguma* of Nakamura Utaemon VI as the spirit of Kiyohime and Matsumoto Kōshirō VIII as the heroic warrior who defeats her in *Musume Dōjōji* (September, 1960). Kabuki-za. (all P. Griffith Collection)

P. 75 *Yanone* (credit p. 7)

P. 77 *Meiboku sendai hagi* (credit p. 70)

P. 81 *Ichinotani futaba gunki* (credit p. 5)

P. 82 *Kanjinchō* (credit pp. 8–9)

P. 83 *Yoshitsune senbon zakura* (1991). Kokingo: Bandō Mitsugorō X. (Tokyo National Theatre)

P. 84 *Kagamiyama gonichi no Iwafuji* (1990). Iwafuji: Onoe Kikugorō VII. (Tokyo National Theatre)

P. 85 *Ichinotani futaba gunki* (credit p. 5)/ *Kanadehon chūshingura* (2002). Kanpei: Nakamura Ganjirō III; Oakaya: Bandō Takesaburō V. (Tokyo National Theatre)

P. 101 *Sonezaki shinjū* (2001). Ohatsu: Yoshida Minosuke; Tokubei: Yoshida Tamao. (Tokyo National Theatre)

P. 107 *Sugawara denju tenarai kagami* (2003). Kan Shōjō: Yoshida Tamao; Kakuju: Yoshida Bunjaku. (Tokyo National Theatre)

P. 111 *Sugawara denju tenarai kagami* (2003). Genzō: Yoshida Tamame; Tonami: Kiritake Kanju; Matsuōmaru: Yoshida Bungo; Chiyo: Yoshida Minosuke; Kan Shūsai: Kiritake Monhide; Midaidokoro: Kiritake Kameji. (Tokyo National Theatre)

P. 113 *Yoshitsune senbon zakura* (2003) Tadanobu, in reality Genkurō kitsune: Yoshida Bungo. (Tokyo National Theatre)

P. 118 *Sugawara denju tenarai kagami* (2003). *Gidayū*: Takemoto Tsunatayū; Shamisen: Tsuruzawa Seijirō V. (Tokyo National Theatre)

p. 120 *Dannoura kabutogunki* (1998) Iwanaga: Yoshida Tamame; Shigetada: Yoshida Bungo; Akoya: Yoshida Minosuke. (Tokyo National Theatre)

p. 163 *Eguchi* (*Tokubetsu kōen*, February 26, 1989). *Nochijite*: Kanai Akira; *Ture*: Kanamori Hidetoshi, Higashikawa Mitsuo. Hōshō School. (National Noh Theatre)

p. 167 *Takasago* (*Fukyū kōen*, March 12, 1988). *Nochijite*: Tomoeda Akiyo. Kita School. (National Noh Theatre)

p. 168 *Okina* (15th Aniversary of National Noh Theatre, September 15, 1998). Okina: Hōshō Fusateru. Hōshō School. (National Noh Theatre)

p. 169 *Kantan* (*Teirei kōen*, December 2, 1987). *Shite*: Asami Masakuni. Kanze School. / *Izutsu* (*Fukyū kōen*, November 11, 1989). *Nochijite*: Kanze Hideo. Kanze School. (both National Noh Theatre)

p. 170 *Funa Benkei* (*Teirei kōen*, December 22, 1996). *Nochijite*: Kanze Hideo; *Waki*: Nakamura Yasaburō; *Wakitsure*: Korekawa Masahiko, Fukuō Kazuyuki; *Kokata*: Umewaka Shintarō; *Ai*: Shigeyama Sennojō. Kanze School. (National Noh Theatre)

p. 173 *Aoi no ue* (credit p. 5) *Waki*: Noguchi Atsuhiro.

p. 175 *Hagoromo* (credit p. 4)

p. 176 *Ataka* (*Teirei kōen*, May 2, 1990). *Waki*: Hōshō Kan. Hōshō School. / *Yashima* (*Teirei kōen*, March 15, 1996). *Nochijite*: Hōshō Fusateru. Hōshō School. (both National Noh Theatre)

p. 177 *Ko-omote* mask (National Noh Theatre)

p. 178 *Heida* and *hannya* masks (National Noh Theatre)

p. 179 *Sotoba Komachi* (*Tokubetsu kōen*, October 30, 1983). *Shite*: Umewaka Manzaburō; *Waki*: Hōshō Yaichi; *Wakitsure*: Kudō Kazuya. Kanze School. (National Noh Theatre)

p. 186 *Tsurigitsune* (1998). Kyoto Kanze Hall. *Kitsune*: Shigeyama Masakuni. / *Susugigawa* (credit p. 13). Both photos by Kawanishi Yoshiki. (both Shigeyama Kyōgen-kai)

p. 187 *Bōshibari* (2002). Kyoto Kanze Hall. Tarōkaja: Shigeyama Shime; Jirōkaja: Shigeyama Sengorō; the master: Shigeyama Akira. Photo by Kawanishi Yoshiki. (Shigeyama Kyōgen-kai)

p. 189 *Tsurigitsune* (credit p. 186). *Ado*: Shigeyama Shime.

p. 192 *Chatsubo* (1999). Hōshō Noh Theatre. *Suppa*: Nomura Mansaku; *Chūgoku no mono*: Nomura Mansai; *Mokudai*: Nomura Mannosuke. Photo by Maejima Yoshihiro. (Mansaku no Kai)

p. 209 *Kamereonzu rippu* (2004). Fukatsu Eri (left), Tsutsumi Shinichi. Photo by Hosono Shinji. (Bunkamura)/ *Okepi!* (2003). Actors: from left front, Kohinata Fumiyo, Kabira Jay, Aijima Kazuyuki, Shirai Akira; from left back, Kobayashi Takashi, Terawaki Yasufumi, Okada Makoto, Fuse Akira. Photo by Yakō Masahiko. (Parco)

p. 210 *Pandora no kane* (1999). Actors: from left, Matsuo Suzuki, Tsutsumi Shinichi, Amami Yūki, Furuta Arata. Photo by Aoki Tsukasa. (NODA MAP)/ *Doro ningyo* (2003). Actors: from left, Kuboi Ken, Toriyama Masakatsu, Kara Jūrō. Photo by Okamoto Yasuko. (Kara-gumi)

p. 211 *Warai no daigaku* (1996). Actors: Kondō Yoshimasa (left), Nishimura Masahiko. Photo by Yakō Masahiko. (Parco)/ *Tōkyō nōto* (2000). Actors: from left, Shiga Kōtarō, Ōtsuka Hiroshi, Matsuda Hiroko, Hirata Yōko, Yamamura Takako, Wada Eriko. Photo by Aoki Tsukasa. /*Mizu no tawamure* (1998). Actors: Higuchi Kanako (left), Takenaka Naoto. Photo by Ōmori Yūki. (Nakamura Stage Production)

p. 212 *Aterui* (2002). Actor: Ichikawa Somegorō VII. (Shochiku Co., Ltd.)/ *Hebunzu sain* (1998). Actors: from left, Abe Sadao, Iguchi Noboru, Miyazaki Tomu, Kudō Kankurō, Ikezu Shōko, Kaoda Kaohiko. Photo by Takimoto Junsuke. (Otona Keikaku)

p. 213 *Toki no monooki* (1999). Actors: from right, Kusamura Reiko, Takahashi Chōei, Sanada Kaoru, Taoka Miyako. Photo by Kirimura Ayasa. (Nitosha)/ *Daruma san ga koronda* (2004). Actors: from left, Pe Yuu, Shimofusa Gentarō, John Oglevee, Kuboshima Takashi. Photo by Ōhara Taku. (RINKO-GUN)/ *Keshō* (2001). Actor: Watanabe Misako. Photo by Yakō Masahiko. (Chijinkai)

p. 214 *Yūrei wa koko ni iru* (1998). Actors: Kushida Kazuyoshi (left), Ogawa Mayumi. Photo by Yakō Masahiko. (New National Theatre).

p. 215 *Shōjo kamen* (1971). Actors: from left, Maro Akaji, Ri Reisen, Kara Jūrō. Photo by Mikoshiba Shigeru. (*Kara-gumi* published by Parco)

p. 216 *Aohigekō no shiro* (2003). Actors: from left, Kosuda Yasuto, Matsumoto Kio, Ri Reisen. Photo by Miyauchi Katsu. (Ryūzanji Jimusho)/ *Sunafukin no tegami* (1994). Actors: from left, Kosuda Yasuto, Nagano Satomi, Yamashita Hiroko, Ikeda Narushi. (THIRDSTAGE)

p. 217 *Doro ningyo* (2003). Actor: Kara Jūrō. Photo by Fujisawa Kunimi. (Kara-gumi)

p. 218 *Hanshin* (1999). Actors: from left, Katō Takako, Noda Hideki, Fukatsu Eri. Photo by Aoki Tsukasa. (NODA MAP)

p. 219 *Akaoni* (1996). Actors: from left, Tomita Yasuko, Noda Hideki, Angus Barnett, Danda Yasunori. Photo by Aoki Tsukasa; *Nokemono kitarite* (1987). Actors: from left, Uesugi Shōzō, Takeshita Akiko, Noda Hideki. (both NODA MAP)

p. 220 *Ningen gowasan* (2003). Actors: from left, Matsuo Suzuki, Nakamura Kankurō V, Kudō Kankurō. Photo by Hosono Shinji. (Bunkamura)

p. 221 *Yabuhara kengyō* (2000). Actors: from right, Fujiki Takashi, Arashi Hironari, Nakamura Tatsu. (Chijinkai)

p. 223 *Atami satsujin jiken montekaruro iryūjon* (1998). Actor: Abe Hiroshi. Photo by Saitō Kazuo. (Parco)/ *Hagike no san shimai* (2000). Actors: from left, Minamitani Asako, Yo Kimiko, Okamoto Yasuyo. Photo by Rin Keisen. (Nitosha)

p. 224 *Matoryōshika* (1999). Actors: from left, Matsumoto Kōshirō IX, Ichikawa Somegorō VII, Matsumoto Kio. Photo by Yakō Masahiko. (Parco)

p. 226 *Tōkyō genshikaku kurabu* (1999). Actors: Nishikawa Tadashi (left), Koichi Mantarō. Photo by Yakō Masahiko. (Parco)/ *Hōōchō no hinin hō* (1996–97). Actors: from left, Yamanishi Atsushi, Hiwatashi Shinji, Okada Tadashi, Uo Yōko. Photo by Sudō Masayuki. (Jitensha Kinqureat's Company)

p. 227 *Ginga senritsu* (1999). Actors: from left, Ōmori Mikiko, Tsuda Shōko, Shinoda Tsuyoshi, Nishikawa Hiroyuki. Photo by Itō Kazunori. (Caramelbox)/ *Dokuro-jō no shichinin* (1997). Actors: Furuta Arata (left), Yoshimoto Miyoko. Photo by Higuchi Hiroaki. (VILLAGE)

p. 228 *Macchi uri no shōjo* (2003). Actors: front, Tezuka Tōru, from left back, Fuji Sumiko, Terashima Shinobu, Inokuma Tsunekazu. Photo by Yakō Masahiko. (New National Theatre)

p. 229 *Frōzun bīchi* (2002). Actors: from left, Imae Fuyuko, Inuyama Inuko, Matsunaga Reiko, Minemura Rie. Photo by Hikiji Nobuhiko. (SILLY WALK)/ *Hinemi* (1995). (U-enchi Saisei Jigyōdan)

p. 230 *Ie ni wa takai ki ga atta* (2004). Actors: from left, Hatasawa Seigo, Fukushi Kenji, Moriuchi Miyuki. Photo by Yokoyama Hideki. (Hirosaki Gekijō)

P. 231 *Natsu hoteru* (2001). Actors: Matsumoto Kōshirō IX (left), Matsu Takako. Photo by Yakō Masahiko. (Parco)

P. 232 *Tennō to seppun* (1999). Actors: from left, Kameron Steele, Kawanaka Kenjirō, Inokuma Tsunekazu, Tezuka Tōru, Josh Fox, Ōnishi Takahiro. Photo by Ōhara Taku. (RINKO-GUN)

P. 233 *Musabori to ikari to orokasa to* (1998). Actors: Satō Orie (left), Kobayashi Katsuya. Photo by Hata Hiromi. (Office Cottone)

P. 234 *Shinjū afururu keihakusa* (2001). Photo by Yakō Masahiko. (Bunkamura)

P. 235 *Dionysos* (1990). Actors: Nishikibe Takahisa (center). Photo by Mori Yasuhiro. (SPAC)

P. 236 *Good Woman of Setsuan* (1999). Actors: Matsu Takako (center); André Pink (right). Photo by Yakō Masahiko. (New National Theatre)/*Shanhai bansu kingu* (1990). Actors: Sasano Takashi (left), Kushida Kazuyoshi (right). (Bunkamura)

P. 237 *Nokutān* (2003). Photo by Yakō Masahiko. (New National Theatre)

P. 238 *Utsukushiki mono no densetsu* (1999). Actors: from left, Hayashi Ryūzō, Mita Kazuyo, Suma Kei. Photo by Yakō Masahiko. (New National Theatre)

P. 239 *Hora zamurai* (1998). Horata Sukeemon: Nomura Mansaku; Tarōkaja: Nomura Mansai; Jirōkaja: Tsukizaki Haruo. (Mansaku no Kai)

P. 240 *Hamlet* (2003). Actors: Nomura Mansai (left), Tsukayama Masane. (Setagaya Public Theater)/*Shigosen no matsuri* (1999). Actors: Nomura Mansai (left), Mita Kazuyo. (New National Theatre). Both photos by Yakō Masahiko.

P. 242 *Mizu no eki* (1983). Actor: Andō Tomoko./*Komachi fūden* (1984). Actor: Satō Kazuyo. Both photos by Furudate Katsuaki. (both Ōta Shōgo)

P. 243 *Kabuki za no kaijin* (2001). Actors: from left, Kanō Yukikazu, Yashiro Shinichi./*Okujochūtachi* (1999). Actors: from left, Matsubara Ayao, Kitazawa Yō, Yamashita Yoshiaki, Morikawa Masafumi, Shimakura Raizō, Mizoguchi Kenji, Kanō Yukikazu. Both photos by Miyauchi Katsu. (both Hanagumi Shibai)

P. 245 *Berusaiyu no bara* (2001). Actors: Hanafusa Mari (left), Wao Yōka. (Takarazuka)

P. 248 *Man of La Mancha* (1970). Actor: Matsumoto Kōshirō IX (then Ichikawa Somegorō VI) (center) (Matsumoto

Kōshirō Jimusho)/*Ri Kōran* (2000). Actor: Nomura Ryōko. Photo by Yamanoue Masanobu. (Gekidan Shiki)

P. 249 *Yuta to fushigi na nakama tachi* (2004). Actor: Tanabe Shinya (center). Photo by Igarashi Shin. (Gekidan Shiki)/ *Ai rabu Botchan* (2000). (ONGAKU-ZA MUSICAL/ R- Company)

P. 250 *Labor of Love* (1991–92). Photo by Hanabusa Shinzō. (Furusato Caravan)/ *Pacific Overture* (2002). Actors: from left front, Sakemoto Akira, Awata Urara; from left back, Ochi Norihide, Hiura Ben, Okada Makohoto by Aoki Tsukasa. (New National Theatre)

P. 251 *The Comedy of Errors* (1988). Actors: from left front , Tamura Yumi, Kobayashi Hiromi, Hoshi Kazutoshi, Yoshizawa Ken. Photo by Ikegami Naoya. (Shakespeare Theatre)

P. 252 Sai no kuni Shakespeare Series 8 *Macbeth* (2001). Actors: Ōtake Shinobu (left), Karasawa Toshiaki. Photo by Yakō Masahiko./Sai no kuni Shakespeare Series 12 *Pericles* (2003). Actors: Uchino Masaaki (left), Tanaka Yūko. Photo by Egawa Masashi. (Saitama Arts Theater)

P. 253 Sai no kuni Shakespeare Series 4 *King Lear* (1999). Actors: Sir Nigel Hawthorne (left), Sanada Hiroyuki. Photo by Yakō Masahiko. (Saitama Arts Theater)/*King Lear* (2002). Actors: from left, Niihori Kiyosumi, Okuno Akihito, Katō Masaharu. (The Japan Performing Arts Foundation)

P. 254 *Broken Hamlet* (1993). Actors: Uesugi Shōzō (left), Enjōji Aya. Photo by Ishikawa Jun./*Sandaime Richādo* (1990). Actor: Noda Hideki./*Ryūzanji Macbeth* (1989). Actor: Shionoya Masayuki. (Ryūzanji Jimusho)

P. 255 Autumn Festival of Performing Arts *Himawari* (1997). Actors: from left, Katagiri Hairi, Ōmori Hiroshi, Kiba Katsumi, Takada Shōko. Photo by Takashima Chigusa. (Saitama Arts Theater)/*Kanadehon Hamlet* (2004). Actors: from left, Oda Yutaka, Honda Tsuginobu, Kiba Katsumi, Hasegawa Atsuo, Uchiyama Morihiko. Photo by Tsuruta Teruo. (Kiyama Jimusho)

P. 256 *La Argentina Shō* (1977). Actor: Ōno Kazuo. Photo by Ikegami Naoya. (Ōno Kazuo Dance Studio)

P. 257 *Kaiin no uma* (2001). Photo by Fukunaga Kōji. (Dairakudakan)

P. 258 *Hibiki* (1999). Photo by Sakamoto Masafumi. (Sankai Juku)

P. 280 *Kaiin no uma* (2001). Photo by Fukunaga Kōji. (Dairakudakan)

Kyoto National Museum Collection

P. 25 Painted screen of *Okuni Kabuki*. Early 17th century.

National Noh Theatre

P. 166 "*Dōjōji*, the picture of old Nō/ Kyōgen in the early Edo period."

P. 183 "*Inuyamabushi*, the picture of old Nō/Kyōgen in the early Edo period."

Prints from the P. Griffith Collection

Jacket: The ghost of Iosaki appears from behind a screen with an extended neck, a staging trick called *rokuro kubi*. In this scene, the same actor took both roles, an example of the *hayagawari*, "quick-change" technique. *Mai ōgi chiyo no Matsuwaka* was performed at the Kawarasaki-za in the 9th month, 1825. (Left) Yukisaki Jinnai, in reality, Yoshida no Matsuwaka and (right) Koshimoto Iosaki: Onoe Kikugorō III. By Utagawa Kunisada I.

P. 20 The hero Sukeroku strikes a *mie* pose as his lover Agemaki looks on in the *kabuki jūhachiban* play *Sukeroku kuruwa no hanamidoki*, performed at the Nakamura-za in the 3rd month, 1799. Agemaki no Sukeroku: Ichikawa Danjūrō VI; Keisei Agemaki: Iwai Kumesaburō I. By Utagawa Toyokuni I.

P. 22 A portrait of Ichikawa Danjūrō VI, probably in the role of Omasa's elder brother Ganpei in the play *Gokusaishiki musume ōgi*, performed at the Miyako-za in the 6th month, 1797. By Utagawa Kunimasa I.

P. 24 The supernatural fox Kuzunoha leaves a farewell poem on the paper doors before abandoning her child to return to the wild. The actor writes from bottom to top, and back to front, all with the brush held in his mouth, an example of *keren* stage trickery in the play *Shinodazuma nagori no kowakare*, staged at the Ichimura-za in the 9th month, 1802. Kuzunoha: Segawa Rokō III (Kikunojō III). By Utagawa Toyokuni I.

P. 55 The scar-faced Yosaburō is now reduced to a life of petty crime and meets his lover again after a long separation, in the *sewamono* play *Genjidana*. Kirare Yosa: Ichikawa Danjūrō IX. From the series *Ichikawa Danjūrō engei hyakuban*, "The One Hundred Best Roles of Ichikawa Danjūrō," 1898. By Toyohara Kunichika.

P. 57 Nakamura Shikan IV dances the role of the *shirabyōshi* Hanako with Sawamura Tosshō II as the foolish priest Seitakabō in *Musume Dōjōji*, performed at the Morita-za in the 5th month, 1870. By Toyohara Kunichika.

P. 70 Bandō Mitsugorō III as Kawagoe Tarō, the ambassador sent to question Yoshitsune about his loyalty to his brother, in Act I of *Yoshitsune senbon zakura* performed at the Nakamura-za in the 8th month, 1804. By Utagawa Kunihisa I.

P. 72 Wearing the *sujiguma* style of makeup, the actor appears as a superhero in the play *Shibaraku*. Usui Aratarō Sadamitsu: Ichikawa Ebizō V (Danjūrō VII). From a series of portraits of famous actors past and present, 1863. By Utagawa Toyokuni III.

P. 75 The actor appears in a variation of the normal wig for this role in which the sidelocks are brushed out and flattened, but he wears the usual stiffened white paper called *chikara gami*, "strength paper." This performance of *Shibaraku* was part of the play *Sewa nidai ōyose Genji*, performed at the Miyako-za in the 11th month, 1796. Usui Aratarō Sadamitsu: Ichikawa Ebizō

(Danjūrō V). This was the actor's retirement performance (*issei ichidai*). By Utagawa Toyokuni I.

P. 76 The wig called *sakaguma*, "thatched bear fur," which covers the crown of the head, produces a rather unkempt appearance and is usually worn by villainous samurai in *jidaimono* plays. With his two swords, the character is almost certainly a *rōnin*, and most probably Sadakurō from Act V of *Kanadehon chūshingura*, performed at the Ichimura-za in the 9th month, 1803. Sadakurō: Ichikawa Omezō I. By Utagawa Kunimasa I.

P. 78 The elegant *shimada* hairstyle is worn by a variety of characters including lower ranking courtesans such as Umegawa in the *Ninokuchi mura* scene of *Koi bikyaku Yamato ōrai*. Umegawa: Sawamura Sōnosuke I, 1922. By Yamamura Kōka, also called Toyonari.

P. 87 A typical pose from a *danmari* scene as three characters grapple in the dark for an important white banner, the symbol of a warrior's house. Such *danmari* were often included in the annual *kaomise* productions. The play *Ise heiji rishō no kaomise* was performed at the Ichimura-za in the 11th

month, 1826. From left, Morihisa: Bandō Mitsugorō III; Gihei: Ichikawa Danjūrō VII; Giheiji's wife Otsuji: Iwai Kumesaburō II. By Utagawa Toyokuni II./The actor as the spirit of the cherry tree bends backwards in the difficult *ebizori* "prawn-bend" pose in the last section of the dance *Seki no to*. Sumizome: Bandō Tamasaburō V, 1997. By Paul Binnie.

Prints from the Ronald Cavaye Collection

P. 76 With his hair oiled and stiffened and with short sidelocks that also stick out, Lord Suketsune cuts a stylish figure in the play *Toshi otoko ehō Soga*, performed at the Ichimura-za in the 1st month, 1803. Kudō Suketsune: Ichikawa Omezō I. By Utagawa Kunimasa I.

P. 78 The *uma no shippo*, "pony-tail" hairstyle, is usually worn by country girls or by *akuba*, "evil women." Here, the role is that of a strong and argumentative boatwoman in the dance *Kaminari sendō*, performed at the Kabuki-za in September, 1997. The boatwoman Oen: Ichikawa Ennosuke III. By Tsuruya Kōkei.

ACKNOWLEDGMENTS

Ningyō Jōruri Bunrakuza, Japan Actors' Association, Japan Playwrights Association, Kabuki-za, Mansaku no Kai, National Bunraku Theatre, National Noh Theatre, Shigeyama Kyōgen-kai, Shochiku Co., Ltd., Tokyo National Theatre, and other theaters, troupes, playwrights, directors, actors, and photographers.

Nomura Mansai (Foreword)
Ōhori Kumiko (assistance with the Foreword)
Tsuruya Kōkei (for some of the Kabuki illustrations)
Ōkawa Yōko (line drawings)
Ichiba Shinji, Yanai Tetsuo (assistance with the translations)

（英文版）日本演劇ガイド   A Guide to the Japanese Stage

2004 年11月25日   第 1 刷発行

著　者　ロナルド・カヴァイエ、ポール・グリフィス、扇田昭彦
序　文　野村萬斎
発行者　畑野文夫
発行所　講談社インターナショナル株式会社
　　　　〒112-8652 東京都文京区音羽 1-17-14
　　　　電話　03-3944-6493（編集部）
　　　　　　　03-3944-6492（営業部・業務部）
　　　　ホームページ　www.kodansha-intl.com

印刷・製本所　大日本印刷株式会社

落丁本、乱丁本は購入書店名を明記のうえ、講談社インターナショナル業務部宛にお送りください。送料小社負担にてお取替えいたします。なお、この本についてのお問い合わせは、編集部宛にお願いいたします。本書の無断複写（コピー）は著作権法上での例外を除き、禁じられています。

定価はカバーに表示してあります。

© ロナルド・カヴァイエ、ポール・グリフィス、扇田昭彦 2004
Printed in Japan
ISBN4-7700-2987-X